REVIEW AND ASSESSMENT OF THE INDONESIA–MALAYSIA–THAILAND GROWTH TRIANGLE ECONOMIC CORRIDORS

MALAYSIA COUNTRY REPORT

Abdul Rahim Anuar

MARCH 2023

© 2023 Asian Development Bank
6 ADB Avenue, Mandaluyong City, 1550 Metro Manila, Philippines
Tel +63 2 8632 4444; Fax +63 2 8636 2444
www.adb.org

Some rights reserved. Published in 2023.

ISBN 978-92-9269-768-6 (print); 978-92-9269-769-3 (electronic); 978-92-9269-770-9 (ebook)
Publication Stock No. TCS220415-2
DOI: http://dx.doi.org/10.22617/TCS220415-2

Notes:
In this publication, "$" refers to United States dollars and "RM" refers to Malaysian ringgit.
ADB recognizes "China" as the People's Republic of China; "Hong Kong" as Hong Kong, China; and "America" as the United States.

This publication is produced by ADB Technical Assistance (TA) 9572: Enhancing Effectiveness of Subregional Programs to Advance Regional Cooperation and Integration in Southeast Asia, which has funding support from the People's Republic of China Regional Cooperation and Poverty Reduction Fund, and the Republic of Korea e-Asia and Knowledge Partnership Fund.

Cover design by Mike Cortes.

CONTENTS

TABLES, FIGURES, BOX, AND MAPS

Tables

Figures

Box

Maps

ACKNOWLEDGMENTS

This technical study was coordinated by a team in the Regional Cooperation and Operations Division (SERC), Southeast Asia Department of the Asian Development Bank (ADB). The technical study forms part of the analytical work produced under the ADB Technical Assistance 9572: Enhancing Effectiveness of Subregional Programs to Advance Regional Cooperation and Integration in Southeast Asia, which has funding support from the People's Republic of China Regional Cooperation and Poverty Reduction Fund, and the Republic of Korea e-Asia and Knowledge Partnership Fund.

The study was conducted by a team of consultants led by Carolina S. Guina, regional cooperation expert and team leader who provided specific guidance in carrying out the study and wrote the integrative report. A team of national consultants conducted the research on economic corridors in Indonesia, Malaysia, and Thailand and wrote the individual country reports. They are Sandy Nur Ikfal Raharjo (Indonesia), Abdul Rahim Anuar (Malaysia), and Pawat Tangtrongjita (Thailand).

Alfredo Perdiguero, director of SERC, and Gary Krishnan, senior country specialist supervised the study team. Maria Theresa Bugayong, senior operations officer (Resource Planning), and Jordana Queddeng-Cosme, consultant, provided technical and logistic support and coordinated the field visits where they also participated.

The Indonesia–Malaysia–Thailand Growth Triangle (IMT-GT) ministers Agus Suparmanto, minister of trade, Republic of Indonesia; Dato' Sri Mustapa Mohamed, minister in Prime Minister's Department (Economy), Malaysia; and Arkhom Termpittayapaisith, minister of finance, the Kingdom of Thailand, at the 26th IMT-GT Ministerial Meeting held in November 2020, provided overall strategic guidance in the course of reviewing the report.

The study benefited from the valuable inputs and insights of the following senior officials: Rizal Affandi Lukman, and Raldi Hendro Koestoer, Coordinating Ministry for Economic Affairs of Indonesia; Saiful Anuar Bin Lebai Hussen, Noor Zari Bin Hamat, Mohd Shafiee B. Mohd Shah, and Sarimah Binti Amran, Economic Planning Unit, Prime Minister's Office of Malaysia; and Danucha Pitchayanan, Pattama Teanravisitsagool, and Wanchat Suwankitti, Office of the National Economic and Social Development Council of Thailand. The national secretariats worked closely with the team, especially the national consultants, in facilitating access to information and data, arranging and participating consultations with various stakeholders and meticulously reviewing the many drafts of the report. They are Netty Muharni, Tri Hidayatno, Sonny Ameriansah Soekoer of the Coordinating Ministry of Economic Affairs in Indonesia; Suhana Binti Md Saleh, Ahmad Zamri Bin Khairuddin, Balamurugan Ratha Krishnan, Nurul Ezzah Binti Md Zin, Mohammad Akhir Abdul Rahman, and Mattias Murphy Lai of the Economic Planning Unit, Prime Minister's Office in Malaysia; and Thuttai Keeratipongpaiboon, Chiraphat Chotipimai, Orachat Sungkhamanee, Potcharapol Prommatat, and Puntasith Charoenpanichpun of the Office of the National Economic and Social Development Council of Thailand. The Centre for IMT-GT Subregional Cooperation headed by Firdaus Dahlan and relevant IMT-GT working groups also provided insights.

The integrative report and country reports were copyedited by Maria Theresa Mercado and proofread by Maria Guia de Guzman and Jess Alfonso Macasaet. Michael Cortes handled typesetting, graphics generation, and designed the cover artwork. Pamela Asis-Layugan, Alona Mae Agustin, Raquel Tabanao, Nicole Marie Afable, Marianne Macabingkil, Cira Rudas, and Camille Genevieve Salvador provided overall assistance in the publications process. Angel Villarez and Rienzi Niccolo Velasco prepared the maps under the supervision of Abraham Villanueva and Carmela Fernando-Villamar. The ADB Department of Communications team provided invaluable assistance in design and publishing.

ABBREVIATIONS

ADB	Asian Development Bank
AH2	Asian Highway 2
ASEAN	Association of Southeast Asian Nations
BCC	Boustead Cruise Centre
BCP	border crossing point
BKHIP	Bukit Kayu Hitam Inland Port
BPCT	Batu Pahat Container Terminal
BRI	Belt and Road Initiative
CIMT	Centre for IMT-GT Subregional Cooperation
CMGF	Chief Ministers and Governors Forum
CPO	crude palm oil
CVIA	Chuping Valley Industrial Area
E1–E2	North–South Expressway
EC	economic corridor
ECE	East Coast Expressway
ECER	East Coast Economic Region
ECERDC	East Coast Economic Region Development Council
ECRL	East Coast Rail Link
EPU	Economic Planning Unit
EU	European Union
FELCRA	Federal Land Consolidation and Rehabilitation Authority
FFB	fresh fruit bunch
FIZ	free industrial zone
FTZ	free trade zone
GDP	gross domestic product
HALMAS	Halal Malaysia
ICT	information and communication technology
IMT-GT	Indonesia–Malaysia–Thailand Growth Triangle
IRDA	Iskandar Regional Development Authority
JAKIM	Department of Islamic Development Malaysia
JBC	Joint Business Council
Jimah	Jimah East Power Sdn Bhd
KLIA	Kuala Lumpur International Airport
KRC	Kedah Rubber City
KTMB	Keretapi Tanah Melayu Berhad or Malayan Railways Limited
MIDA	Malaysian Investment Development Authority
MITI	Ministry of International Trade and Industry
MOU	Memorandum of Understanding
NBCT	North Butterworth Container Terminal
NCER	Northern Corridor Economic Region
NCIA	Northern Corridor Implementation Authority

NIP	Nilai Inland Port
NPP	National Physical Planning
NS Malaysia	National Secretariat of Malaysia
PBCT	Padang Besar Cargo Terminal
PIP	Perlis Inland Port
PKFZ	Port Klang Free Zone
Plan Malaysia	Federal Department of Town and Country Planning
PRC	Peoples' Republic of China
RBD	refined, bleached, and deodorized
RDD	Regional Development Division
Ro-Ro	roll on, roll off
RTS	Rapid Transit System
SAPULA	Sabang–Phuket–Langkawi
SBEZ	Special Border Economic Zone
SEPU	State Economic Planning Unit
SEZ	special economic zone
SIP	Segamat Inland Port
SITC	Standard International Trade Classification
SKRL	Singapore–Kunming Rail Link
SOM	Senior Officials Meeting
SRT	State Railway of Thailand
SSP	State Structure Plan
TEU	twenty-foot equivalent unit
UNESCO	United Nations Educational, Scientific and Cultural Organization
WCE	West Coast Expressway
WGTI	Working Group Trade and Industry

CHAPTER

1

INTRODUCTION

Overview

On 1 October 2018 in Melaka, Malaysia, the 24th Indonesia–Malaysia–Thailand Growth Triangle (IMT-GT) Ministerial Meeting directed a review of existing IMT-GT economic corridors (ECs), and a study of the proposed sixth corridor linking Pattani–Yala–Narathiwat in Thailand with Perak and Kelantan in Malaysia, and with southern Sumatera in Indonesia. The countries requested technical assistance from the Asian Development Bank (ADB) in conducting this review.

The economic corridor (EC) approach to development was first emphasized in the IMT-GT Road Map 2007–2011 as a key anchor for clustering major economic activities in the subregion. The IMT-GT Implementation Blueprint 2012–2016 (IB 2012–2016)—the successor to the road map—included economic corridor development programs and projects among the flagship initiatives in the transport and energy sector. The importance of economic corridors was carried over to the IB 2017–2021 which reaffirmed the importance of economic corridors as a spatial framework to help achieve the IMT-GT 2036 Vision.

The IMT-GT strategic framework documents over the past years indicate the absence of a definitive framework for economic corridor development at a subregional level. The progress achieved so far has resulted from independent national initiatives vetted through the IMT-GT platform, rather than from deliberate, evidence-based, corridor-wide planning at the subregional level. This review is the first endeavor that looks at economic corridors from a wider perspective since it became a focus of IMT-GT economic cooperation in 2007.[1]

Study Objectives

In assessing the IMT-GT economic corridors, this review aims to:
(i)   analyze the corridors' connections by road, rail, sea, and air;
(ii)   identify gaps in such connections, and recommend new routes for expansion of economic opportunities;
(iii)   review the proposed sixth EC, and recommend its configuration;
(iv)   review links between ECs and the emerging subregional corridor network;
(v)   review ECs from a value chain perspective;
(vi)   recommend ways to improve EC development.

Methodology

As an initial activity, the study identified specific nodes in each corridor to establish the role of different economic units in relation to the major transport backbone and gateways. The nodes provided the reference points for assessing connectivity in the corridor. It also provided the basis for identifying linkages with potential nodes by way of expanding the corridor configuration based on emerging national strategies and economic opportunities. The nodes were classified according to the roles they perform: capital cities and urban areas, commercial nodes, border crossing point (BCP), maritime gateway ports, tourism nodes, and interlink nodes.

[1]   C. S. Guina. 2023. *Review and Assessment of the Indonesia–Malaysia–Thailand Growth Triangle Economic Corridors: Integrative Report.* Manila: Asian Development Bank. The introduction was based on the integrative report, which is published as a separate publication.

The study considered possibilities for expanding existing corridors to other provinces and states. The motivation was to loop in strategically positioned areas in the government's spatial strategy into the regional economic corridors to derive additional benefits from continuity and scale effects. The expanded corridor would optimize regional spatial use by taking advantage of new production, growth, and logistics centers located in a wider area; enhance supply chain opportunities; and contribute to a more equitable distribution of benefits. The additional provinces and states can upgrade to the main logistics routes that connect to other corridor networks, thus diversifying economic and social outcomes.

The study also looked at the value chain[2] of three major products in IMT-GT—palm oil, rubber, and halal foods—to get a broad perspective on the geography of their production, processing, and distribution components in the economic corridors. The geography of value chain components is a basis for determining the appropriate interventions to make the chain more efficient and their products more competitive.

The study is qualitative and draws its observations and findings from inferences and interpretation of data collected from official and other sources. Desk research was conducted on IMT-GT documents, reports of meetings, references, and research materials. Fieldwork in Malaysia was conducted with the team leader on 3–8 November 2019. The ministries and agencies involved in providing relevant information during the fieldwork were:

(i)   Economic Planning Unit, Putrajaya

(ii)   Ministry of Transport, Putrajaya

(iii)   Royal Malaysian Customs Department, Putrajaya

(iv)   Ministry of Tourism, Arts and Culture Malaysia, Putrajaya

(v)   Perak State Economic Planning Unit, Perak

(vi)   Melaka State Economic Planning Unit, Melaka

(vii)   East Coast Economic Region Development Council, Putrajaya

(viii) Port Klang Authority, Port Klang

(ix)   Penang Port Commission, Penang

(x)   Tanjung Bruas Port, Melaka

The consultations covered many of the corridor provinces and states and involved meetings with the national secretariats, relevant line ministries, bodies responsible for spatial development programs or national corridors, provincial and state planning units, ports authorities, and customs houses at BCPs and the private sector (including representatives from the IMT-GT Joint Business Council [JBC]).

Several consultations with the IMT-GT National Secretariat of Malaysia (NS Malaysia) were also conducted in the course of the study. Representatives from the following ministries and agencies were also interviewed:

(i)   Centre for IMT-GT Subregional Cooperation, Putrajaya

(ii)   Northern Corridor Implementation Authority, Penang

---

[2]   In this study, the distinction between the terms **value chain** and **supply chain** is not strictly applied. It is noted that a value chain is the process by which a company adds value to its raw materials to produce products eventually sold to consumers; while the supply chain represents all the steps required to get the product to the customer. https://www.investopedia.com/ask/answers/043015/what-difference-between-value-chain-and-supply-chain.asp#:~:text=The%20value%20chain%20is%20a,the%20product%20to%20the%20customer.

(iii)   Malaysia Investment Development Authority, Kuala Lumpur

(iv)   Royal Malaysian Customs Department, Putrajaya

(v)   Ministry of Works, Kuala Lumpur

(vi)   Ministry of Transport, Putrajaya

(vii)   Ministry of Home Affairs, Putrajaya

(viii)   Federal Department of Town and Country Planning, Putrajaya

(ix)   Kedah State Economic Planning Unit, Kedah

(x)   Kedah State Economic Development Corporation, Kedah

(xi)   Melaka Public Works Department, Melaka

(xii)   Melaka State Economic Development Corporation, Melaka

(xiii)   Lumut Port (Lumut Maritime Terminal Sdn. Bhd.), Perak

Structure of the Report

The Malaysia Country Report, which has been incorporated into the integrative report, is divided into eight chapters as follows:

(i)   Introduction (Chapter 1)

(ii)   Development Context (Chapter 2)

(iii)   Review of Economic Corridors in Malaysia (Chapter 3)

(iv)   Proposed Route for the Sixth Economic Corridor (Chapter 4)

(v)   The Network of IMT-GT Economic Corridors (Chapter 5)

(vi)   Economic Corridors from a Value Chain Perspective (Chapter 6)

(vii)   Addressing Gaps in Institutional Mechanisms for Economic Corridor Development (Chapter 7)

(viii)   Summary of Findings and Recommendations (Chapter 8)

The study comes in four separate publications—the integrative report, which presents the overall findings from a subregional perspective, and individual county reports for Indonesia, Malaysia, and Thailand, which reflect the national perspectives.

Existing Economic Corridors

There are five existing IMT-GT economic corridors. The new EC6 corridor was proposed at the 24th IMT-GT Ministerial Meeting in Melaka in October 2018. Malaysia is involved in ECs 1, 2, 4, and the proposed EC6. EC3 is a national corridor in Sumatera and EC5 covers only Thailand and Indonesia. Langkawi was proposed to be included in the reconfigured EC5 due to its strategic location along the cruise tourism routes of the Strait of Malacca and the Andaman Sea. Map 1 presents the existing economic corridors.

The five existing ECs are described briefly below:

(i) **Extended Songkhla–Penang–Medan Economic Corridor (EC1)**. EC1 consists of three main sections: two overland routes and a maritime route. The two overland routes connect (i) the Southern Thailand provinces of Nakhon Si Thammarat, Phatthalung, and Pattani with the international gateway port in Songkhla, Yala, and Narathiwat; (ii) an overland route from Songkhla to Penang; and (iii) the maritime route that links Penang to Medan, the capital of North Sumatera, across the Strait of Malacca. Within North Sumatera, the important land connectivity is between Medan City and Belawan Port. Belawan Port in Medan is currently the main international port that supports this maritime connectivity segment. EC1 hosts some of the most agriculture-rich provinces in Southern Thailand that trade with Malaysia, Sumatera, and Singapore and plays an important role in the supply chain of traded goods outside the subregion. EC1 covers several provinces in the border areas of Malaysia and Thailand and serves as the anchor for clustering major economic activities through the development of industrial hubs and special economic zones.

(ii) **Strait of Malacca Economic Corridor (EC2)**. EC2 is a coastal corridor connecting Thailand's southern provinces of Trang and Satun with Malaysia's states of Perlis, and on to Port Klang, Penang, and Melaka along the western coast. The maritime gateways in EC2 under the existing configuration are Tammalang Port (Satun), Port Klang (Selangor), Penang Port (Penang), and Tanjung Bruas Port (Melaka). The approach to corridor connectivity is multimodal, with land and coastal linkages. Due to the proximity of this corridor to Sumatera, there is considerable potential to complement the various stages of the production chain with the island, especially if a series of economic and industrial zones are established at strategic points along the corridor. This corridor has the potential to serve as a food hub, especially for halal, since a number of food terminals and integrated food centers are being planned within the corridor.

(iii) **Banda Aceh–Medan–Pekanbaru–Palembang Economic Corridor (EC3)**. EC3 is a national corridor in Sumatera. Connectivity among these provinces is envisaged to build traffic volume leading to Sumatera's international ports along its eastern coast—Banda Aceh, Medan, Pekanbaru, Dumai, and Jambi—complementing coastal connectivity with ports in Penang and Melaka. This corridor, which is part of the Association of Southeast Asian Nations (ASEAN) Highway Network, is of critical importance for developing Sumatera, as well as an important building block for further enhancing connectivity within the IMT-GT subregion. Its development is closely linked with that of the other three corridors.

(iv) **Melaka–Dumai Economic Corridor (EC4)**. EC4 is a maritime corridor linking Riau Province in Sumatera to the state of Melaka in Peninsular Malaysia.[3] The underpinning economic rationale for this link is based on the strategic location of Dumai Port and Tanjung Bruas Port located opposite each other in one of the narrowest stretches of the Strait of Malacca thus having the shortest distance between them across the strait. The corridor includes the development of land connectivity to Dumai Port, as well as the development of Tanjung Bruas Port. EC4 has a long tradition of freight and passenger traffic between Sumatera and Malaysia. Dumai is the gateway port of Riau Province, one of the richest provinces of Indonesia with abundant palm oil plantations and on–shore oil and gas resources. Dumai is principally a palm oil-related export port with general cargo, fertilizer, cement, and rice being the main import traffic.

---

[3]   Peninsular Malaysia consists of 11 out of the 13 states, and two out of the three federal territories of Malaysia. The capital city, Kuala Lumpur is also in Peninsular Malaysia. Melaka is part of the Peninsular's southern region, which also includes Johor and Negeri Sembilan. Apart from the southern region, Peninsular Malaysia is divided into the central (Kuala Lumpur, Putrajaya, and Selangor), eastern (Kelantan, Pahang, and Terengganu), and northern (Kedah, Penang, Perak and Perlis) regions.

(v)   **Ranong–Phuket–Aceh Economic Corridor (EC5)**. EC5 is mainly a maritime corridor linking ports in the northern part of Sumatera (mainly Ulee Lheue and Malahayati in Aceh Province) with Southern Thailand along its western coast facing the Andaman Sea, with the aim of exploiting tourism potentials. In Sumatera, Aceh Province is part of the corridor and Banda Aceh, the capital, and Sabang (located in the adjacent We Island) are the gateway and tourism nodes, respectively. EC5 is envisaged to enhance the connectivity between Sumatera and Southern Thailand primarily through the maritime mode. Connectivity was envisaged to be established through the development of facilities in key ports in Sumatera.

In Malaysia, there are eight states participating in the IMT-GT namely: Kedah, Kelantan, Melaka, Negeri Sembilan, Penang, Perak, Perlis, and Selangor. Seven states are involved in three existing corridors—ECs 1, 2, and 4. These states are Kedah, Melaka, Negeri Sembilan, Penang, Perak, Perlis, and Selangor. The state of Johor was included under the reconfigured EC4. The proposed EC6 includes Kelantan, Pahang, and Terengganu. However, the states of Johor, Pahang, and Terengganu are not participating states under the IMT-GT and their inclusion in the economic corridors would require a decision from the federal government. The state of Johor is currently part of the subregional Singapore–Johor–Riau Islands Growth Triangle. Meanwhile, Terengganu and Pahang are not involved in any subregional cooperation program. With the inclusion of these three states, all states in the Peninsular Malaysia would be involved in the development of the IMT-GT economic corridors.

Map 1: Five Indonesia–Malaysia–Thailand Growth Triangle Economic Corridors

Source: Asian Development Bank.

CHAPTER

2

DEVELOPMENT CONTEXT

IMT-GT Regional Development

The IMT-GT IB 2017–2021 outlines the IMT-GT economic development cooperation strategy with economic corridor development as one of the enablers to reduce the regional development gap among member countries. Economic projects, which have a transcending border effect, planned by the IMT-GT member countries, will create new business and employment opportunities in the economic corridors. These projects in the ECs can be classified into the following sectors: (i) roads, railways, and bridges; (ii) dry port and seaports; (iii) economic projects; and (iv) trade facilitation.

Majority of IMT-GT projects in Malaysia (Table 1) are located near the borders of neighboring Thailand and Indonesia, taking advantage of interlink corridors such as Kelantan–Narathiwat, Kedah–Songkhla, Perlis–Satun, and Melaka–Dumai. The northern states of Kedah, Perlis, and Kelantan are less-developed states. The IMT-GT projects are expected to strengthen the economies of the states and address regional imbalances consistent with IMT-GT's goal of promoting growth in less-developed areas through the economic corridor development.

Table 1: IMT-GT Projects under Implementation Blueprint 2017–2021

IMT-GT Projects	State	Economic Corridor	Direct Transcending Border Effect to IMT-GT	Economic Sectors Expected to Benefit
Road, Railways, and Bridges				
Tak Bai–Pengkalan Kubor	Kelantan	EC6*	Narathiwat in Southern Thailand	Border trade
Second Bridge Link at Su-ngai Kolok–Rantau Panjang	Kelantan	EC6*	Narathiwat in Southern Thailand	Border trade
East Coast Railway Link	Kelantan, Terengganu,* Pahang*	EC6*	*Indirect impact to Southern Thailand*	Logistics and border tourism
Dry Ports, Seaports, and Airports				
Perlis Inland Port	Perlis	EC2	Satun in Southern Thailand	Logistics and border trade
Melaka–Dumai Ro-Ro Project	Melaka	EC4	Riau in Sumatera	Border trade and tourism
Upgrading of Kota Bharu Airport	Kelantan	EC6*	*Indirect impact to Narathiwat in Southern Thailand*	Border tourism and logistics
Economic Projects				
Kedah Rubber City	Kedah	EC1	Satun in Southern Thailand and Riau in Sumatera	Border trade and rubber industry
Kedah Science Technology Park	Kedah	EC1	Songkhla in Southern Thailand	Hi-tech industries
Chuping Value Industrial Area	Perlis	EC2	Satun in Southern Thailand	All economic sectors
Trade Facilitation				
New Bukit Kayu Hitam CIQ Project	Kedah	EC1	Songkhla in Southern Thailand	Border trade and tourism
Upgrading of Padang Besar ICQS	Perlis	EC1/2	Satun in Southern Thailand	Border trade and tourism

* = proposed economic corridor; CIQ = customs, immigration, and quarantine; EC = economic corridor; ICQS = immigration, customs, quarantine, and security; IMT-GT = Indonesia–Malaysia–Thailand Growth Triangle; Ro-Ro = roll on, roll off.
Source: Centre for IMT-GT Subregional Cooperation (CIMT). 2016. *Implementation Blueprint 2017–2021*. Putrajaya: CIMT.

Macroeconomic Indicators

Malaysia's gross domestic product (GDP) averaged $314 billion a year during 2014–2018 (Table 2). With a population of 32 million, the country is classified by the World Bank as an upper middle-income country that aspires to become a high-income economy in the near future. The development of economic corridors is a strategy aimed at helping Malaysia to achieve the status of a high-income economy. From 2014 to 2018, the Malaysian economy grew at a rate of 5% per year, with an average per capita income of about $10,000 per year.

Table 2: Malaysia: Selected Macroeconomic Indicators, 2014–2018

Selected Macroeconomic Indicators	2014	2015	2016	2017	2018	Average (2014–2018)	CAGR* (2014–2018), %
GDP (constant at 2015 prices, $ million)*	336,823	296,285	296,342	302,271	337,420	313,828	5.4
GDP per capita (constant 2015 prices, $)*	10,968	9,501	9,368	9,439	10,420	9,939	5.5
Population (million)	30.7	31.2	31.6	32.0	32.4	31.6	1.3
Population Density (population/square kilometer)	93	95	96	97	98	96	

CAGR = compound annual growth rate, GDP = gross domestic product.
*The CAGR was calculated using the local currency (Malaysian ringgit) to avoid erratic fluctuations in foreign exchange rates.
Sources: Department of Statistics Malaysia. 2021. *National Accounts 2015–2020. Gross Domestic Products.* Putrajaya: DOS Malaysia; Department of Statistics Malaysia. 2019. Current Population Estimates: Malaysia 2019. Putrajaya: DOS Malaysia.

Gross Domestic Product

Selangor contributed the most to the nation's GDP (23%), while Perlis contributed the least (0.5%) for 2014–2018 (Table 3). The difference in GDP typically reflects interstate development gaps. Based on Malaysia's development composite index,[4] the states of Johor, Melaka, Negeri Sembilan, Penang, Perak, and Selangor were grouped as the more-developed states. Kedah, Kelantan, Pahang, Perlis, and Terengganu were clustered as less-developed states.

All states recorded positive economic growth for the 2014–2018 study period (Table 4). The growth rates, which varied among the states, reflected regional imbalances. The individual state's factor endowment, which influences its competitive edge, as well as investment inflows into the host economy, both in terms of quantity and quality, contributed to Malaysia's GDP performance. Among the states, Selangor recorded the highest economic growth, while Perlis registered the least.

---

[4]   Government of Malaysia. 2006. *9th Malaysia Plan 2006–2010.* Kuala Lumpur.

Table 3: Malaysia: Gross Domestic Product by State, 2014–2018

(at constant 2015 prices, $ million)

States	2014	2015	2016	2017	2018	Average (2014–2018)	Average Share to Malaysia GDP (Average 2014–2018), %
Existing IMT-GT states							
Selangor	76,075	67,405	67,941	70,207	79,946	72,315	23
Penang	22,061	19,499	19,886	20,170	22,595	20,842	7
Perak	18,086	16,055	15,900	16,113	18,077	16,846	5
Negeri Sembilan	10,108	10,551	11,030	11,566	12,055	11,062	4
Kedah	11,075	9,796	9,921	10,013	11,104	10,382	3
Melaka	10,264	9,072	9,091	9,491	10,504	9,684	3
Kelantan	6,273	5,443	5,418	5,463	5,972	5,714	2
Perlis	1,588	1,361	1,343	1,324	1,458	1,415	1
Existing IMT-GT states	155,530*	139,183	140,530	144,345*	161,711	148,260	47
Proposed IMT-GT States							
Johor	30,866	27,306	28,128	28,722	32,338	29,472	9
Pahang	14,278	12,493	12,264	12,685	13,926	13,129	4
Terengganu	9,108	7,886	7,746	7,899	8,629	8,254	3
Proposed IMT-GT states	54,252	47,685	48,138	49,305	54,893	50,855	16
Peninsular Malaysia	**209,782**	**186,868**	**188,668**	**193,650**	**216,604**	**199,115**	**63**
Malaysia	**336,823**	**296,285**	**296,342**	**302,271**	**337,420**	**313,828**	

GDP = gross domestic product, IMT-GT = Indonesia–Malaysia–Thailand Growth Triangle.
Notes: Peninsular Malaysia or West Malaysia, consists of 11 states and 2 federal territories, 8 of which are participating in the IMT-GT states. While Terengganu, Pahang, and Johor are nonparticipating IMT-GT states. Malaysia comprises West Malaysia, Sabah, and Sarawak.
* Totals may not sum precisely because of rounding.
Sources: Department of Statistics Malaysia. 2010. *Gross Domestic Product (GDP) by State, 2005–2009*. Putrajaya: DOS Malaysia; Department of Statistics Malaysia. 2016. *GDP by State: National Accounts 2010–2015*. Putrajaya: DOS Malaysia; Bank Negara Malaysia. 2019. *Monthly Highlights and Statistics: November 2019*. Kuala Lumpur: BNM.

Table 4: Malaysia: Gross Domestic Product by State, Annual Growth Rate

(at constant 2015 prices, %)

State	2014	2015	2016	2017	2018	CAGR (2014–2018)
Existing IMT-GT States						
Selangor	6.7	5.7	7.1	7.1	6.9	6.7
Penang	8.0	5.5	8.3	5.2	5.1	6.1
Melaka	7.7	5.5	6.5	8.2	3.9	6.0
Kedah	4.2	5.6	7.6	4.6	4.1	5.4
Perak	4.6	5.9	5.2	5.1	5.3	5.4
Negeri Sembilan	3.1	4.4	4.5	4.9	4.2	4.5
Kelantan	5.0	3.5	5.7	4.5	2.6	4.1
Perlis	5.1	2.3	4.8	2.2	3.3	3.2
Proposed IMT-GT States						
Johor	6.5	5.6	9.4	5.9	5.6	6.6
Pahang	4.1	4.4	4.3	7.2	3.0	4.7
Terengganu	6.1	3.3	4.3	5.7	2.5	4.0
MALAYSIA	**6.0**	**5.0**	**6.2**	**5.7**	**4.7**	**5.4**

CAGR = compound annual growth rate, IMT-GT = Indonesia–Malaysia–Thailand Growth Triangle.
Note: The CAGR was calculated using the local currency (Malaysian ringgit) to avoid erratic fluctuations in foreign exchange rates.
Sources: Department of Statistics Malaysia. 2010. *Gross Domestic Product (GDP) by State, 2005–2009*. Putrajaya: DOS Malaysia; Department of Statistics Malaysia. 2016. *GDP by State: National Accounts 2010–2015*. Putrajaya: DOS Malaysia; Bank Negara Malaysia. 2019. *Monthly Highlights and Statistics: November 2019*. Kuala Lumpur. BNM.

GDP per Capita

The development gap in Malaysia is also reflected in the level of GDP per capita among the states. The GDP size and population affect the GDP per capita. The state of Penang recorded the highest GDP per capita while Kelantan, which is a less-developed state, recorded the lowest GDP per capita (Table 5).

Table 5: Gross Domestic Product per Capita by State, 2014–2018
(at constant 2015 prices, $)

States	2014	2015	2016	2017	2018	Yearly Average (2014–2018)	Monthly Average (2014–2018)
Existing IMT-GT States							
Penang	13,147	11,483	11,577	11,564	12,818	12,118	1,010
Selangor	12,572	10,910	10,799	11,003	12,347	11,526	961
Melaka	11,774	10,204	10,089	10,394	11,388	10,770	897
Negeri Sembilan	9,363	9,691	10,033	10,383	10,735	10,041	837
Perak	7,356	6,508	6,406	6,463	7,221	6,791	566
Perlis	6,479	5,478	5,349	5,254	5,753	5,663	472
Kedah	5,362	4,673	4,680	4,670	5,134	4,905	409
Kelantan	3,640	3,092	3,016	2,987	3,210	3,189	266
Proposed IMT-GT States							
Pahang	8,971	7,770	7,539	7,702	8,365	8,069	672
Johor	8,671	7,563	7,702	7,769	8,625	8,066	672
Terengganu	7,987	6,793	6,546	6,539	7,025	6,978	581
Peninsular Malaysia	**10,907**	**9,356**	**8,982**	**8,621**	**9,498**	**9,473**	**789**
Malaysia	**10,968**	**9,501**	**9,368**	**9,439**	**10,420**	**9,939**	**828**

IMT-GT = Indonesia–Malaysia–Thailand Growth Triangle.
Sources: Department of Statistics Malaysia. (2010). *Gross Domestic Product (GDP) by State, 2005-2009*. Putrajaya: DOS Malaysia; Department of Statistics Malaysia (2016). *GDP by State: National Accounts 2010-2015*. Putrajaya: DOS Malaysia; Bank Negara Malaysia (2019). *Monthly Highlights and Statistics*: November. Kuala Lumpur: BNM.

Population

The size of the population reflects the market size of a state. A large population indicates a high demand for goods and services. These demands can create opportunities for business and investment in the state. States with development projects could attract foreign and domestic investments. The availability and quality of labor also influence investors' decisions to invest in a particular region. This investment inflow will create employment opportunities for the local population.

Malaysia had a population of around 32 million people in 2018 (Table 6). Selangor has the most number of inhabitants, while Perlis, a small state, has the least. In 2018, the eight participating states in IMT-GT accounted for 53% of the country's population, while the states proposed for inclusion in the IMT-GT economic corridors—Johor, Pahang, and Terengganu—accounted for 21%.

Table 6: Malaysia: Population by States, 2018
(million people)

State	2018 (million)	Share to Malaysia's total population (%)	CAGR (2014–2018) (%)
Existing IMT-GT states			
Selangor	6.5	20	1.7
Perak	2.5	8	0.5
Kedah	2.2	7	1.2
Kelantan	1.9	6	1.9
Penang	1.8	5	1.2
Negeri Sembilan	1.1	3	0.1
Melaka	0.9	3	1.4
Perlis	0.3	1	0.9
Subtotal	17.1	53	1.4
Proposed IMT-GT states			
Johor	3.7	12	1.3
Pahang	1.7	5	1.1
Terengganu	1.2	4	1.9
Subtotal	6.6	21	1.4
Peninsular Malaysia	**23.7**	**73**	**1.4**
Malaysia	**32.4**	**100**	**1.3**

CAGR = compound annual growth rate. IMT-GT = Indonesia–Malaysia–Thailand Growth Triangle.
Note: Peninsular Malaysia or West Malaysia, consists of 11 states and 2 federal territories, 8 of which are participating in the IMT-GT States. While Terengganu, Pahang, and Johor are nonparticipating IMT-GT states. Malaysia comprises Peninsular Malaysia, Sabah and Sarawak.
Source: Department of Statistics Malaysia. 2019. *Current Population Estimates: Malaysia 2019*. Putrajaya: DOS Malaysia.

Regional Imbalances

There is a development gap between the states in the economic corridors, with Penang as the most developed state and Kelantan, the least-developed state. To address the regional imbalances, the federal and state governments have prioritized more development projects in the less-developed regions under the State Development Blueprint and the Malaysia Five-Year Plan. The federal government is also assisting the state governments by setting up regional development authorities such as the Northern Corridor Implementation Authority (NCIA) for the northern regions (Perlis, Kedah, Penang, and Perak), the East Coast Economic Region Development Council (ECERDC) for the east coast region (Kelantan, Terengganu, Pahang, and North Johor), and the Iskandar Regional Development Authority (IRDA) for South Johor. The IMT-GT economic corridors are consistent with the spatial development concept under the National Physical Planning (NPP) designed by Federal Department of Town and Country Planning (Plan Malaysia).

Development Strategy in the Economic Corridors

The goal of the State's development blueprint is to achieve a high-income economy status. Hence, the state has identified growth nodes to attract investments that could generate jobs and business opportunities for the local people. Poverty would be reduced as a result of increased employment and income. Business opportunities can also create forward and backward linkages between industries.

Projects in growth nodes have the following characteristics:[5]

- Catalytic projects that create significant positive economic multiplier effects to the surrounding areas and generate optimal social impact as a by-product.

- Projects that create economic centers identified to reduce regional imbalances by expanding the development to promoted areas.

- Projects that are developed in areas with limited ability to attract investments but has the potential to tap into the available natural resources, existing industries or linkages to larger urban centers.

Agencies Responsible for Planning

State planning agencies. The development policies of each state are designed by their respective State Economic Planning Unit (SEPU). The state's development blueprints are, however, required to take into account the NPP designed by the Plan Malaysia. The most recent NPP is the Third NPP (NPP3) with a planning period from 2016 to 2040. Besides NPP3, each state needs to adopt the development plans at the state structure plan, local plan, and local special area plans, prepared by Plan Malaysia for each state.

Federal development planning agencies. The federal government has established regional development authorities to oversee the state's economy. The NCIA was created in 2007 to plan and monitor the development of the Northern Corridor Economic Region (NCER), which includes the states of Kedah, Penang, Perlis, and Perak. On the east coast of the Peninsular Malaysia, the ECERDC was established in 2008 to design and oversee development in the East Coast Economic Region (ECER), covering Kelantan, Mersing, Pahang, Segamat (Johor), and Terengganu.[6] The IRDA was established in 2006 to plan and govern development in southern Johor.[7] Specifically, for Johor, there are two regional development agencies—IRDA and ECERDC—which oversee development of Johor, especially in the northern and southern parts of the state.[8] The economic development of Melaka, Negeri Sembilan, and Selangor, on the other hand, are governed by the SEPU. Table 7 summarizes the relationship between economic corridors and the development planning agencies involved in the development blueprint.

---

[5]   Northern Corridor Implementation Authority. 2017. *The Northern Corridor Economic Region Development Blueprint 2016–2025 (Blueprint 2.0)*. Penang: NCIA.

[6]   East Coast Economic Region Development Council. 2019. *ECER Master Plan 2.0: The Next Leap 2018–2015 (Blueprint 2.0)*. Kuala Lumpur: ECERDC.

[7]   Khazanah Malaysia. 2006. *The First Comprehensive Development Plan for South Johor Economic Region 2006–2025 (CDP 1.0)*. Kuala Lumpur: Khazanah Malaysia.

[8]   Khazanah Malaysia. 2015. *The Second Comprehensive Development Plan for Iskandar Malaysia 2014–2025 (CDP 2.0)*. Kuala Lumpur: Khazanah Malaysia.

Table 7: Development Blueprint Matrix According to Development Agencies and Economic Corridors

IMT-GT Economic Corridor/State	Development Authority		Development Plan	
	Regional Development Agency (RDA)	State Development Agency	RDA Blueprint	State Development Blueprint / Plan Malaysia
1 EC2: Perlis	Northern Corridor Implementation Authority	Perlis Economic Planning Unit	• NCER Blueprint 2.0 (2016–2025)	• Perlis Strategic Development Plan 2012–2030
2 EC1: Kedah		Kedah Economic Planning Unit		• Kedah Transformation Plan 2013–2018; Kedah Development Plan 2020–2035
3 EC1 and 2: Penang		Penang Economic Planning Unit		• Penang Paradigm 2023 and Penang 2030 (2018–2030)
4 EC2: Perak		Perak Economic Planning Unit		• Perak Amanjaya Development Plan (2016–2020); Perak Development Plan 2030 (2021–2030)
5 EC2: Selangor	–	Selangor Economic Planning Unit	–	• Selangor Planning and Development Plan 2025
6 EC2: Negeri Sembilan	–	Negeri Sembilan Economic Planning Unit	–	• Negeri Sembilan Structure Plan 2045 • Negeri Sembilan Strategic Development Plan 2010–2020 • Comprehensive Development Plan Malaysian Valley Vision 2045
7 EC2 and EC4: Melaka	–	Melaka Economic Planning Unit	–	• Melaka Strategic Plan 2035 (2020–2035)
8 EC4: Johor (North)	East Coast Economic Region Development Council (ECERDC) for Northern Johor (Mersing)	Johor Economic Planning Unit	• ECER Blueprint 2.0 (2018–2025)	• Johor Sustainable Development Plan 2015–2030
EC4: Johor (South)	Iskandar Regional Development Authority for Southern Johor (Johor Bahru)		• The 1st Comprehensive Development Plan (2006–2025) • The 2nd Comprehensive Development Plan (2014–2025)	
9 EC6: Kelantan*	ECERDC	Kelantan Economic Planning Unit	• ECER Blueprint 2.0 (2018–2025)	• Kelantan Sustainable Development Masterplan 2019–2023
10 EC6: Terengganu*		Terengganu Economic Planning Unit		• Terengganu Prosperity Masterplan 2030 (2019–2030)
11 EC6: Pahang*		Pahang Economic Planning Unit		• Pahang Strategic Development Plan 2020–2025 and Pahang Strategic and Economic Transformation Plan 2016–2020

– = not applicable, EC = economic corridor, ECER = East Coast Economic Region, IMT-GT = Indonesia–Malaysia–Thailand Growth Triangle, NCER = Northern Corridor Economic Region.
* Proposed EC6 states.
Source: Compiled by author from various state development blueprints, regional development blueprints, and state structure plans.

Table 8 shows selected growth nodes identified by state governments as part of their efforts to develop their state into a high-income economy, which are located in the existing IMT-GT economic corridors and the proposed EC6.

Table 8: Selected Growth Node Projects, by State

IMT-GT Corridor	State	Selected Key Growth Node Project
EC1 and 2	Perlis	Chuping Valley Industrial Area
		Perlis Inland Port
	Kedah	Bukit Kayu Hitam Special Border Economic Zone
		Kedah Science Technology Park
		Kedah Rubber City
		Baling–Pengkalan Hulu–Betong Border Zone
	Penang	Batu Kawan Development
EC2	Perak	Greater Kamunting Conurbation
		Manjung Aman Jaya Maritime City
		Baling–Pengkalan Hulu–Betong Border Zone
	Selangor	Port Klang – Maritime and Port Support Industries Cluster (Port Klang–Pulau Indah–Teluk Gong–Sijangkang)
	Negeri Sembilan	Malaysian Vision Valley 2.0 (Port Dickson-Seremban)
EC2 and 4	Melaka	Melaka Gateway
EC4	Johor*	Iskandar Malaysia (Southern Johor/Johor Bahru)
		Mersing–Segamat KDA
EC6	Kelantan	Cross-Border Development: Kota Bharu–Jeli–Besut
		Central Spine Development: Gua Musang–Kuala Lipis KDA
	Terengganu**	ECER Special Economic Zone: Kerteh–Kuantan–Pekan
		Kuala Terengganu City Center–Kenyir–Dungun Triangle
	Pahang**	ECER Special Economic Zone: Kertih–Kuantan–Pekan
		West Pahang Growth Area: Bentong–Raub
		Rural–Urban Integration: Development Authority of Pahang Tenggara and Jengka Regional Development Authority

EC = economic corridor, ECER = East Coast Economic Region, IMT-GT = Indonesia–Malaysia–Thailand Growth Triangle, KDA = key development area.
Notes:
* Proposed state for inclusion in EC4.
** Proposed states for inclusion in EC6.
Source: Compiled by author from various state development blueprints and regional development blueprints.

In summary, with the collaboration of regional development authorities, each state identifies growth nodes to help spur its economy. These growth nodes create spillover effects on neighboring regions, promoting development in the economic corridors. Connectivity between economic corridors via transport infrastructure will facilitate mobility of resources, capital, and labor for industrial development and, ultimately, will further support the development of the state's economy.

REVIEW OF THE ECONOMIC
CORRIDORS IN MALAYSIA

This chapter reviews the three existing IMT-GT economic corridors where Malaysia is participating:

(i)   Economic Corridor (EC) 1: The Extended Songkhla–Penang–Medan Economic Corridor (Surat Thani–Nakhon Si Thammarat–Songkhla–Narathiwat–Kedah–Penang–North Sumatera).

(ii)   EC2: The Strait of Malacca Economic Corridor (Trang–Satun–Perlis–Penang–Perak–Port Klang–Melaka).

(iii)   EC4: The Melaka–Dumai Economic Corridor (Melaka–Dumai–Johor–Batam–Riau Islands).

It also includes EC5: The Ranong–Phuket–Aceh Economic Corridor, where Malaysia is not participating under the existing corridor but has added Langkawi (Kedah) in the reconfigured corridor.

Economic Corridor 1. The Extended Songkhla-Penang-Medan Economic Corridor

Overview

EC1 consists of three main routes (Map 2): (i) the Southern Thailand provinces of Nakhon Si Thammarat, Phatthalung, and Pattani with the international gateway port in Songkhla, Yala, and Narathiwat; (ii) an overland route from Songkhla to Penang; and (iii) the maritime route that links Penang to Medan, the capital of North Sumatera, across the Strait of Malacca. Within North Sumatera, the important land connectivity is between Medan City and Belawan Port. Belawan Port in Medan is currently the main international port which supports this maritime connectivity segment.

The states in Malaysia covered by EC1 are Kedah, Penang, and Perlis (Table 9 and Map 3). The border towns between the northern states of Malaysia and Songkhla Province (Southern Thailand) are (i) Padang Besar (Perlis)–Padang Besa (Songkhla), (ii) Bukit Kayu Hitam (Kedah)–Sadao (Songkhla), and (iii) Durian Burung (Kedah)–Ban Prakop (Songkhla). The Asian Highway 2 (AH2) route connects the Songkhla Province to the state of Kedah via the Bukit Kayu Hitam–Sadao BCPs.

Table 9: Economic Corridor 1: Existing Nodes in Malaysia, by Type

State	Node	Type				
		CAP	COM	BCP	MGP	TOUR
Penang	Penang Port • Butterworth • George Town		✓		✓	✓
Kedah	Bukit Kayu Hitam		✓	✓		✓
	Durian Burung		✓	✓		
	Alor Setar	✓				
Perlis	Padang Besar		✓	✓		✓

BCP = border crossing point, CAP = capital, COM = commercial, MGP = maritime gateway port, TOUR = tourism.
Source: Author.

**Map 2: Extended Songkhla–Penang–Medan Economic Corridor
(Economic Corridor 1)**

Source: Asian Development Bank.

Socioeconomic Profile

Penang had the highest growth rate and GDP per capita among the EC1 states during 2014–2018. Kedah is the EC1 state with the largest population while Penang has the highest population density (Table 10).

Table 10: Economic Corridor 1: Gross Domestic Product, Gross Domestic Product per Capita, and Population of Participating States in Malaysia, 2014–2018

Selected Macroeconomic Indicators	2014	2018	Average (2014–2018)	Average Share to Malaysia (2014–2018), %	CAGR* (2014–2018), % (based in RM)
GDP (at constant 2015 prices, $ million)*					
Penang	22,061	22,595	20,842	6.6	6.0
Kedah	11,075	11,104	10,382	3.3	5.4
Perlis	1,588	1,458	1,415	0.5	3.2
Malaysia	336,823	337,420	313,828	–	5.4
GDP per capita (at constant 2015 prices, $)*					
Penang	13,146	12,818	12,118	–	4.7
Kedah	5,369	5,134	4,905	–	4.2
Perlis	6,479	5,753	5,663	–	2.3
Malaysia	10,968	10,420	9,939	–	4.0
Population (million)					
Penang	1.7	1.8	1.7	5.4	1.2
Kedah	2.1	2.2	2.1	6.7	1.2
Perlis	0.2	0.3	0.3	0.8	0.8
Malaysia	30.7	32.4	31.6	–	1.3
Population Density (population/square kilometer)					
Penang	1,629	1,711	1,670	–	1.2
Kedah	219	229	225	–	1.2
Perlis	308	319	314	–	0.2
Malaysia	93	98	96	–	

– = not applicable, CAGR = compound annual growth rate, GDP = gross domestic product, RM = Malaysian ringgit.
* The CAGR was calculated using the local currency (Malaysian ringgit) to avoid erratic fluctuation in foreign exchange rates.
Source: Department of Statistics Malaysia. 2019. *State's Socioeconomic Report (various states)*. Putrajaya: DOS Malaysia.

The disparity in the State's GDP reflects the development gap in EC1. This stems from the difference in economic fundamentals. The economic structure of Penang is led by the manufacturing sector, especially the electrical and electronics industry, while Perlis is an agriculture-based economy. Kedah has developed its economy based on a combination of manufacturing and agriculture sectors (Table 11).

**Map 3: Extended Songkhla–Penang–Medan Economic Corridor
(Economic Corridor 1) - Malaysia**

Source: Asian Development Bank.

Table 11: Economic Corridor 1: Share of Sector Value-Added to Gross Domestic Product by Economic Activities, 2018 (%)

State	Agriculture (%)	Mining and Quarrying (%)	Manufacturing (%)	Construction (%)	Services (%)
Penang	2.2	0.2	43.3	2.8	50.6
Kedah	12.2	0.3	28.6	2.3	56.0
Perlis	21.5	0.6	7.9	2.5	65.9
Malaysia	7.3	7.6	22.4	4.9	56.7

Source: Department of Statistics Malaysia. 2019. *State's Socioeconomic Report (various states)*. Putrajaya: DOS Malaysia.

Each state under EC1 has its long-term development blueprint that identifies potentially significant growth nodes as part of the development strategy to further advance its economy. The development of the growth nodes, supported by transport connectivity, has the potential to reduce the development gap between regions and states. Table 12 shows the development blueprints guiding the three states.

Table 12: Economic Corridor 1: State and Regional Development Blueprints

Economic Corridor 1	State Development Blueprint	Regional Development Blueprint
Perlis	Perlis Strategic Development Plan 2012-2030	NCER Blueprint 2.0 (2016-2025)
Kedah	Kedah Development Plan 2020-2035	
Penang	Penang 2030 (2018-2030)	

NCER = Northern Corridor Economic Region.
Source: Compiled by author from various state development blueprints.

Key Nodes in the Existing EC1

Perlis. The Padang Besar BCP is the main gateway between Perlis and Southern Thailand. These border regions are connected by road and railway networks. There is a rail link between Hat Yai and Butterworth, which directly links to North Butterworth Container Terminal (NBCT) in Penang.

- Padang Besar is under the Perlis–Kedah–Thailand Strategic Border Zone. As an important border gateway for cargo movement, Padang Besar Cargo Terminal (PBCT) will be expanded to resolve the bottleneck congestion of cargo from Southern Thailand, thus improving trade facilitation at BCP. The cargo terminal will also be transformed into the Regional Rail Freight Consolidation Centre for the northern states of Malaysia.

Kedah. Bukit Kayu Hitam and Durian Burung are key nodes supporting the proposed Bukit Hitam Special Border Economic Zone (SBEZ) and Kedah Rubber City (KRC). These BCPs also serve as transit nodes connecting the northern states of Malaysia and Southern Thailand via the North–South Expressway (E1–E2) and Asian Highway 2 (AH2) in Songkhla, Southern Thailand. Under the NCER Blueprint 2.0, both BCPs served as growth nodes to further enhance the less-developed border regions in EC1.

- Bukit Kayu Hitam SBEZ. This SBEZ consists of two main development projects, namely, the Kedah Science and Technology Park (KSTP) and Kota Perdana SBEZ (KPSBEZ). This development projects would be a catalyst to stimulate economic growth in the northern region. KPSBEZ is planned to be the most efficient and sustainable integrated logistics services hub in the region, offering an excellent business environment, and focusing on the development of sustainable and efficient logistics chains, clusters, and modes of transport. KSTP focuses on two components, namely the Global Research Centre and Modern Industrial Park as economic drivers for Kedah's development.

- Kedah Rubber City. The project, which is located at Bukit Ketapang Estate (Padang Terap), is to promote the global competitiveness of the Malaysian rubber industry. Spanning across an area of nearly 505.86 hectares, seven key clusters have been identified for KRC, which are advanced latex products, tire and tire-related products, automotive rubber products, engineering rubber products, advanced rubber materials, biotechnology, and services and support. At the IMT-GT level, the project is a synergistic effort supported by Indonesia and Thailand to stimulate socioeconomic development in the border region. It will be developed into a "Rubber Belt" that would link together the region's major rubber producers in the IMT-GT.

Penang. Penang Port is the country's second premier port and an important trade gateway for the EC1 states and Southern Thailand. There is good road and railway connectivity between commercial nodes and industrial parks in EC1 with Penang Port. This enables industry players operating in EC1 to utilize Penang Port as a trade gateway for their products to the international market.

- Butterworth is located in mainland Penang. This city is a significant economic center and also a major transportation hub for EC1 and EC2. Keretapi Tanah Melayu Berhad (KTMB) or Malayan Railways Limited and the E1–E2 expressway traverse through the city.
- The Swettenham Pier Cruise Terminal has since evolved into Malaysia's busiest harbor for cruise ships and one of the major entry points into Penang. The terminal is one of the ports that will benefit most from the rise in cruise tourism and has undergone an upgrade in 2020. With the project scheduled for completion by 2023, the terminal will be able to increase its passenger capacity by 50% as it can accommodate 12,000 passengers in comparison with the present 8,000 passengers.[9]

State capitals. The state capitals that are involved in the EC1 are Kangar (Perlis), Alor Setar (Kedah), and George Town (Penang). These major cities are commercial and administrative centers that provide services to the public, business communities, and industry players to facilitate economic activities in the states.

Status of Physical Connectivity

Road Connectivity

The road network in EC1 begins from Surat Thani and continues toward Nakhon Si Thammarat, Songkhla, and Hat Yai. Hat Yai is the entry point to states in northern Malaysia. There are three major routes from Hat Yai to northern Malaysia that traverse the following BCPs (Table 13): (i) Bukit Kayu Hitam–Sadao, (ii) Durian Burung–Ban Prakop, and (iii) Padang Besar–Padang Besa. The road and expressway networks within EC1 are well-connected. The EC1/2, which is also the route for the AH2, connects Bukit Kayu Hitam (Kedah) to Penang Port in Butterworth and George Town (Penang). The towns of Kangar and Alor Setar, which are capital cities connect the BCP nodes with Penang Port.

---

9   The information on EC1's key nodes was compiled from Northern Corridor Implementation Authority (NCIA). 2020. *Northern Corridor Economic Region Strategic Development Plan 2021-2025.* Penang: NCIA. The information on Penang was compiled from Penang Institute. 2019. *Penang Economic Development Report 2019/2020.* George Town: Penang Institute.

Table 13: Economic Corridor 1: Key Routes between Nodes

Start Point	End Point	Route	Distance (km)	Traffic Lanes	Road Class
Padang Besar Perlis	Kangar	5	35	2–4	Federal road
Kangar		5	47	2–4	Federal road
Bukit Kayu Hitam	Alor Setar	E1/AH2	48	4	Expressway
Durian Burung		K11/175	65	2–4	State and federal road
Alor Setar	Penang Port, Butterworth, Penang	E1/AH2	103	4	Expressway
Penang Port, Butterworth, Penang	Penang Port, George Town, Penang	E17, E36, 3133	26	4	Federal road and expressway

km = kilometer.
Source: Author.

Rail Connectivity

KTMB is the main railway operator in Peninsular Malaysia. KTMB's North Line covers the railway networks from Butterworth Railway Station to Padang Besar Railway Station. KTMB North Line links with Southern Thailand via the State Railway of Thailand (SRT) Southern Line, which runs from Bangkok to Hat Yai, connects to the Padang Besar Railway Station in Perlis, and continues to Butterworth, Johor Bahru, and Singapore (Woodlands Customs, Immigration, and Quarantine). The Hat Yai train station is the interchange node to Padang Besar Station and Su-ngai Kolok (Narathiwat).

Butterworth–Padang Besar Station. The railway line to the north from Penang begins at Butterworth and ends at Padang Besar, Perlis (Table 14). Thai manufacturers and traders operating in Southern Thailand utilize KTMB's cargo services to export their products through Penang Port (NBCT), via Padang Besar (PBCT), due to lower logistics costs compared to using ports in Bangkok.

Table 14: Economic Corridor 1: Perlis, Kedah, and Penang: KTMB North Line

Region/State	Start Point	to	End Point	km	Cargo Station/Inland Port
North Line					
Perlis	Padang Besar	→	Arau Station	28	Padang Besar Container Terminal
Perlis/Kedah	Arau	→	Anak Bukit	26	
Kedah	Anak Bukit	→	Alor Setar	12	
	Alor Setar	→	Gurun Station	36	
	Gurun	→	Sungai Petani	22	
Kedah/Penang	Sungai Petani	→	Tasek Gelugor	18	
Penang	Tasek Gelugor	→	Butterworth	15	North Butterworth Container Terminal
	Butterworth	→	Bukit Mertajam	12	
Subtotal Distance (Padang Besar–Bukit Mertajam)				**169**	

km = kilometer, KTMB = Keretapi Tanah Melayu Berhad or Malayan Railways Limited.
Source: Compiled by author from KTMB's various publication sources. Retrieved from http://www.ktmb.com.my/index.html.

Maritime Connectivity

An important port in EC1 is the Penang Port, which is strategically located along the Strait of Malacca, and one of the busiest shipping routes in the world. The port serves as the primary gateway for EC1 and Southern Thailand.

The port is a deep-water seaport consisting of seven terminals along the Penang Strait—six of the terminals in mainland Seberang Perai, particularly in Butterworth and Perai, and one in George Town in Penang Island as Swettenham Pier Cruise Terminal. Penang Port Sdn is fully owned by the Malaysia Mining Corporation (MMC) Berhad. The NBCT enables Penang Port to be the focal point for shipping and transshipment activities.

Penang Port is fully equipped to handle all types of cargo such as containers, liquid, dry bulk, break bulk, and others; and provides a multitude of services to cater to their safe and efficient transit via the port's various terminals and facilities. The expansion of Penang Port will further enhance its importance as the maritime gateway for trade and tourism in NCER, as well as Southern Thailand. As of 2019, the port was capable of handling 2.3 million twenty-foot equivalent unit (TEU) of cargo annually and it is well positioned to capture more cargo in the future. With the port expansion and infrastructure development, Penang Port will be positioned as a smart, modern port that is capable of handling 7.5 million TEUs of cargo per year by 2030 onward.[10]

Penang Port has extensive trading links with ports in Sumatera (Table 15). The port also has trading relations with Songkhla Port via a land bridge from Songkhla to Butterworth and the main export gateway of choice for manufacturers in Southern Thailand.

Table 15: Economic Corridor 1: Penang Port: Connectivity with Ports in Sumatera and Southern Thailand

Links to Ports in Sumatera and Thailand:	Type of Marine Activities	Remarks
Sumatera		
Aceh: Banda Aceh Port (Port Malahayati), Kuala Idi, Kuala Langsa, Lhokseumawe, Sabang	Cargo	
North Sumatera: Belawan (Medan), Pangkalan Dodek, Tanjung Balai	Cargo and container	EC1 Route: Penang Port to Belawan Port
Riau: Dumai, Perawang Riau	Cargo	
Bangka Belitung: Pangkal Balam, Bangka		
Southern Thailand		
Songkhla (Railway Mode)	Cargo	EC1 Route: Land Bridge Link–Hat Yai Padang Besar–Penang Port Butterworth (North Butterworth Container Terminal)

EC = economic corridor.
Source: Compiled by author from information provided by Penang Port Commission on 22 January 2020.

---

[10] The information was compiled from NCIA. 2020. *Northern Corridor Economic Region Strategic Development Plan 2021–2025.* Penang: NCIA.

The Swettenham Pier Cruise Terminal is the busiest port-of-call in Malaysia for cruise shipping. The terminal plays a vital role as a major entry point for international tourists into Penang, apart from the Penang International Airport and overland connectivity. It also caters to ferry services that ply between Penang and the islands of Langkawi and Pulau Payar in Kedah. Since 2020, plans have been in the works to expand the terminal to accommodate larger cruise ships. The terminal will benefit from the increase in international cruise travel.[11]

Air Links

Within the EC1 region, there are several airports located across two states: the Penang International Airport (Bayan Lepas, Penang), Langkawi International Airport (Langkawi, Kedah), and Sultan Abdul Halim Airport (Alor Setar, Kedah). Perlis does not have an airport. Within EC1, air connectivity is limited, i.e., only between Penang and Langkawi (Kedah). This is attributed to the proximity of the major cities in the EC1—Alor Setar, Butterworth, George Town, and Kangar—and can be easily accessed by the road networks. Penang–Langkawi connectivity is provided by low-cost carriers, such as Firefly and Air Asia, that operate out of Penang and Langkawi International Airports (Table 16).

Table 16: Economic Corridor 1: Flight Routes to Sumatera and Southern Thailand

Airports	Airlines	Destinations
Langkawi International Airport, Langkawi, Kedah	Air Asia, Firefly	• Penang (EC1)
Sultan Abdul Halim Airport, Alor Setar, Kedah	Air Asia, MAS, Firefly, Malindo Air	• Air Asia: Kuala Lumpur, Johor Bahru • MAS: Kuala Lumpur • Firefly: Subang • Malindo Air: Subang • (Note: No flights within EC1 from Alor Setar)
Penang International Airport, Bayan Lepas, Penang	Air Asia	• Langkawi (Kedah) • Medan (EC1)
	MAS	• Phuket (EC2)
	Firefly	• Langkawi (Kedah) • Banda Aceh (EC3) • Phuket (EC2)
	Malindo Air	• Banda Aceh (EC3)
	Sriwijaya Air (Indonesia)* Lion Air (Indonesia)	• Medan (EC1)

EC = economic corridor, MAS = Malaysian Airlines.
* International airlines.
Source: Compiled by author from the websites of relevant domestic and international airlines.

In terms of international connectivity within EC1, only Penang International Airport provides air connectivity to northern Sumatera, specifically Medan and Banda Aceh, and Southern Thailand, namely Phuket. However, Banda Aceh is under EC2, and Phuket under EC3. The good air connectivity between countries within EC1 indirectly promotes the tourism industry in Langkawi, Medan, and Penang.

---

11   O. Mok. 2019. Penang's Swettenham Pier Cruise Terminal expansion to start in early 2020. *Malay Mail*. 18 November. https://www.malaymail.com/news/malaysia/2019/11/18/penangs-swettenham-pier-cruise-terminal-expansion-to-start-in-early-2020/1810920.

Trade

Thailand and Indonesia are Peninsular Malaysia's top 10 trading partners in 2018. Thailand contributed 6%, and Indonesia 4%, to the Peninsular Malaysia's total trade with the rest of the world (Table 17). The development of the IMT-GT economic corridors has the potential to increase trade even more with Thailand and Indonesia.

Total trade between Peninsular Malaysia and Thailand shows a positive growth trend, which was 7% per year for the period 2015–2018 (Table 18). For Indonesia, a lower growth trend of 6% per annum was registered in the same period. As for Peninsular Malaysia–Thailand's bilateral trade, a part of the trade was through the BCPs of Padang Besar–Padang Besa, Wang Kelian–Wang Prachan, Bukit Kayu Hitam–Sadao, Durian Burung–Ban Prakop, Bukit Bunga–Ban Buketa, Rantau Panjang–Su-ngai Kolok, and Pengkalan Kubor–Tak Bai.

Table 17: Peninsular Malaysia's Top 10 Trading Partners, 2018

Rank	Partner Economy	Export, 2018 ($ million)	Share To Total Peninsular Malaysia's Exports, %	Partner Economy	Import, 2018 ($ million)	Share To Total Peninsular Malaysia's Imports, %
1	Singapore	33,415	15	People's Republic of China	41,352	20
2	People's Republic of China	30,403	14	Singapore	24,649	12
3	United States	21,755	10	United States	15,838	8
4	Hong Kong, China	18,359	8	Taipei,China	15,606	7
5	**Thailand**	**12,827**	**6**	Japan	15,280	7
6	Japan	10,771	5	**Thailand**	**11,764**	**6**
7	Viet Nam	7,743	4	**Indonesia**	**9,478**	**5**
8	**Indonesia**	**7,010**	**3**	Republic of Korea	9,364	4
9	Germany	6,827	3	India	6,411	3
10	Australia	6,128	3	Germany	6,376	3
	Grand Total (including RoW)	**217,287**		**Grand Total (including RoW)**	**209,986**	

RoW = rest of the world.
Source: Department of Statistics Malaysia. 2021. Malaysia External Trade Statistics Online. https://metsonline.dosm.gov.my/ (accessed 1 June 2021).

Table 18: Peninsular Malaysia's Trade with Thailand and Indonesia, 2015 and 2018

Regional Partner	2015 ($ million)	2018 ($ million)	CAGR 2015–2018, % (based in RM)	2018 Share to Peninsular Malaysia's Trade, %
Thailand				
Export	10,016	12,827	9.8	5.9
Import	10,480	11,764	5.1	5.6
Total Trade	20,496	24,591	7.4	5.8
Balance of Trade	**(465)**	**1,063**	–	–
Indonesia				
Export	6,870	7,010	1.8	3.2
Import	7,500	9,478	9.3	4.5
Total Trade	14,370	16,488	5.8	3.9
Balance of Trade	**(629)**	**(2,467)**	–	–
Peninsular Malaysia's Trade with the RoW				
Export	171,419	217,287	9.4	–
Import	168,943	209,986	8.7	–
Total Trade	**340,363**	**427,273**	**9.1**	–

– = not applicable, ( ) = negative, CAGR = compound annual growth rate, RoW = rest of the world.
Notes: The CAGR was calculated using the local currency (Malaysian ringgit) to avoid erratic fluctuation in foreign exchange rates. Totals may not sum precisely because of rounding.
Source: Department of Statistics Malaysia. 2021. Malaysia External Trade Statistics Online. https://metsonline.dosm.gov.my/ (accessed 1 June 2021).

In the EC1, cross-border trade takes place between the northern states of Malaysia (Perlis and Kedah) and Southern Thailand (Songkhla) through BCPs of Padang Besar–Padang Besa, Bukit Kayu Hitam–Sadao, and Durian Burung–Ban Prakop. The Penang Port serves as a key trade gateway for manufacturers located in EC1 and Southern Thailand. The port is easily accessible by road and railway networks for exporting their merchandise to the international market.

The cross-border total trade between Malaysia and Thailand accounted for 27% of the overall Malaysia–Thailand total trade in 2018 (Table 19). The cross-border trade balance however was in favor of Thailand. During 2015–2018, the growth of cross-border total trade was sluggish (2%) compared to the overall trade between Peninsular Malaysia and Thailand (7%). This was partly due to the economic slowdown in the border regions, particularly in Southern Thailand.

Table 19: Peninsular Malaysia's Border Trade with Thailand, 2015–2018

($ million)

Malaysia–Thailand Cross-Border Trade	2015	2016	2017	2018	Average (2015–2018)	2018 Share to Peninsular Malaysia's Trade with Thailand, %	CAGR (2015–2018), % (based in Ringgit)
Import ($ million)	3,723	3,572	3,670	3,634	3,650	31	0.3
Export ($ million)	2,792	2,848	2,904	2,985	2,882	23	3.4
Total Border Trade ($ million)	6,515	6,420	6,574	6,619	6,535	27	1.6
Trade Balance ($ million)	(932)	(724)	(766)	(649)	(768)	–	–

– = not applicable, ( ) = negative, CAGR = compound annual growth rate.
Notes: The CAGR was calculated using the local currency (Malaysian ringgit) to avoid erratic fluctuations in foreign exchange rates. Totals may not sum precisely because of rounding.
Source: Royal Malaysian Customs Department. 2019. Putrajaya: RMCD.

Kedah–Thailand trade. Bukit Kayu Hitam BCP is the main trade gateway between the northern states of Malaysia and Thailand. In terms of total trade, the Bukit Kayu Hitam accounted for 73% of all BCP's total trade with Thailand. This is in contrast to cross-border trade through Durian Burung BCP which accounted for only 1% of all BCP's total trade with Thailand (Table 20).

Table 20: Economic Corridor 1: Kedah–Thailand Trade, 2015–2018

($ million)

BCP	2015	2016	2017	2018	Average (2015–2018)	Average Share to all Malaysia–Thai BCPs Trade (2015–2018), %	CAGR (2015–2018), % (based in RM)
Kedah	4,890	4,744	4,779	4,882	4,824	74	1.0
Export	1,904	1,895	1,986	2,101	1,971	68	4.5
Import	2,986	2,849	2,793	2,781	2,852	78	(1.3)
Bukit Kayu Hitam	4,824	4,669	4,729	4,840	4,765	73	1.2
Export	1,898	1,891	1,974	2,095	1,964	68	4.5
Import	2,926	2,778	2,755	2,745	2,801	77	(1.0)
Durian Burung	66	75	51	42	58	1	(13.1)
Export	6	5	12	6	7	0.2	3.6
Import	60	71	39	36	51	1	(15.0)
All Malaysia–Thai BCPs	6,515	6,420	6,574	6,620	6,532	–	1.6
Export	2,792	2,848	2,904	2,985	2,882	–	3.4
Import	3,723	3,572	3,670	3,634	3,650	–	0.3

( ) = negative, – = not applicable, BCP = border crossing point, CAGR = compound annual growth rate.
Notes: The CAGR was calculated using the local currency (Malaysian ringgit) to avoid erratic fluctuations in foreign exchange rates. Totals may not sum precisely because of rounding.
Source: Royal Malaysian Customs Department. 2019. Putrajaya: RMCD.

Export and import products. The main products traded through Bukit Kayu Hitam BCP were machinery and electrical and rubber and plastic products. In Durian Burung, the main products traded were vegetable and animal-based products (Tables 21 and 22).

Table 21: Economic Corridor 1: Bukit Kayu Hitam Border Crossing Point: Top Five Products Traded with Thailand, 2018

Rank	Product Description	Export ($ million)	Share %	Rank	Product Description	Import ($ million)	Share %
1	Machinery and electrical	1,213	58	1	Rubber and plastics	809	29
2	Rubber and plastics	245	12	2	Mineral products	651	24
3	Metals	233	11	3	Machinery and electrical	649	24
4	Chemicals	140	7	4	Metals	100	4
5	Foodstuff	68	3	5	Transportation	100	4
	Others	196	9		Others	436	16
	Total	**2,095**	**100**		**Total**	**2,745**	**100**

Note: Totals may not sum precisely because of rounding.
Source: Royal Malaysian Customs Department. 2019. Putrajaya: RMCD.

Table 22: Economic Corridor 1: Durian Burung Border Crossing Point: Top Five Products Traded with Thailand, 2018

Rank	Product Description	Export ($ million)	Share, %	Rank	Product Description	Import ($ million)	Share, %
1	Vegetable products	6.0	93	1	Animal and animal products	19.0	54
2	Foodstuff	0.2	4	2	Vegetable products	9.0	24
3	Animal and animal products	0.1	2	3	Foodstuffs	7.0	20
4	Rubber and plastics	0.04	1	4	Mineral products	0.5	1
5	Textiles	0.01	0	5	Chemicals	0.2	0
	Others	0.03	1		Others	0.1	0
	Total	**6.0**	**100**		**Total**	**36.0**	**100**

Note: Totals may not sum precisely because of rounding.
Source: Royal Malaysian Customs Department. 2019. Putrajaya: RMCD.

Perlis–Thailand trade. Perlis–Thailand bilateral trade was conducted via Padang Besar and Wang Kelian BCPs. Under EC1, the Padang Besar was the main trade gateway between Perlis and Thailand. The bilateral trade was in favor of Perlis. The Perlis–Thailand's total trade accounted for 11% of all BCPs' total trade with Thailand for 2015–2018. Compared to other BCPs in the EC1, this percentage was lower than Bukit Kayu Hitam BCP, which accounted for 73% of the total trade of all Malaysia–Thai BCPs (Table 23).

Table 23: Economic Corridor 1: Perlis–Thailand Trade, 2015–2018
($ million)

BCP	2015	2016	2017	2018	Average (2015–2018)	Average Share to all Malaysia–Thai BCPs Trade (2015–2018), %	CAGR[a] (2015–2018), % (based in RM)
Perlis–Total[b] Trade	1,400	1,445	1,549	1,507	1,475	23	3.6
Export	797	850	816	790	813	28	0.8
Import	603	594	733	716	662	18	7.1
Padang Besar (road and rail mode)	1,344	1,322	1,422	1,424	723	11	3.1
Export	742	728	689	708	717	25	(0.5)
Import	602	594	733	716	656	18	7.1
All Malaysia–Thai BCPs: Total Trade	6,515	6,420	6,574	6,620	6,532	–	1.6
Export	2,792	2,848	2,904	2,985	2,882	–	3.4
Import	3,723	3,572	3,670	3,634	3,650	–	0.3

– = not applicable, ( ) = negative, BCP = border crossing point, CAGR = compound annual growth rate.
Note: Totals may not sum precisely because of rounding.
[a] The CAGR was calculated using the local currency (Malaysian ringgit) to avoid erratic fluctuations in foreign exchange rates.
[b] Including trade through Wang Kelian BCP.
Source: Royal Malaysian Customs Department. 2019. Putrajaya: RMCD.

Trade between Perlis and Thailand is via the road and rail transport modes. Trading through road transport mode is more preferred by traders between the two regions. In 2018, more than 90% of the trading volume in Padang Besar utilized the road transport mode (Table 23). This suggests that the railway as a transportation mode for the distribution of goods is underutilized. However, the proposal to establish the Perlis Inland Port (PIP) in Chuping Valley Industrial Area (CVIA) under the NCER Blueprint 2.0 is expected to increase the use of the railway as an important transportation mode for cross-border trade between Perlis and Thailand.

Export and import products. The leading products traded with Thailand using roads through the Padang Besar BCP were machinery and electrical products. Products traded via rail were transport products and wood and wood products (Tables 24 and 25).

Table 24: Economic Corridor 1: Padang Besar: Top Five Products Traded with Thailand, 2018
(Road Mode)

		Exports				Imports	
Rank	Product Description	($ million)	Share, %	Rank	Product Description	($million)	Share, %
1	Machinery and electrical	262	37	1	Machinery and electrical	185	26
2	Transportation	87	12	2	Transportation	165	23
3	Metals	78	11	3	Foodstuffs	109	15
4	Rubbers and plastics	73	10	4	Rubber and plastics	66	9
5	Foodstuffs	54	8	5	Vegetable products	47	7
	Others	149	21		Others	142	20
	Total	**703**	**100**		**Total**	**714**	**100**

Note: Totals may not sum precisely because of rounding.
Source: Royal Malaysian Customs Department. 2019. Putrajaya. RMCD.

Table 25: Economic Corridor 1: Padang Besar: Top Five Products Traded with Thailand, 2018
(Rail Mode)

		Export				Import	
Rank	Product Description	($ million)	Share %	Rank	Product Description	($ million)	Share %
1	Transportation	4.00	84	1	Wood and wood products	0.7	43
2	Vegetable products	0.40	8	2	Stone and glass	0.5	30
3	Foodstuffs	0.40	8	3	Rubber and plastics	0.3	16
4	Metals	0.00*	0	4	Mineral products	0.2	11
5	Chemicals and allied industries	0.00*	0	5	Animal and animal products	0	0
	Others	0.01	0		Others	0	0
	Total	**5.00**	**100**		**Total**	**1.6**	**100**

* very negligible.
Note: Totals may not sum precisely because of rounding.
Source: Royal Malaysian Customs Department. 2019. Putrajaya: RMCD.

Tourism

At the national level, tourists from Thailand and Indonesia have consistently been among the top five countries visiting Malaysia from 2015 to 2018 (Tables 26 and 27).[12] Over the same period, the growth of tourist arrivals from Thailand was about 13% per year higher than the growth of arrivals from Indonesia at 6%. This was partly due to the well-connected road and railway networks as well as the air connectivity between Malaysia and Thailand.

---

[12]   Calculated from data retrieved at Ministry of Tourism, Arts and Culture, 2021. MyTourism Data Portal. http://mytourismdata.tourism. gov.my/?page_id=14#!range=year&from=2015&to=2018&type=55872e6e2bd39&destination=34MY.

Table 26: Top Five Tourist Arrivals by Origin in Malaysia, 2018

Rank	Origin	2018 (million)	Share to Total Tourist Arrivals %
1	Singapore	10.6	41
2	Indonesia	3.3	13
3	People's Republic of China	2.9	11
4	Thailand	1.9	7
5	Brunei Darussalam	1.4	5
	Total (including RoW)	**25.8**	–

– = not applicable. RoW = rest of the world.
Note: Totals may not sum precisely because of rounding.
Source: Ministry of Tourism, Arts and Culture. 2021. MyTourism Data. http://mytourismdata.tourism.gov.my/?page_id=14#!range=year&from=2015&to=2018&type=55872e6e2bd39&destination=34MY (accessed 1 June 2021).

Table 27: Malaysia: Tourist Arrivals from Thailand and Indonesia, 2015–2018
(million)

Origin	2015	2016	2017	2018	Average 2015–2018	Average Share to Total Tourist Arrivals (2015–2018), %	CAGR (2015–2018), %
Thailand	**1.3**	**1.8**	**1.8**	**1.9**	**1.7**	**6.6**	**12.5**
Indonesia	2.8	3.0	2.8	3.3	3.0	11.4	5.5
Grand Total (including RoW)	25.7	26.8	25.9	25.8	26.1	–	0.1

– = not applicable, CAGR = compound annual growth rate, RoW = rest of the world.
Source: Ministry of Tourism, Arts and Culture , 2021. Retrieved from MyTourism Data Portal. http://mytourismdata.tourism.gov.my/?page_id=14#!range=year&from=2015&to=2018&type=55872e6e2bd39&destination=34MY (accessed 1 June 2021).

The tourism industry has contributed to the growth of EC1 states. Each state plans its tourism policy by identifying iconic tourism products to attract international and domestic visitors.

Penang. The tourism sector has always been an integral part of Penang's economy. As a key tourist destination, the state attracts millions of tourists annually, with its scenic beaches, diverse cultures, and delicious local food are among the main attractions. The inauguration of George Town as a United Nations Educational, Scientific and Cultural Organization (UNESCO) World Heritage Site in 2007 heightened Penang's appeal as a holiday destination. Tourism in Penang has expanded into several subsectors such as medical tourism, cruise tourism, and ecotourism. Penang International Airport is the main entry point for travelers and tourists to Penang.[13] In 2018, Indonesia was ranked first in terms of international tourist arrivals in Penang, as compared with Thailand that was ranked 10th (Table 28). This was aided partly by a well-connected air network in EC1 between Penang and Medan, as well as Banda Aceh (EC3). Air transport connectivity is provided by low-cost carriers, such as Air Asia, Firefly, Sriwijaya Air (Indonesia), and Lion Air (Indonesia) that operate in Penang International Airport.

[13] The information was abridged from Penang Institute. 2019. Penang Economic Development Report 2017/2018. George Town: Penang Institute.

Table 28: Economic Corridor 1: Penang: Top 5 International Tourist Arrivals, 2018

Ranking	Origin	2018 (million)	Share to Total Tourist Arrival, %
1	Indonesia	0.3	9.0
2	Singapore	0.1	3.7
3	People's Republic of China	0.1	2.7
4	India	0.0*	1.4
5	Australia	0.0*	0.8
	Total (including RoW)	3.0	–
10	Thailand	0.0*	0.7

* = very negligible, – = not applicable, RoW = rest of the world.
Note: The statistics only captured international visitors who have come through the immigration crossing points via Penang International Airport and Penang Swettenham Port.
Source: Penang State Exco Office for Tourism and Creative Economy. 2012. *Penang Tourism Masterplan 2021–2030*. George Town: PETACE Office.

Swettenham Pier Cruise Terminal, established in 1904, also represents one of the major entry points for tourists into Penang. Cruise tourism has always been vital to Penang's tourism industry, and this subsector experienced significant growth from 2016 to 2018 (Tables 29 and 30). The Cruise Terminal has undergone an upgrade in 2020, with the project scheduled for completion within 2–3 years. Upon completion, the pier will be able to increase its passenger capacity by 50% as it will be able to accommodate 12,000 passengers in comparison with the present 8,000 passengers.[14]

Table 29: Economic Corridor 1: Penang: Number of Cruise Passengers at the Swettenham Pier Cruise Terminal

	2016	2017	2018	Average (2015–2018)	CAGR (2015–2018), %
Number of Cruise Passengers	213,566	426,140	341,028	326,911	16.9
Number of Vessels	136	267	185	196	10.8

CAGR = compound annual growth rate.
Source: Ministry of Tourism, Arts and Culture, 2020. Putrajaya. MOTAC Malaysia.

Kedah. The growth of Kedah's tourism industry began when the island of Langkawi was granted duty-free zone status in 1987. Under the Langkawi Tourism Blueprint (2016–2020), Langkawi has been planned as an international tourist destination. Over 2014–2017, the growth rate of tourists arriving in Langkawi was significantly higher (10%) than that of mainland Kedah which registered a negative growth trend of –0.7%.

---

[14]   The information was compiled from Penang Institute. 2019. *Penang Economic Development Report 2019/2020*. George Town. Penang.

Table 30: Tourist Arrivals in Kedah by Origin, 2014–2017
(million)

Destination	Tourist Origin	2014	2015	2016	2017	Average (2014–2017)	CAGR (2016–2018), %
Mainland Kedah	Domestic	1.1	1.0	1.0	1.0	1.0	(0.7)
	International	0.1	0.1	0.1	0.1	0.1	(0.5)
	Subtotal	1.1	1.1	1.1	1.1	1.1	(0.7)
Langkawi	Domestic	1.0	1.3	1.4	1.6	1.3	15.2
	International	1.2	1.2	1.2	1.4	1.2	5.1
	Subtotal	2.2	2.5	2.7	2.9	2.6	10.0
Mainland Kedah and Langkawi	**Total**	**3.3**	**3.5**	**3.8**	**4.0**	**3.7**	**6.6**

( ) = negative, CAGR = compound annual growth rate.
Notes: Data for 2018 are not available. Totals may not sum precisely because of rounding.
Source: Tourism Malaysia Kedah. 2019. *Tourist Arrivals in Kedah.* Retrieved from Malaysian Open Data Portal. https://www.data.gov.my/data/dataset/faaa069a-142a-4d21-8992-627d5789cbcc/resource/18061bdb-12e4-45c0-9ce8-bcd757c64ada/download/kemasukan-pelancong-ke-negeri-kedah-2014-2017.xlsx (accessed 1 May 2020).

Langkawi was accorded the UNESCO Global Geopark status in June 2007. The Langkawi Geopark comprises Machincang Cambrian geoforest parks, Kilim Karst Geoforest Park, and Dayang Bunting Marble Geoforest Park. These geoforest parks have become popular tourist sites for both domestic and international visitors. Under the Kedah Development Blueprint 2035, tourism sectors that are being prioritized are archaeotourism, geotourism, and ecotourism.[15]

Table 31 illustrates examples of tourism products that are being promoted to spur the growth of tourism industry in Kedah.

Table 31: Economic Corridor 1: Kedah: Selected Existing Key Tourism Products

Nature Tourism	Tourism Product
Langkawi	Pulau Payar Marine Park, Cenang Beach, Telaga Tujuh Waterfall, Dayang Bunting Island
Mainland Kedah	Bukit Hijau Eco Forest Park (Kulim), Jerai Geopark (Kuala Muda and Yan), Ulu Legong (Baling), Lata Bayu Eco Forest Park (Baling), Sungai Sedim Recreational Forest (Kulim)
Cultural Heritage	
Langkawi	Mahsuri's Tomb (Padang Matsirat)
Mainland Kedah	Gunung Keriang Recreational Park (Kota Setar); People's Republic of China and Malay Town (Kota Setar); Bujang Valley Archaeological Museum (Kuala Muda); Balai Besar, Alor Star (Kota Setar); Nobat Tower, Alor Star (Kota Setar)
Artificial	
Langkawi	Gunung Machinchang Cable Car; Galeria Perdana, Langkawi Eagle Suare; Langkawi Underwater World'; Langkawi Crystal; Telaga Harbor Park
Mainland Kedah	The Carnival, Sungai Petani (Sungai Petani); Alor Star Tower (Kota Setar); Pekan Rabu, Alor Star (Kota Setar)

Source: Compiled by author.

---

[15]   Kedah State Economic Planning Unit. 2020. *Kedah Development Blueprint 2035.* Alor Setar. BPEN. https://www.kedah.gov.my/wp-content/uploads/2021/01/BUKU-PELAN-PEMBANGUNAN-KEDAH-2035.pdf.

Perlis is a small state situated at the confluence of major tourism hotspots, namely Langkawi and Southern Thailand. Perlis's tourism industry focuses on nature tourism, agrotourism, wellness tourism, transit tourism, cross-border tourism, and recreational tourism. Tourism locations are centered at Nakawan Range, Timah-Tasoh Lake, and Perlis State Park to attract domestic and international tourists. The Timah-Tasoh Lake has always been referred to as "Malaysia's Guilin" due to its beautiful hilly backdrop.[16] In 2017, a total of 4.1 million tourists arrived in Perlis. Kuala Perlis was the most popular entry point, especially for visitors from Southern Thailand (Table 32).[17]

Table 32: Economic Corridor 1: Perlis: Foreign Tourist Arrivals by Entry Points, 2017

	Kuala Perlis	Padang Besar BCP (road mode)	KTMB (Padang Besar rail mode)	Wang Kelian BCP	Total Foreign Tourist
Foreign Tourists Arrivals 2017 (million)	2.2	1.2	0.2	0.4	4.1
Share of Entry Points to Total Foreign Tourist, %	53.6	29.2	4.8	9.8	100.0

BCP = border crossing point, KTMB = Keretapi Tanah Melayu Berhad or Malayan Railways Limited.
Source: Malaysia Open Government Data . Bilangan Kedatangan Pelancong (PINTU MASUK) Negeri Perlis. https://www.data.gov.my/data/ms_MY/dataset/bilangan-kedatangan-pelancong-pintu-masuk-negeri-perlis-2017 (accessed 1 May 2020).

Industrial Activities

Since the 1980s, the state and federal governments have established industrial parks to attract investments in line with the government's policy to transform Malaysia from an agriculture-based to a diversified, industrial, and service-based economy. Industries in Malaysia are mainly located in over 200 industrial parks and 18 free industrial zones (FIZs) throughout the country.[18] These industrial parks and special economic zones (SEZs) also function as commercial and growth nodes. In 2018, there were 215 industrial parks in the Peninsular Malaysia, including 43 industrial parks in EC1 (Table 33).[19]

---

[16]   The information was compiled from Perlis Economic Planning Unit. 2013. *Perlis Strategic Development Plan 2012–2030*. Kangar. Perlis.

[17]   There are no tourism statistics for Perlis in 2018. However, the trend for entry into Perlis can be based on the 2008 trend where it was observed that almost 80% of the tourists originated from Thailand (Perlis Economic Planning Unit. 2013. *Perlis Strategic Development Plan 2012–2030*. Kangar. Perlis).

[18]   FIZs are export processing zones that have been developed to cater to the needs of export-oriented industries. Companies in FIZs are allowed duty free imports of raw materials, components, parts, machinery and equipment, directly required in the manufacturing process. In areas where FIZs are not available, companies can set up licensed manufacturing warehouses, which are accorded facilities similar to those enjoyed by establishments in FIZs.

[19]   Malaysian Investment Development Authority (MIDA). 2018. *Map of Major Infrastructural Facilities*. Retrieved from https://www.mida.gov.my/publications/map-of-malaysia/.

Table 33: Economic Corridor 1: Industrial Parks by State
(as of end December 2018)

Perlis	Kedah	Penang
1. Chuping Valley Industrial Area*	1. Gurun Industrial Park	1. Batu Kawan Industrial Park
2. Chuping Industrial Park	2. Kuala Ketil Industrial Park	2. Bayan Lepas Industrial Park
3. Jejawi Industrial Park	3. Kulim Industrial Park	3. Bayan Lepas Technoplex
4. Kuala Perlis Industrial Park	4. Mergong Barrage Industrial Park	4. Bukit Minyak Industrial Park
5. Padang Besar Industrial Park	5. Mergong Industrial Park	5. Bukit Tengah Industrial Park
6. Pauh Putra Technology Park	6. Padang Meha Industrial Park	6. Mak Mandin Industrial Park
	7. Sungai Petani Industrial Park	7. Prai Industrial Park
Specialized Park	8. Tikam Batu industrial Park	8. Seberang Jaya Industrial Estate
7. Perlis Halal Park	9. Mergong Barrage Industrial Park	
8. MARA Halal Park Kuala Perlis	10. Mergong Industrial Park	**Special Economic Zone**
	11. Padang Meha Industrial Park	9. Bayan Lepas Free Industrial Zone Phase 1
	12. Sungai Petani Industrial Park	10. Bayan Lepas Free Industrial Zone Phase 2
	Special Economic Zone	11. Bayan Lepas Free Industrial Zone Phase 3
	13. Bukit Kayu Hitam Special Border Economic Zone*	12. Bayan Lepas Free Industrial Zone Phase 4
	14. Kota Perdana Special Border Economic Zone*	
		Specialized Park
	Specialized Park	13. Penang Science Park,
	15. Kedah Rubber City*	14. Penang Science Park North
	16. Kedah Halal Park	15. Penang Science Park South
	17. Kulim Hi-Tech Park	16. Prai Free Industrial Zone
		17. Penang International Halal Park
		18. PERDA Halal Park

* Proposed industrial park
Source: Malaysian Investment Development Authority. 2018. *Industrial Park in Malaysia*. Kuala Lumpur: MIDA.

The location of industrial parks and the availability of local resources are among the main determinants in attracting investment. The industrial parks are equipped with infrastructure facilities, such as road connectivity, electricity, water supply, and telecommunications, to attract manufacturers to invest in the parks. Firms operating in the industrial parks have easy access to raw materials from nearby primary industries via transport connectivity.

The E1–E2 and the KTMB North Line form the transport backbone for the EC1, specifically between Padang Besar and Penang Port. The Penang Port serves as a trade gateway for manufacturers in the EC1, as well as Thai traders from Southern Thailand. For manufacturers that operate in the EC1, they can use a combination of road and rail transport modes to reach Penang Port for exporting or importing their products to and from international markets.

There are well-connected rail links between PBCT and NBCT and Butterworth Railway Station and Hat Yai Railway Station, with Padang Besar Railway Station as the transit station. This well-connected rail transport mode attracts Thai traders to utilize PBCT, which has links with Penang Port, as the trade gateway to market their products to international markets.

The PBCT is the first inland port established within the EC1 region. It has commenced operations in 1984 and is a mid-range inland port for Penang Port and a long-distance inland port for Port Klang.[20] This inland port encourages domestic and international container transactions, especially in Southern Thailand and the northern states of Malaysia. Perishable goods, rubber, wood, timber, and raw materials are the main cargo handled by the PBCT.

The PBCT, which facilitates cross-border container cargo between the northern states of Malaysia and Thailand, has been upgraded and expanded to accommodate more cargo coming from Thailand, which would then head for onward shipment via Penang Port. Its main objective is to optimize the cargo terminal's efficiency in handling the cargo shipment from Southern Thailand to NBCT, which in turn improves its capacity in handling a larger volume of cargo annually.[21]

The Bukit Kayu Hitam Inland Port (BKHIP) has been proposed to be built in Bukit Kayu Hitam SBEZ, as planned under the Kedah Development 2035 and NCER Blueprint 2.0. The BKHIP, which would become the third inland port in the EC1, will facilitate cross-border container cargo movement between Malaysia and Thailand that is anticipated to increase in the near future. The BKHIP also eases logistics services for industry players operating within the Bukit Kayu Hitam SBEZ by providing a direct rail link to Penang Port.

- The role played by BKHIP, as a logistics hub, will become even more significant if the proposal to build a rail land bridge from Songkhla Port to Penang Port can be realized. Thus, there are suggestions from industry players in Thailand to build a railway spur line from Songkhla Port to Hat Yai, and Hat Yai to Bukit Kayu Hitam. On the Malaysian side, there has been a proposal to build a railway spur line from Bukit Kayu Hitam to Arau Railway Station for connectivity to Penang Port.[22]

- The Penang–Songkhla land bridge will significantly improve efficiency and lower transportation costs. Shippers in Thailand see the geographical advantages of Penang Port. Via rail or road, the distance between Hat Yai and Penang is around 230 kilometers (km) or about a 4-hour drive. However, haulers will take 12–13 hours to drive from Hat Yai to Thailand's main ports like Bangkok Port and Laem Chabang Port. The Songkhla Port does not cater to big ships due to its limited water draft and handling capacity. Thus, it is only logical for them to load and ship the containers in Penang. Penang serves the Thai shippers' requirements in terms of meeting their logistics demands. Penang Port is fully equipped to handle all types of cargo such as containers, liquid, dry bulk, and break bulk.[23]

- If the proposed BKHIP is fully realized, it will further facilitate cross-border container cargo between the northern states of Malaysia and Thailand, which is expected to grow in the near future. With good connectivity between inland ports and seaports, logistics services to industry players in EC1's industrial parks will be more efficient.

---

[20] Nizamuddin Zainuddin, et al. 2019. Inland Port Logistical Issues in Northern Region of Peninsular Malaysia. *Journal of Humanities, Language, Culture and Business* (HLCB) 3(12).

[21] *Malay Mail.* 2021. Perlis, NCIA outline development priorities for Northern Corridor Economic Region amid Covid-19. 21 January. Retrieved from https://www.malaymail.com/news/malaysia/2021/01/21/perlis-ncia-outline-development-priorities-for-northern-corridor-economic-r/1942762.

[22] Invest Kedah. 2018. *Exclusive Update: Best Invest-In-Kedah Hotspot 2018. Kota Perdana Special Border Economic Zone.* Alor Setar. Kedah.

[23] *The Malaysian Reserve.* 2018. Penang Port Taps Southern Thailand's Booming Economy. 25 January. https://themalaysianreserve.com/2018/01/25/penang-port-taps-southern-thailands-booming-economy/.

Overall Assessment

There are regional disparities in EC1 which stems from the differences in economic fundamentals. The economic structure of Penang is mainly based on manufacturing, especially the electrical and electronics industry, as compared to Perlis that is agriculture-based. In contrast, Kedah has developed its economy based on a combination of manufacturing and agriculture. Under the NCER Blueprint 2.0, several growth nodes have been identified to enhance the respective state economies and address the development gaps. Tourism is one of the economic drivers that can help boost the state's GDP.

The federal and state roads as well as expressways, which are well-connected, form the EC1's transportation networks. The urban and hinterland areas of EC1 are accessible by federal and state roads. The E1–E2 form the transport backbone within the EC1. The road and rail networks link important nodes within the EC1 from Padang Besar to Penang Port, which passes through major economic centers like Kangar, Alor Setar, Butterworth, and George Town.

Penang Port is an important trade gateway for the EC1 and can be easily accessed using the railway and road transport systems. Manufacturers and traders within the EC1 as well Thai traders in Southern Thailand utilize the Penang Port to export and/or import their products to and from the international markets.

Inland ports like the PBCT and NBCT, as well as the proposed BKHIP, play a significant role in providing access for manufacturers and producers in the hinterland to seaports which act as gateways to the nation's trade. The transit points provided by inland ports enable the exporters and importers in the nation's hinterlands to connect with the nearest transshipment seaports. They also provide linkages between exporters and end-users of products.

Flight connectivity in the EC1 is only between Penang and Langkawi, with flights departing from Penang International Airport and Langkawi International Airport. This is attributed to the proximity of the major cities in the EC1—Butterworth, George Town, Alor Setar, and Kangar —that can be accessed easily by the road and railway networks.

Adequate and well-functioning transport connectivity in EC1 has assisted in the development of the states and supported supply chain activities in the primary, secondary, and tertiary industries. Even though the air connectivity is limited, it has contributed to the development of the tourism industry in EC1, specifically in Langkawi and Penang. These spillover effects have contributed indirectly to narrowing the development gaps in the EC1 states.

Connectivity between Malaysia and Thailand in EC1 is through the E1 or E2 that connects with AH2 through the Bukit Kayu Hitam BCP. The KTMB North Line–SRT Southern Line traverses Hat Yai, Padang Besar, and Penang Port. Thai traders in Southern Thailand use Penang Port as their main trade gateway. Regarding connectivity with EC1 Sumatera, Penang Port has trading links with ports in EC1 Sumatera. Low-cost airlines, namely Air Asia, Sriwijaya Air (Indonesia), and Lion Air (Indonesia) provide air links between Penang and Medan. The Penang–Medan air links indirectly promote the tourism industry in both regions.

The NCER Blueprint 2.0 supports the IMT-GT ECs' objective by expanding transport connectivity and establishing growth centers. The blueprint focuses on transportation infrastructure to achieve better connectivity between growth nodes and promote supply chain flows between industries in the primary, secondary, and tertiary sectors located within the EC1 region. The EC1's logistics services have been enhanced to improve connectivity between PBCT and Penang Port. The proposed BKHIP is to meet the increasing demand for cargo movement between Malaysia and Thailand following the anticipated increase in cross-border trade in the near future.

Reconfiguration of EC1

Indonesia and Thailand have included additional provinces in EC1 based on their development strategies (Map 4). The inclusion of additional provinces has taken into account the countries' development plans, the role of existing nodes, and emerging opportunities for greater synergy within the corridor (Table 34). To complement the roles of Belawan Port and Medan under the existing configuration, Indonesia has added three nodes in North Sumatera: (i) Kuala Tanjung Port and industrial zone, (ii) Sibolga Port and Sibolga City, and (iii) Lake Toba. Indonesia's strategy for EC1 aligns with the development of Sumatera Island that leverages on the ongoing construction of the Trans-Sumatera Toll Road, the planned expansion of ports and airports, and the establishment of industrial parks and SEZs. The focus is on the development of downstream products for agriculture, fisheries, and mining-based industries and catalyzing export-oriented growth centers to create increased value-added.

Thailand has added three provinces in EC1: (i) Chumphon, (ii) Surat Thani, and (iii) Phatthalung, based on the Southern Economic Corridor (SEC) development strategy. The SEC aims to integrate production networks for rubber and rubber products (rubber latex, rubber wood, seafood, and halal food) with supply chains along EC1 and the proposed EC6, through multimodal connectivity and industrial clusters (industrial parks, SEZs).

Malaysia's strategy in EC1 centers on Penang Port as the country's second premier port and key maritime gateway for Thailand and North Sumatera exports to international markets. No additional nodes have been proposed in EC1 in as much as the existing nodes in the three states are well aligned with the development plans of national economic corridors in northern Malaysia. Major developments in the border areas in Bukit Kayu Hitam, Durian Burung, and Padang Besar will likely have significant impact on the economic activities in the corridor in the near to medium term (Map 5).

The existing EC1 has been renamed the **Southern Thailand–Northern Malaysia–North Sumatera Economic Corridor**.

Table 34: Economic Corridor 1: Existing and Additional Provinces and Nodes, by Type

Province/State	Node	CAP	COM	BCP	MGP	TOUR
INDONESIA						
North Sumatera	Belawan Port				✓	
	Medan	✓				
	Kuala Tanjung Port*		✓		✓	
	Sibolga*		✓		✓	
	Lake Toba*					✓
MALAYSIA						
Penang	Penang Port • Butterworth • George Town		✓		✓	✓
Kedah	Bukit Kayu Hitam		✓	✓		✓
	Durian Burung		✓	✓		
	Alor Setar	✓				
Perlis	Padang Besar		✓	✓		✓
	Kangar*	✓				
THAILAND						
Songkhla	Songkhla	✓				
	Songkhla Port*				✓	
	Hat Yai		✓			
	Sadao			✓		
	Padang Besa			✓		
	Ban Prakop			✓		
Nakhon Si Thammarat	Nakhon Si Thammarat	✓				
Chumphon*	Chumphon*	✓				
Surat Thani*	Surat Thani *	✓	✓			
	Ko Samui*					✓
Phatthalung*	Phatthalung City*	✓				
Pattani**	Pattani City	✓				
Yala**	Yala City	✓				
Narathiwat**	Narathiwat City	✓	✓			

BCP = border crossing point, CAP = capital, COM = commercial, MGP = maritime gateway port, TOUR = tourism.
Notes:
* Denotes additional provinces and nodes.
** Pattani, Yala, and Narathiwat were part of the extended EC1 but these provinces have been integrated with the proposed route for EC6 to link with the eastern part of Malaysia.
Source: Study team.

**Map 4: Southern Thailand–Northern Malaysia–North Sumatera Economic Corridor
(Reconfigured Economic Corridor 1)**

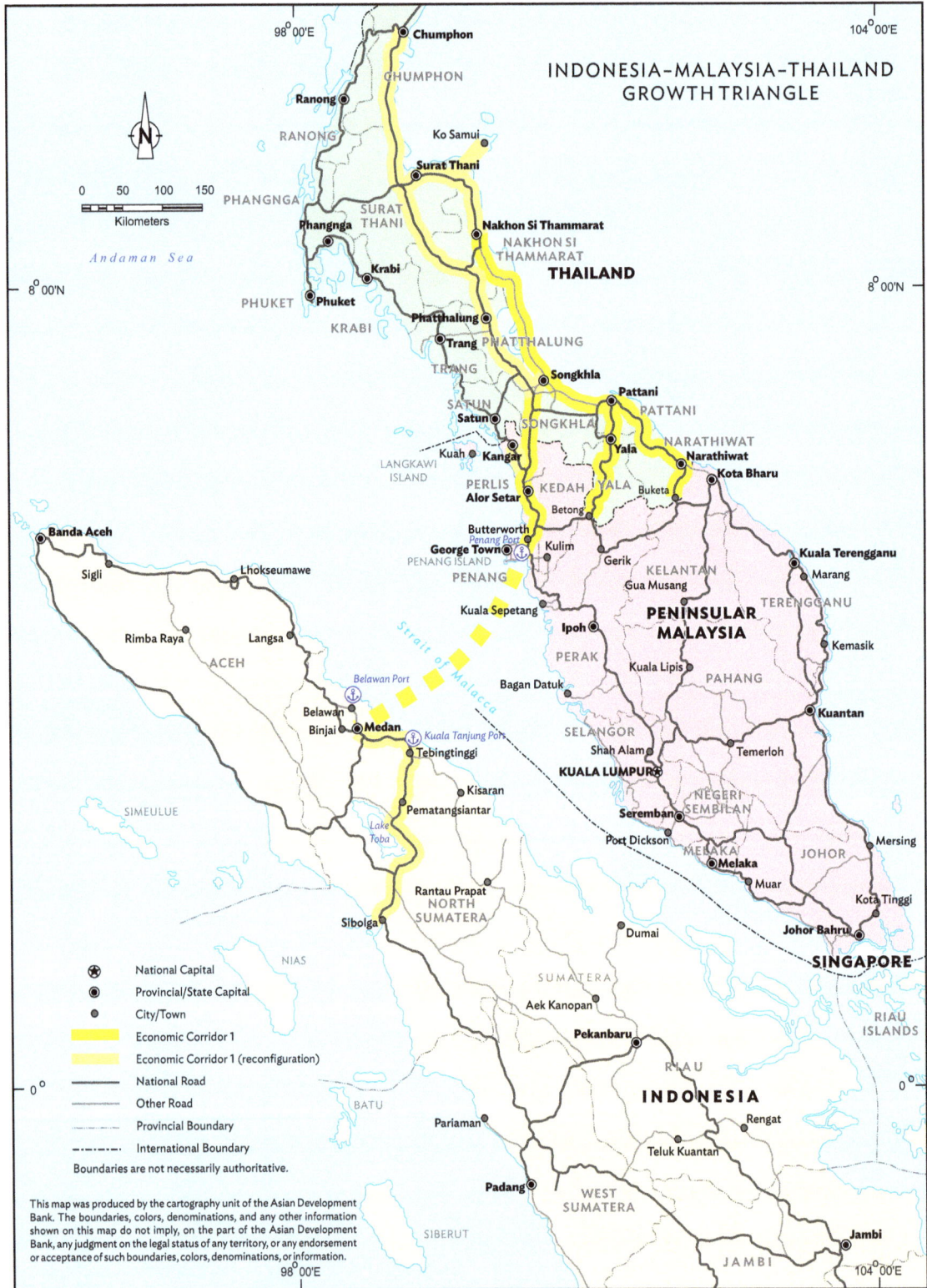

Source: Asian Development Bank.

**Map 5: Southern Thailand–Northern Malaysia–North Sumatera Economic Corridor
(Reconfigured Economic Corridor 1) - Malaysia**

Source: Asian Development Bank.

Economic Corridor 2. The Strait of Malacca Economic Corridor

Overview

EC2 is a coastal corridor connecting Thailand's southern provinces of Trang and Satun with Malaysia's states of Perlis, and on to Port Klang, Penang, and Melaka along the western coast (Map 6). The maritime gateways in EC2 under the existing configuration are Tammalang Port (Satun), Port Klang (Selangor), Penang Port (Penang), and Tanjung Bruas Port (Melaka). The approach to corridor connectivity is multimodal, with land and coastal linkages.

The existing EC2 nomenclature indicates that the states of Melaka, Penang, Perlis, and Selangor are under its coverage. The EC2, however, also includes the states of Kedah, Negeri Sembilan, and Perak. The EC2 is an extended version of the EC1 that covers seven states—Kedah, Melaka, Negeri Sembilan, Penang, Perak, Perlis, and Selangor—which are contiguously bordered along the west coast of the Peninsular Malaysia (Map 7).

The existing nodes in EC2 include Melaka City, Padang Besar, Penang Port, Pengkalan Hulu, and Wang Kelian (Table 35). There are no nodes for the states of Kedah and Negeri Sembilan. Padang Besar, which is under EC1, also performs an important role in the EC2 because it serves as a rail land bridge connecting Port Klang with ports in Bangkok. Penang Port also serves as a trade gateway for Thai traders and industry players within the northern region of the EC1 and EC2.

Table 35: Economic Corridor 2: Existing Nodes in Malaysia, by Type

| Province/State | Node | Type | | | | |
		CAP	COM	BCP	MGP	TOUR
MALAYSIA						
Perlis	Wang Kelian			✓		✓
	Padang Besar			✓		✓
Perak	Pengkalan Hulu			✓		✓
Penang	Penang Port				✓	✓
	• Butterworth					
	• George Town					
Selangor	Port Klang				✓	✓
Melaka	Melaka City	✓				✓

BCP = border crossing point, CAP = capital, COM = commercial, MGP = maritime gateway port, TOUR = tourism.
Source: Author.

Pengkalan Hulu is one of the eight main BCPs between the northern states of Malaysia and Southern Thailand. It connects Perak with Yala (Southern Thailand). Cross-border trade and individual movements take place at the Pengkalan Hulu–Betong BCP. Pengkalan Hulu is also known as "The Gateway to Thailand" under the IB 2012–2017.[24]

---

[24]   CIMT. 2017. *Implementation Blueprint 2017–2021*. Putrajaya: CIMT.

Map 6: Strait of Malacca Economic Corridor
(Economic Corridor 2)

Source: Asian Development Bank.

Map 7: Strait of Malacca Economic Corridor
(Economic Corridor 2) - Malaysia

Source: Asian Development Bank.

Wang Kelian, which is the start point for EC2, is the BCP that connects Perlis and Satun via road connectivity. Padang Besar BCP links Perlis with Sadao–Songkhla through both road and rail connectivity. Penang Port and Port Klang are the maritime gateways to the EC2. Melaka City, the state capital of Melaka, is the end point for EC2.

Socioeconomic Profile

Among the EC2 states, Selangor contributed the most to the nation's GDP, while Perlis contributed the least for 2014–2018 (Table 36). The difference in GDP typically reflects interstate development gaps. The states of Melaka, Penang, Perak, and Selangor are the more-developed states, while Kedah and Terengganu are the less-developed states. As in EC1, the regional disparities stem from the difference in economic fundamentals. The more-developed states are driven by the manufacturing sector, whereas the less-developed states are agriculture-led (Table 37).

The development path for the states of Kedah, Penang, Perak, and Perlis is monitored by the NCER Blueprint 2.0. Meanwhile, the development of Melaka, Negeri Sembilan, and Selangor are under the respective state development blueprints. There is no regional development agency that has been set up by the federal government to cluster these states (Melaka, Negeri Sembilan, and Selangor) into one region. There are also specific development blueprints that are planned by the private sector, such as the Comprehensive Development Plan Malaysian Valley Vision 2045 (MVV 2.0) that has been prepared by Sime Darby Property Sdn. Bhd. for Negeri Sembilan (Table 38).[25]

---

[25]   C. Y. Hoong. 2018. Malaysia Vision Valley 2.0 to Take Off with High-Tech Industrial Park. *The Edge Malaysia* . 31 December. https://www.theedgemarkets.com/article/malaysia-vision-valley-20-take-hightech-industrial-park.

Table 36: Economic Corridor 2: Selected Macroeconomic Indicators, 2014–2018

States in EC2	2014	2018	Average (2014–2018)	Average Share to Malaysia (2014–2018), %	CAGR* (2014–2018), % (based in RM)
GDP (at constant 2015 prices, $ million)*					
Perlis	1,588	1,458	1,415	0.5	3.2
Penang	22,061	22,595	20,842	6.6	6.0
Perak	18,086	18,077	16,846	5.4	5.4
Selangor	76,075	79,946	72,315	23.0	6.7
Melaka	10,264	10,504	9,684	3.1	6.0
Kedah	11,075	11,104	10,382	3.3	5.4
Negeri Sembilan	10,108	12,055	11,062	3.5	4.5
Malaysia	336,823	337,420	313,828	–	5.4
GDP per capita (at constant 2015 prices, $ million)*					
Perlis	6,479	5,753	5,663	–	2.3
Penang	13,146	12,818	12,118	–	4.7
Perak	7,356	7,221	6,791	–	4.9
Selangor	12,572	12,347	11,526	–	4.9
Melaka	11,774	11,388	10,770	–	4.5
Kedah	5,369	5,134	4,905	–	4.2
Negeri Sembilan	9,363	10,735	10,041	–	3.5
Malaysia	10,968	10,420	9,939	–	4.0
Population (million)					
Perlis	0.2	0.3	0.3	0.8	0.8
Penang	1.7	1.8	1.7	5.4	1.2
Perak	2.5	2.5	2.5	7.9	0.5
Selangor	6.1	6.5	6.3	19.9	1.7
Melaka	0.9	0.9	0.9	2.8	1.4
Kedah	2.1	2.2	2.1	6.7	1.2
Negeri Sembilan	1.1	1.1	1.1	3.5	1.0
Malaysia	30.7	32.4	31.6	–	1.3
Population Density (population/square kilometer)					
Perlis	308	319	314	–	0.2
Penang	1,629	1,711	1,670	–	1.2
Perak	117	119	118	–	0.6
Selangor	763	817	791	–	1.8
Melaka	528	558	544	–	0.8
Kedah	219	229	225	–	1.2
Negeri Sembilan	162	169	165	–	1.0
Malaysia	93	98	96	–	1.3

– = not applicable, CAGR = compound annual growth rate..
*The CAGR was calculated using the local currency (Malaysian ringgit) to avoid erratic fluctuations in foreign exchange rates.
Source: Department of Statistics Malaysia. 2019. *State's Socioeconomic Report (various states)*. Putrajaya: DOS Malaysia.

Table 37: Economic Corridor 2: Share of Sector Value-Added to Gross Domestic Product by Economic Activity, 2018

State	Agriculture (%)	Mining and Quarrying (%)	Manufacturing (%)	Construction (%)	Services (%)
Perlis	21.5	0.6	7.9	2.5	65.9
Penang	2.2	0.2	43.3	2.8	50.6
Perak	15.1	0.6	18.1	3.2	62.8
Selangor	1.4	0.2	28.3	5.8	62.0
Melaka	10.8	0.1	38.6	3.5	46.6
Kedah	12.2	0.3	28.6	2.3	56.0
Negeri Sembilan	7.3	0.5	37.7	4.2	48.4
Malaysia	**7.3**	**7.6**	**22.4**	**4.9**	**56.7**

Source: Department of Statistics Malaysia. 2019. State's Socioeconomic Report (various states). Putrajaya: DOS Malaysia.

Table 38: Economic Corridor 2: State and Regional Development Blueprint

EC2	State Development Blueprint	Regional Development Blueprint
Perlis	• Perlis Strategic Development Plan 2012–2030	NCER Blueprint 2.0 (2016–2025)
Kedah	• Kedah Development Plan 2020–2035	
Penang	• Penang 2030 (2018–2030)	
Perak	• Perak Development Plan 2030 (2021–2030)	
Selangor	• Selangor Planning and Development Plan 2025 • Selangor Structure Plan 2035	
Negeri Sembilan	• Negeri Sembilan Structure Plan 2045 • Negeri Sembilan Strategic Development Plan 2010–2020 • Comprehensive Development Plan Malaysian Valley Vision 2045	No regional development blueprint
Melaka	• Melaka Strategic Plan 2035 (2020–2035)	

NCER = Northern Corridor Economic Region.
Source: Compiled by author from various state development blueprints and Plan Malaysia's State Structure Plan.

Under the State Development Blueprint and NCER Blueprint 2.0, several strategic growth nodes have been identified for enhancing the state economies. Within EC2, new nodes identified in Perlis are Chuping Valley and Kuala Perlis. For Perak, the new nodes are Kamunting and Lumut. The town of Batu Kawan and Tanjung Bruas Port are new nodes for Penang and Melaka, respectively. Other new nodes that have been identified are Kuah for Kedah, and Port Dickson and Seremban for Negeri Sembilan.

The addition of new nodes will enhance and widen the connectivity with the existing nodes to achieve seamless connectivity and overcome the developmental gaps between regions in EC2. The trade gateways that are related to the addition of nodes in the EC2 are the Port of Port Dickson (Negeri Sembilan), Lumut Port (Perak), and Tanjung Bruas Port (Melaka).

Existing Nodes

State capitals. The state capitals that are involved in the EC2 are George Town (Penang) and Melaka City (Melaka). These state capitals are important economic nodes performing the role of the commercial and administrative centers that provide services to the public, business communities, and industry players in order to facilitate economic activities in the state. George Town and Melaka City were declared as UNESCO World Heritage sites in 2008. These historical cities have become popular tourist destinations for both local and international visitors and travelers.

Perlis. Wang Kelian and Padang Besar are the main BCPs between Perlis and Southern Thailand. Cross-border trade activities take place at BCPs of Wang Kelian–Wang Prachan (Satun) and Padang Besar–Padang Besa (Sadao).

Perak. Pengkalan Hulu is the main BCP between Perak and Yala (Southern Thailand). There are cross-border trade activities at the Pengkalan Hulu–Betong BCP.

Penang. Penang Port is the main trade gateway for EC2 (specifically for the northern region). Butterworth is a major economic center on the mainland of Penang. It connects the EC1 and EC2 via the E1 and E2 and KTMB rail lines, which run from Johor Bahru to Bangkok.

Selangor. Port Klang is the premier port in the country and is also the main trade gateway for the EC2. As Malaysia's premier port and national loading center, Port Klang plays a pivotal role as the national maritime gateway and regional logistics hub. The port has trading links with over 130 countries and deals with more than 600 ports around the world. It is the first port-of-call for eastbound ships and the last port-of-call for westbound ships on the Asia–Europe route. Port Klang is the 12th busiest port in the world.

Status of Physical Connectivity

Road Connectivity

The road network in EC2 begins in Trang, passes through the Wang Prachan (Satun)–Wang Kelian (Perlis) BCP and continues to Butterworth (Penang), Port Klang (Selangor), Seremban, and ends at Melaka City (Melaka). An alternative route from Trang to Melaka City is via the Padang Besar BCP. Perlis, which is a small state, has two BCPs, Wang Kelian and Padang Besar (Table 39).

From Yala Province, the route to Perak is via Pengkalan Hulu (Perak) BCP. Pengkalan Hulu (Perak) is 866 km from Tanjung Bruas Port, via Penang Port (Butterworth), Kamunting, Lumut Port, Port Klang, Seremban, and Melaka City. The road networks from Wang Kelian and Pengkalan Hulu to Tanjung Bruas Port are well-connected with federal and state roads as well as expressways. The E1 and E2 serve as the transport backbone for connectivity between the nodes along the EC2.

Table 39: Economic Corridor 2: Wang Kelian and Pengkalan Hulu–Tanjung Bruas Port Route

Start Point	End point	Route	Distance (km)	Traffic Lanes	Road Class
Wang Kelian, Perlis (Main route from Satun)	Chuping, Perlis	R15, R123, 7, R116, R129, R122	38	2	Federal and state road
Chuping, Perlis	Kuala Perlis Jetty, Perlis	194	37	2	Federal and state road
Kuala Perlis Jetty, Perlis	Kuah Jetty, Langkawi, Kedah	Ferry Link	33 (18 nm)	Ferry links	–
Kuala Perlis Jetty, Perlis	Penang Port, Butterworth	7, E1/AH2	143	2–4	Federal road and expressway
Pengkalan Hulu, Perak (alternative route from Yala)	Penang Port, Butterworth	77, 76, 67, 4, E15	97	2–4	Federal road and expressway
Penang Port, Butterworth, Penang	Batu Kawan, Penang	E17, E1/AH2, E28	32	4	Expressway
Batu Kawan, Penang	Kamunting, Perak	E28, E1/AH2, A2	64	2–4	Federal road and expressway
Kamunting, Perak	Lumut Port, Perak	A2, E1/AH2,	159	2–4	State and expressway
Lumut Port, Perak	Port Klang, Selangor	5, 109, E1/AH2, 2	250	2–4	Federal road and expressway
Port Klang, Selangor	Seremban (NS)	181, E5, E37, E2/AH2	95	2–4	Federal road and expressway
Seremban (NS)	Port Dickson (NS)	E2/AH2, E29, 5	32	2–4	Federal road and expressway
Port Dickson (NS)	Melaka City, Melaka	E29/E2/AH2	109	4	Expressway
Melaka City, Melaka	Tanjung Bruas Port, Melaka	195, 5	13	2	Federal road
Tanjung Bruas Port, Melaka	Port of Bandar Sri Junjungan, Dumai, Riau, Sumatera	Ferry roll on, roll off	177 (96 nm)	Shipping route	–

– = not applicable, km = kilometer, nm = nautical miles, NS= Negeri Sembilan.
Source: Compiled by author.

The West Coast Expressway (WCE) is a 233 km highway connecting Banting in Selangor with Taiping, Perak. The WEC's construction began in 2014 and is expected to be completed by 2024. Upon completion, it is projected to enhance the accessibility and connectivity of the areas along the alignment. The WCE will potentially open up the west coast corridor as the travel time to the coastal areas will be reduced, thus spurring the growth of development in these areas. WCE also facilitates access to Lumut Port via an interchange node in Lekir (Perak).

Rail Connectivity

The KTMB's North, Central, and South Lines serve as the transport backbone for the EC2 by providing passenger and cargo services linking Padang Besar (Perlis) with Butterworth, Kuala Lumpur, Port Klang, and to Tampin/Pulau Sebang (Melaka). The distance between Padang Besar Railway Station and Tampin Railway Station is 724 km (Table 40).

Table 40: Economic Corridor 2: Butterworth (Penang)**–Pulau Sebang and Tampin** (Melaka)

Region/State	Start Point	to	End Point	km	Inland Port
North Line					
Perlis/Penang/Perak	Padang Besar	→	Butterworth	157	**Padang Besar Container Terminal**: Facilitates cross-border container cargo between Malaysia and Thailand
	Butterworth	→	Ipoh Station	181	**Ipoh Cargo Terminal**: Facilitates import–export for Kinta Valley businesses, distribute imports from Port Klang, Penang Port, and Johor Port
Central Line					
Selangor/ Kuala Lumpur/ Port Klang	Ipoh Station	→	Kuala Lumpur	207	**Port Klang**: Major trade gateway to international market
	Kuala Lumpur	→	Port Klang	43	
South Line					
Negeri Sembilan/ Melaka	Port Klang	→	Tampin/Pulau Sebang	136	**Nilai Inland Port**: Provides road and/or rail links and logistics services to industries in Central Region
			Total (km)	**724**	

km = kilometer.
Source: Compiled by author from KTMB's various publication sources. http://www.ktmb.com.my/index.html.

Maritime links. All seaports located along the EC2 have trade links with ports in Sumatera. For Thailand, only Penang Port and Port Klang have trading links via rail land bridge with Bangkok Port and Laem Chabang Port that traverse Padang Besar Railway Station. Major ports like Port Klang and Penang Port have wider trading relations with ports located in Sumatera as compared with secondary ports like Lumut Port, Port of Port Dickson, and Tanjung Bruas Port. The secondary ports in Sumatera utilize the services of Port Klang and Penang Port for the transshipment of goods to other international markets. For secondary ports in the EC2, a large part of their trading relations with the ports in Sumatera focuses on coal commodities. Coal is primarily used as fuel to generate electrical power in Malaysia.

Penang Port, Penang. The Penang Port, which is a deep-water seaport, consists of seven terminals along the Penang Strait—six of them in mainland Seberang Perai, particularly the towns of Butterworth and Perai, and one in George Town, on Penang Island, as the Swettenham Pier Cruise Terminal. Within Penang Port, the NBCT is the main terminal for container handling and has the capacity to handle 2 million TEUs per year. The Swettenham Cruise Terminal receives some of the world's largest cruise vessels carrying over 2,000 passengers. The Cruise Terminal is the second most important port-of-call in the country.[26]

---

[26]   The information about Penang Port was compiled from Penang Port Commission found at https://penangport.gov.my/en/port-installation and World Port Source found at http://www.worldportsource.com/ports/commerce/MYS_Port_Klang_273.php.

Penang Port, which is the second-largest port in Malaysia, has trade links with ports in Sumatera, in the provinces of Aceh, North Sumatera, Riau, and Bangka Belitung. Its shipping links are concentrated in the ports in Aceh Province. Penang Port's maritime activity is to export and import various types of cargo and containers to/from the port in Sumatera. The closest port to Penang Port is Belawan Port (Medan, North Sumatera) and the farthest is the Pangkal Balam Port (Bangka) in Bangka Belitung province (Table 41).

Table 41: Economic Corridor 2: Connectivity of Malaysian Ports with Ports in Sumatera and Thailand

Ports in EC2	Links to Ports in Sumatera and Thailand	Type of Marine Activities
Penang Port, Penang	Aceh: Banda Aceh Port (Port Malahayati), Kuala Idi, Kuala Langsa, Lhokseumawe, Sabang	Cargo and container
	North Sumatera: Belawan; Pangkalan Dodek; Tanjung Balai	
	Riau: Dumai; Perawang	
	Bangka Belitung: Pangkal Balam	
	Thailand: Laem Chabang Port Bangkok *Note: Land bridge: Butterworth to Bangkok*	Cargo and container (Laem Chabang Port however it is not under the IMT-GT Economic Corridor)
Port Klang, Selangor	North Sumatera: Belawan, Tanjung Balai	
	Riau: Buatan, Dumai, Pekanbaru, Perawang	
	West Sumatera: Teluk Bayur	Cargo and container
	Jambi: Jambi	
	South Sumatera: Palembang	
	Lampung: Panjang	
	Thailand: Bangkok Port, Laem Chabang Port *Note: Land bridge: Port Klang to Bangkok*	Cargo and container (both ports however are not under the IMT-GT Economic Corridor)
Lumut Port, Perak	Riau: Pelintung	
	Riau Islands: Batu Ampar (Batam)	
	Jambi: Jambi, Kuala Tunggal	Barge (coal)
	Bengkulu: Bengkulu	
	South Sumatera: Muara Lematang, Palembang	
Port of Port Dickson, Negeri Sembilan	Riau: Dumai	Passenger ferry
	South Sumatera: Tarahan	Barge (coal)
Tanjung Bruas Port, Melaka	Riau: Dumai	Ro-Ro cargo ferry
	South Sumatera: Palembang	Barge (coal)
	Aceh: Lhokseumawe	Barge (ammonia)

IMT-GT = Indonesia-Malaysia-Thailand Growth Triangle; Ro-Ro = roll on, roll off.
Source: Compiled by author from respective Port Authority.

Port Klang, Selangor. Since it commenced in 1901, Port Klang, which is a deep-water port, has been Malaysia's premier port. With links to over 500 ports worldwide, Port Klang is the 12th busiest container port in the world. In 1993, the government selected Port Klang to be the National Load Center and a regional hub. Port Klang, Malaysia's largest port, has trading links with ports in Sumatera. Its trading is concentrated in the Jambi, Lampung, North Sumatera, Riau, South Sumatera, and West Sumatera regions.[27]

Port Klang consists of Westports Terminal, Northport Terminal, and Port Klang Free Zone (PKFZ):

- **Northport Terminal**. The terminal can be considered the largest port in Port Klang and the largest container port serving Malaysia. Most of Malaysia's imports and exports are handled through Northport. It also serves the domestic and coastal trade routes, linking Port Klang to ports in Sabah, Sarawak, and Brunei Darussalam as well as short-sea port destinations in Indonesia, Thailand, and Viet Nam. Northport is focused on intra-Asian trade.

- **Westports Terminal**. Westports is a multi-cargo terminal and handles all types of cargoes in containers, breakbulk, dry bulk, liquid bulk, vehicles (Ro-Ro) and other conventional cargoes. The terminal handles international transit cargo at Port Klang. It is the leading mega transshipment hub in Malaysia for the main shipping lines. The terminal also serves as the main gateway for manufacturers located in the central region of the Peninsular Malaysia.[28]

- **Port Klang Free Commercial Zone**. This commercial zone was established to promote entreport trade and manufacturing industries involved in producing goods primarily for export. It also offers consolidated facilities where factories and logistics firms can be located in the same zone, so as to allow for easier coordination and smoother supply chain management.[29]

Port Klang has two terminals dedicated to serving passengers. The Boustead Cruise Centre (BCC) serves cruise vessels, while Asa Niaga Harbor City Terminal is dedicated to ferries.

- BCC is a dedicated cruise terminal in Port Klang. It is the cruise terminal for Kuala Lumpur, one of the world's most visited cities. Many of the world's leading cruise lines like Royal Caribbean, Cunard, Princess Cruises, and Star Cruises visit the Port Klang Cruise Centre each year. The terminal has all the modern conveniences and services today's cruise passengers expect.

- Asa Niaga Harbor City Terminal is a regional passenger ferry terminal that serves high-speed passenger ferries plying between Port Klang and the ports of Dumai and Tanjung Balai in Sumatera, Indonesia.

Port Klang rail and intermodal connections. Port Klang can be accessed by federal and state roads as well as the expressway along the EC2. The KTMB, in collaboration with SRT, provides land bridge services between Port Klang and Hat Yai (Songkhla), Map Ta Phut (Bangkok), and Bangsue (Bangkok). The land bridge from Port Klang, which traverses Padang Besar BCP to Thailand will be part of the Singapore–Kunming Rail Link (SKRL). The advantages of the land bridge from Port Klang to Bangkok include shorter travel time; 60 hours by land bridge compared to 5–7 days by sea (Port Klang to Bangkok), or 3–4 days (Port Klang to Bangkok) by truck.[30]

---

27   The information about Port Klang was compiled from Port Klang Authority found at https://www.pka.gov.my/index.php/en/ and World Port Source found at http://www.worldportsource.com.

28   The information about Westports Terminal was compiled from Westports Malaysia found at https://www.westportsholdings.com/ and World Port Source found at http://www.worldportsource.com/.

29   The information about Port Klang Free Commercial Zone was compiled from Port Klang Free Zone Malaysia found at https://www.pkfz.com/.

30   The information about land bridge from Port Klang to Thailand was abridge from KTMB found at http://www.ktmb.com.my/kargo.html.

Lumut Port, Perak. Lumut Port, which is located in Perak, is strategically located off the Strait of Malacca. The port is positioned for transshipments of dry and liquid bulk cargo moving within Southeast Asia and between the Indian subcontinent, the Middle East, the People's Republic of China (PRC), Australia, and the Atlantic Basin. Lumut Port comprises Lumut Maritime Terminal, Lekir Bulk Terminal, and Lumut Port Industrial Park:[31]

- The Lumut Maritime Terminal is designed to handle dry bulk, liquid bulk, break bulk, and conventional cargo. Pipelines connect the Lumut Port Maritime Terminal to the Lumut Port Industrial Park for the import and export of liquid bulk cargoes.

- The Lumut Port Lekir Bulk Terminal is a deep-water seaport and is currently Southeast Asia's largest dry bulk unloading facility. The terminal is capable of berthing an entire range of vessels in Panamax and Capemax ships. It also handles coal for Sultan Azlan Shah Power Plant Station in Seri Manjung.

- Lumut Port Industrial Park is adjacent to Lumut Port and covers an area of 358 hectares suitable for all types of industry. With ample utilities, the Lumut Port Industrial Park is designed for semiconductor, medium, and heavy industry. Industries currently operating in the Lumut Port Industrial Park include processors for minerals, non-minerals, feed meal, and vegetable oils as well as metal work, metal fabrication, biodiesel, grain import and reexport preparation, and shipbuilding.

Lumut Port, which is a secondary port, carries out trading activities with ports in Sumatera, mainly in Bengkulu, Jambi, Riau, Riau Islands, and South Sumatera. Unlike the maritime activities in Penang Port and Port Klang, Lumut Port employs barges to transport dry bulk loads, specifically coal, from ports in Sumatera for local industrial use in Perak. The port is also a port-of-call for cruise liners passing through the Strait of Malacca. A frequently visited ship is the Seabourn Sojourn.[32]

Lumut Port can only be accessed by federal and state roads as well as the expressway along the EC2. However, there is no railway connectivity between Lumut Port and the closest train station is the Ipoh Railway Station.

Port of Port Dickson, Negeri Sembilan. The Port of Port Dickson is an oil terminal and a minor port for general cargo. Port Dickson has two refineries and a coal-fired power plant, which make significant contributions to the local economy. The industry has generated employment and business opportunities for locals. Hengyuan Refining Company (HRC) Berhad (formerly known as Shell Refining Company) has been operating since 1962, while Petron (formerly ExxonMobil Malaysia) operates another refinery that began operations in 1963. Meanwhile, the coal power plant is owned and operated by Jimah East Power Sdn Bhd (Jimah), which is a subsidiary of Tenaga Nasional Berhad. The plant was commissioned in 2019. Accordingly, the Port of Port Dickson is an important maritime gateway port for HRC, Petron, and Jimah.[33]

The Port of Port Dickson has maritime connectivity with the Port of Tarahan (Lampung, South Sumatera) through the coal trade imported by the Jimah company for power generation, while the connectivity with Dumai is through the passenger ferry link. Port Dickson is the main entry point for Dumai residents to Malaysia.

---

[31] The information on Lumut Port was compiled from Lumut Port found at https://www.lumutport.com/ and World Port Source found at http://www.worldportsource.com.

[32] The information about Seabourn Sojourn's route was abridged from Cruise Watch found at https://www.cruisewatch.com/cruise-ports/lumut/1356.

[33] The information about Port of Port Dickson was compiled from Sea Seek found at https://www.sea-seek.com/en/Port-Dickson-Harbour-Selangor-Malaysia-.

The federal and state governments also plan to upgrade the Port of Port Dickson jetty into a port-of-call for cruise liners passing through the Strait of Malacca. This will promote the tourism industry in Negeri Sembilan. Port Dickson is a tourist destination for local and international tourists.[34]

Tanjung Bruas Port, Melaka. Tanjung Bruas Port (or Port of Melaka), which commenced in the early 1980s, is strategically located along one of the world's busiest trade routes at the center and narrowest point of the Strait of Malacca. Situated within a large developed hinterland drawn from Melaka, Negeri Sembilan, and Northern Johor, the port is surrounded by more than 500 companies operating in Melaka's industrial parks. This enables the port to be developed as a major gateway to handle both containers and conventional cargoes to serve the growing industries in Melaka.[35]

The strategic location of the port also provides an opportunity to tap into marine services such as ship husbandry, ship supplies, bunkering services, and ship-to-ship transfers. The port provides port facilities and services to the local business communities and handles the exportation of hinterland goods as well as the importation of raw materials.

As of 2021, there was no trade link between Tanjung Bruas Port and Dumai. The Melaka–Dumai roll on, roll off (Ro-Ro) Ferry Project, which is in an advanced stage of preparation, is envisaged to establish this trade link. Tanjung Bruas has maritime trade links with other ports in Palembang (South Sumatera) and Lhokseumawe (Aceh). Commodities imported from Palembang are gypsum and coal; from Aceh, ammonia gas. Tanjung Bruas Port also has trade links with Bangkok Port (Thailand); Kaohsiung (Taipei,China); Jurong (Singapore); Saiki (Japan); and Humen (the PRC).[36]

Tanjung Bruas Port can be easily accessed via federal and state roads as well as the expressway within the EC2. However, there is no railway connectivity between the port and the closest railway station, which is the Pulau Sebang or Tampin Railway Station.

Air Links

Air connectivity with Sumatera and Thailand is through airports in Penang, Selangor, and Melaka. Air Asia services various destinations in Sumatera and Southern Thailand compared to other local carriers. Flights departing from Kuala Lumpur International Airport (KLIA) are available for Banda Aceh, Medan, Padang, Palembang, and Pekanbaru. Concerning links with Thailand, Air Asia provides flights to Hat Yai, Krabi, Phuket, and Surat Thani. Within the EC2, flight connectivity is adequate between the major cities in the EC2. Low-cost carriers support tourism activities within the EC2 and IMT-GT provinces (Table 42).

---

[34]   *Malay Mail*. 2019. Putrajaya mulls expanding Port Dickson jetty to lure tourists. 23 May. Retrieved from https://www.malaymail.com/news/malaysia/2019/05/23/putrajaya-mulls-expanding-port-dickson-jetty-to-lure-tourists-video/1755673.

[35]   The information about Tanjung Bruas Port was abridged from Malaysia Mining Corporation (MMC) found at https://www.mmc.com.my/tbp.html.

[36]   The information on Tanjung Bruas Port's links was compiled from consultation with Mohammad Amyrul, Business Development and Commercial Department, Tanjung Bruas Port Authority on 21 August 2020.

Table 42: Economic Corridor 2: Flight Routes to Sumatera, Thailand, and Singapore

Airports	Airlines	IMT-GT Destinations	Within EC2 Destinations
Penang International Airport, Bayan Lepas, Penang (with EC1)	Air Asia, Sriwijaya Air, Lion Air Firefly, Malindo Air MAS, Firefly	Medan Banda Aceh Phuket	• Air Asia: Kuala Lumpur, Langkawi, Melaka • MAS: Kuala Lumpur • Firefly: Subang, Langkawi • Malindo Air: Kuala Lumpur, Subang, Melaka
Langkawi International Airport, Langkawi, Kedah	Air Asia, MAS, Firefly, Malindo Air	No air links with Sumatera and Thailand	• Air Asia: Kuala Lumpur, Penang • MAS: Kuala Lumpur • Firefly: Subang, Penang • Malindo Air: Kuala Lumpur, Subang
Sultan Abdul Halim Airport, Alor Setar, Kedah	Air Asia, MAS	No air links with Sumatera and Thailand	• Air Asia: Kuala Lumpur, Johor Bahru • MAS: Kuala Lumpur • Firefly: Subang
Sultan Azlan Shah Airport, Ipoh, Perak	Air Asia, Malindo Air	No links with Sumatera and Thailand	• No air links with EC2 airports
Kuala Lumpur International Airport 1 and 2, Selangor	Air Asia (KLIA2) MAS (KLIA1), Air Asia (KLIA2) Air Asia (KLIA2), MAS (KLIA1), Citilink* (KLIA2) Air Asia (KLIA2) Air Asia (KLIA2), MAS (KLIA1), Malindo (KLIA1) Bangkok Airways* (KLIA1)	Banda Aceh, Padang, Palembang Medan Pekanbaru Hat Yai, Krabi, Surat Thani Phuket Koh Samui	 • Air Asia and MAS: Penang, Alor Setar, Langkawi • Malindo Air: Penang, Langkawi
Subang Airport, Subang, Selangor	Malindo Air	Pekanbaru, Batam	• Firefly and Malindo Air: Penang, Alor Setar, Langkawi
Melaka International Airport, Batu Berendam, Melaka	Malindo Air	Pekanbaru	• Air Asia and Malindo Air: Penang

* International airlines.
EC=economic corridor, IMT-GT = Indonesia–Malaysia–Thailand Growth Triangle, KLIA = Kuala Lumpur International Airport, MAS = Malaysian Airlines.
Source: Compiled by author from the websites of relevant domestic and international airlines.

Trade

Strong bilateral trade exists between Malaysia and Indonesia, and Malaysia and Thailand (Tables 17 and 18 of EC1's trade section). Trade between the EC2 states and Sumatera is via existing maritime links. The seaports along the EC2—namely Port Klang, Penang Port, Lumut Port, Port of Port Dickson, and Tanjung Bruas Port—are the trade gateways for manufacturers and traders to export their products to Sumatera.

Meanwhile, trade with Southern Thailand is supported by the road and rail connectivity network through the BCPs along the northern states of Malaysia–Southern Thailand border. These BCPs are located in Wang Kelian, Padang Besar, Bukit Kayu Hitam, Durian Burung, and Pengkalan Hulu, and serve as trade gateways for manufacturers and traders in the EC2 to market their products to Southern Thailand.

For 2015–2018, border trade between northern states of Malaysia and Southern Thailand via the Wang Kelian BCP and Pengkalan Hulu was marginal, each accounting for 1% of all BCP's total trade. This demonstrates that the main cross-border trade routes between the Peninsular Malaysia and Southern Thailand are via the Padang Besar and Bukit Kayu Hitam BCPs (Table 43).

Table 43: Border Trade at Wang Kelian (Perlis) and Pengkalan Hulu (Perak) with Thailand, 2015–2018
($ million)

BCP/CIQ	2015	2016	2017	2018	Average (2015–2018)	Average Share to All Malaysia–Thai BCPs Trade (2015–2018), %	CAGR[a] (2015–2018), %, (based in RM)
Perlis–Total[b] Trade	1,400	1,445	1,549	1,507	1,475	23	3.6
Export	797	850	816	790	813	28	0.8
Import	603	594	733	716	662	18	7.1
Wang Kelian Total Trade	55	123	127	82	97	1	15.5
Export	55	122	127	82	97	3	15.6
Import	0.21	0.28	0.16	0.22	0.22	0	3.0
Perak Pengkalan Hulu (Total Trade)	79	80	100	86	86	1	4.3
Export	5	6	7	7	6	0.2	13.8
Import	73	74	94	79	80	2.2	3.5
All Malaysia–Thai BCPs–Total Trade	6,515	6,420	6,574	6,620	6,532	–	1.6
Export	2,792	2,848	2,904	2,985	2,882	–	3.4
Import	3,723	3,572	3,670	3,634	3,650	–	0.3

– = not applicable; BCP = border crossing point; CAGR = compound annual growth rate; CIQ = customs, immigration, and quarantine.
[a] The CAGR was calculated using the local currency (Malaysian ringgit) to avoid erratic fluctuations in foreign exchange rates
[b] Including trade at Padang Besar BCP.
Source: Royal Malaysian Customs Department. 2019. Putrajaya: RMCD.

The main export products to Southern Thailand via Wang Kelian BCP were vegetable products, while the main imports were textiles, and machinery and electrical products. As for Pengkalan Hulu BCP, the main export products were textile and chemicals products, while the main imports were rubber and plastics products (Table 44).

Table 44: Economic Corridor 2: Top Five Products Traded at Wang Kelian (Perlis) and Pengkalan Hulu (Perak) with Thailand, 2018

Rank	Product Description	Exports ($ million)	Share (%)	Rank	Product Description	Imports ($ million)	Share (%)
Wang Kelian							
1	Vegetable products	53	65	1	Textiles	46	21
2	Foodstuffs	12	15	2	Machinery and electrical	37	17
3	Transportation	10	12	3	Animal and animal products	15	7
4	Machinery and electrical	2	2	4	Metals	10	5
5	Chemicals and allied industries	1	2	5	Foodstuffs	4	2
	Others	4	4		Others	108	49
	TOTAL	**82**	**100**		**TOTAL**	**220**	**100**
Pengkalan Hulu							
1	Textiles	2	29	1	Rubber and plastics	68	87
2	Chemicals and allied industries	1	19	2	Vegetable products	5	6
3	Vegetable products	1	17	3	Foodstuffs	3	4
4	Foodstuffs	0.9	12	4	Wood and wood products	1	2
5	Rubbers and plastics	0.7	9	5	Textiles	0.7	1
	Others	1	14		Others	0.8	1
	TOTAL	**7**	**100**		**Total**	**79**	**100**

Note: Totals may not sum precisely because of rounding.
Source: Royal Malaysian Customs Department. 2019. Putrajaya: RMCD.

Tourism

Every state in the EC2 have their own respective tourism policy to advance the tourism industry and thus generate state economic growth. However, for the states under the NCER—Kedah, Penang, Perak, and Perlis—the direction of the state tourism industry is outlined in the NCER Blueprint 2.0 in conjunction with the state government. Under the NCER Blueprint 2.0, the tourism industries that are being given emphasis are the archaeotourism, ecotourism, heritage tourism, and geotourism sectors. These four tourism sectors are also the focus of the state governments of Melaka, Negeri Sembilan, and Selangor. This focus on these tourism sectors is in line with the National Ecotourism Plan 2016–2025 and the National Tourism Policy 2020–2030. Table 45 shows examples of regional ecotourism clusters as established under the National Ecotourism Plan 2016–2025. The regional cluster concept for the sectors of archaeotourism, heritage tourism, and geotourism has also been designed under Plan Malaysia's State Structure Plan (SSP) for states covered by the EC2.[37]

---

[37] For details on tourism spatial development planning, refer to SSP Perlis 3030, SSP Kedah 2035, SSP Penang 2030, SSP Perak 2040, SSP Selangor 2035, SSP Negeri Sembilan 2045, and SSP Melaka2035.

Table 45: Economic Corridor 2: Regional Ecotourism

State	Regional Ecotourism Cluster
Perlis	Kangar–Timah–Tasoh–Sungai Batu Pahat–Cuping Hill–Perlis State Park
Kedah	Jitra–Alor Setar–Gunung Jerai
	Sungai Petani–Ulu Muda
	Langkawi Geoparks–Pulau Payar
Penang	Penang National Park–George Town–Pulau Jerejak
	Sedim–Seberang Perai
Perak	Taiping–Batu Kurau–Bukit Merah
	Ulu Geroh–Gua Tempurung–Gopeng–Batu Gajah
	Royal Belum–Lenggong–Kuala Kangsar
	Pulau Sembilan–Teluk Senangin–Segari Melintang
Selangor	Selangor State Heritage Park
	Sepang–Putrajaya–Shah Alam
	Kuala Selangor–Bukit Malawati–Sabak Bernam
Melaka	Melaka Urban Ecotourism Cluster (Melaka Historical City–Ayer Keroh)
	Tanjung Keling–Pengkalan Balak–Sungai Linggi–Tanjung Tuan
	Jasin–Selandar–Tebong–Asahan
Negeri Sembilan	Rantau–Port Dickson–Sungai Menyala–Sungai Timun
	Jelebu Ecotourism Valley (Jelebu–Kenaboi–Seremban)
	Seremban–Kuala Pilah–Jempol
	Rembau–Tampin

Source: Ministry of Tourism and Culture Malaysia. 2016. *National Ecotourism Plan 2016–2025: Executive Summary*. Putrajaya: MOTAC Malaysia.

Melaka City (Melaka) and George Town (Penang) in 2008, and Lenggong Valley (Perak) in 2012, have been designated as a UNESCO World Heritage sites. Malaysia has proposed other locations to UNESCO for consideration as World Heritage Sites in Selangor, namely FRIM Selangor Forest Park, Gombak Selangor Quartz Ridge, and Sungai Buloh Leprosarium. The Royal Belum State Park in Perak has also been proposed as a World Heritage Site. This will further promote the heritage tourism industry in Selangor and Perak.[38]

Concerning niche tourism, Pulau Pangkor, which is in proximity to Lumut, has been given duty-free island status on 1 January 2020 by the federal government to enhance the shopping tourism sector in Perak.[39] There are also suggestions by the Melaka state government to establish Pulau Besar as a duty-free island to further enhance its tourism industry.[40] Besides shopping tourism, the state of Penang and Melaka are popular destinations for medical tourists, particularly those from Indonesia, seeking better medical care.

Cross-border tourism is promoted by the state governments bordering the provinces of Southern Thailand. In the NCER, border tourism is promoted under the Perlis–Kedah–Thailand Strategic Border Zone and the Baling–Pengkalan Hulu–Betong Border Zone, which give focus on the shopping tourism sector at BCPs like

---

38   The information on Malaysia's UNESCO Heritage sites was compiled from UNESCO. World Heritage Convention found at https://whc.unesco.org/en/statesparties/my.

39   Bernama. 2020. Duty-Free Status Will Revive Pangkor Tourism. *New Straits Times*. 2 January. https://www.nst.com.my/news/nation/2020/01/552734/duty-free-status-will-revive-pangkor-tourism.

40   *The Star*. 2018. Big Plans for Pulau Besar. 6 August. https://www.thestar.com.my/metro/metro-news/2018/08/06/big-plans-for-pulau-besar-cm-melaka-will-develop-and-rebrand-island-as-a-tourist-resort-and-free-tra/.

Padang Besar-Padang Besa, Wang Kelian–Wang Prachan, Bukit Kayu Hitam–Danok, Durian Burung–Ban Prakop, and Pengkalan Hulu–Betong.

Cross-border shopping tourism with Sumatera is generated through the passenger ferry links between Dumai and Tanjung Balai with Port Klang (Asa Niaga Harbour City), and Dumai with Port of Port Dickson and the Melaka International Ferry Terminal (MIFT). The ferry links between Tammalang Pier or Ko Lipe and Kuah Jetty (Langkawi) have promoted shopping tourism in Langkawi with the influx of tourists from Satun and Phuket provinces.

For the states that have cruise ports like Swettenham Pier Cruise Terminal, Star Cruise Jetty Langkawi, Lumut Port, BCC, and MIFT, the respective state governments have given attention to the cruise tourism sector by upgrading their port facilities to attract cruise liners passing through the Strait of Malacca and the Andaman Sea (Table 46).

Table 46: Malaysia: Ship Calls and Cruise Passenger Arrivals in Selected Ports, 2016–2018

Port-of-Call	EC2 States	Passengers (number)				Ship Calls (number)			
		2016	2017	2018	Average (2016–2018)	2016	2017	2018	Average (2016–2018)
Boustead Cruise Centre, Port Klang	Selangor	251,499	305,420	364,511	307,143	142	165	249	185
Swettenham Pier Cruise, Penang Port	Penang	213,566	426,140	341,028	326,911	136	267	185	196
Star Cruise Jetty	Langkawi, Kedah	126,786	110,946	131,160	122,964	77	86	91	85
Melaka International Ferry Terminal	Melaka	56,476	50,680	13,455	40,204	45	49	43	46
Lumut Port	Perak	349	387	190	309	1	2	1	1
TOTAL		**648,676**	**893,573**	**850,344**	**797,531**	**401**	**569**	**569**	**513**

EC = economic corridor.
Source: Ministry of Tourism, Arts and Culture. 2020. Putrajaya: MOTAC Malaysia.

The intensity of the tourism industry can be highlighted by the number of tourist arrivals as hotel guests in each of the states that they visit. Penang hosted the highest number of hotel guests for 2014–2018, averaging 7 million guests per annum, half of which were international tourists. Perlis received the most domestic hotel guests. Among the factors that influence the pattern of hotel guests are tourists' income, the global and local economic situations, transport connectivity, and the attractiveness of tourism products (Table 47).[41]

---

[41]   There is no information published related to international tourists' country of origin that stayed in hotels by state.

Table 47: Economic Corridor 2: Hotel Guests by State, 2014 and 2018
(million)

EC2 States	2014	2018	Average (2014–2018)	Average Share to State (2014–2018), %	CAGR (2014–2018), %
Pulau Pinang	6.8	6.7	6.5	100	(0.7)
Foreign	3.2	3.0	3.0	46	(1.7)
Domestic	3.6	3.6	3.5	54	0.2
Melaka	4.4	4.9	4.7	100	2.6
Foreign	1.8	1.6	1.7	37	(3.0)
Domestic	2.7	3.4	2.9	63	5.9
Selangor	4.1	5.6	4.5	100	8.0
Foreign	1.7	2.0	1.7	39	4.7
Domestic	2.5	3.6	2.7	61	10.1
Kedah	3.3	4.3	3.8	100	6.5
Foreign	1.2	1.6	1.3	36	6.8
Domestic	2.1	2.7	2.4	64	6.4
Negeri Sembilan	2.2	2.5	2.4	100	2.3
Foreign	0.5	0.5	0.5	20	(4.2)
Domestic	1.7	2.0	1.9	80	4.2
Perak	2.5	2.9	2.7	100	3.5
Foreign	0.3	0.3	0.3	10	3.6
Domestic	2.3	2.6	2.4	90	3.5
Perlis	0.2	0.2	0.2	100	1.1
Foreign	0.01	0.01	0.01	3	4.7
Domestic	0.2	0.2	0.2	97	1.0
Malaysia	71.7	82.4	75.0	100	3.6
Foreign	26.3	30.0	27.2	36	3.4
Domestic	45.4	52.4	47.9	64	3.7

CAGR = compound annual growth rate, EC = economic corridor.
Source: My Tourism Data Portal. http://mytourismdata.tourism.gov.my/ (accessed 1 June 2021).

Industrial Activities

Industrial parks. Industrial parks in each state, for the large part, has been developed by the respective state economic development corporations. The industrial parks and SEZs for Perlis, Kedah, and Penang has been discussed in the section titled Economic Corridor 1: Industrial Activities and SEZs. Table 48 lists the industrial parks in those states.

As of the end of 2018, the states of Melaka and Selangor each had 21 industrial parks despite the GDP of Melaka being relatively smaller than Selangor. Negeri Sembilan has 14 industrial parks. The industrial parks developed by the state governments aim to attract foreign and domestic investments to their respective states. Investing in the state economy, especially in the export-oriented manufacturing sector, could create a spillover effect on the state's economy through new business and job opportunities.

Table 48: Economic Corridor 2: Industrial Parks by State
(as of end December 2018)

Selangor	Negeri Sembilan	Melaka
1. Bandar Sultan Sulaiman Industrial Park	1. Arab Malaysia Industrial Estate	1. Alor Gajah Industrial Estate
2. Banting Industrial Park	2. Chembong Industrial Park	2. Ayer Keroh Business Industrial Park
3. Bukit Changgang Industrial Park	3. College Heights industrial Park	3. Ayer Keroh Industrial Estates
4. Bukit Raja Industrial Park	4. Malaysia Vision Valley	4. Bukit Rambai Industrial Park
5. Eco Business Park V, Bandar Puncak Alam	5. Nilai Industrial Park	5. Cheng Technology Park
6. Elmina Industrial Park, Shah Alam	6. Nilai Utama Industrial park	6. Composite Technology City
7. Kapar Bestari Industrial Park	7. Oakland Industrial Park	7. Elkay Industrial Park
8. Kota Seri Langat Industrial Park	8. Senawang Industrial Estate	8. HICOM Pegoh Industrial Park
9. Lagong Industrial Park	9. Senawang Industrial park	9. Jasin Industrial Park
10. Mahkota Industrial Park, Banting	10. Sendayan TechValley	10. Krubong Industrial Park
11. Pulau Indah Industrial Park	11. Sungai Gadut Industrial Park	11. Masjid Tanah Industrial Estate
12. Selangor Bio Bay	12. Techpark @ Enstek	12. Melaka World Solar Valley
13. Selangor Vision City	13. Tuanku Jaafar Industrial Park	13. Merlimau Industrial Estate
14. Serena Industrial Park		14. Rembia Industrial Estate
15. Subang Aerotech Park	**Specialized Park**	15. Smart Industrial Center, Bukit Rambai
16. Tanjung Industrial Park	14. Pedas Halal Park	16. Taman Tasik Utama Industrial Park
17. Technology Park Malaysia		17. Tangga Batu Industrial Estate
18. UMW High Value Manufacturing Park		18. Telok Gong Industrial Estate
19. Zurah Industrial Park		19. Telok Mas Industrial Estate
Special Economic Zone		**Special Economic Zone**
20. Port Klang Free Zone		20. Batu Berendam Free Trade Zone
Specialized Park		**Specialized Park**
21. Selangor Halal Hub, Pulau Indah		21. Melaka Halal Hub, Serkam

Source: Malaysian Investment Development Authority. 2018. Industrial Park in Malaysia. Kuala Lumpur: MIDA.

Industrial parks in EC2 have good connectivity with the seaports through a network of road and railway. The E1 and E2 highways and KTMB railway form the transport backbone along the west coast of the EC2. Port Klang and Penang Port, which are classified as major seaports, are the main trade gateways for EC2.

Manufacturers in the industrial parks have direct access to the markets in Southern Thailand through the road transport network. The E1 and E2 are joined with the AH2 via interchange node Bukit Kayu Hitam BCP. There is also the well-established rail link between the KTMB railway main line with SRT Southern Line, via Padang Besar BCP, which provides a land bridge from Port Klang to ports in Bangkok. This will significantly lower transportation costs to both traders and shippers.

Inland ports. Inland ports play a significant role in providing access for manufacturers and producers in the hinterland to seaports which act as gateways to the nation's trade. The existing inland ports within the EC2 are PBCT (Perlis), Ipoh Cargo Terminal (ICT) (Perak), and Nilai Inland Port (NIP) (Negeri Sembilan). Meanwhile, the newly recommended inland ports are the PIP (Perlis) and BKHIP (Kedah). Inland ports in Perlis and Kedah will facilitate cross-border container cargo movement between Malaysia and Thailand that is anticipated to increase in the near future.

The PBCT is a mid-range inland port for Penang Port and a long-distance inland port for Port Klang. This inland port facilitates cross-border container cargo between Malaysia and Thailand, which would then head for onward shipment via Penang Port (NBCT) (Table 49) (footnote 20).

Table 49: Economic Corridor 2: Features of Inland Port

Inland Ports	Functions	Connection to Seaport
Padang Besar Cargo Terminal	• Facilitates cross-border container cargo between Malaysia and Thailand • Focus mode rail transport	Penang Port and Port Klang
Ipoh Cargo Terminal	• Facilitates import-export for Kinta Valley businesses, distribute import from Port Klang • Focus mode rail and road	Penang Port, Port Klang and Tanjung Pelepas Port
Nilai Inland Port	• Provides road and/or rail links and logistics services to industries in the Central region	Port Klang and Tanjung Pelepas Port

Source: Adapted from Nizamuddin, Zainuddin, et al. 2019. Inland Port Logistical Issues in Northern Region of Peninsular Malaysia. *Journal of Humanities, Language, Culture and Business* (HLCB). 3(12).

The ICT, the second inland port in Malaysia, was established in 1989. It is a mid-range inland port for Penang and a long-distance inland port for Port Klang and Tanjung Pelepas Port. This inland port is connected with all Malaysian container seaports by means of road and rail links. While the NIP is considered as a short-range inland port for Port Klang, it offers a range of value-added services, facilities, and spaces to support the growing container volumes at Port Klang in the central region (Melaka and Negeri Sembilan) (footnote 20).

Land bridges. The KTMB, in collaboration with SRT, provides land bridge service from Port Klang (Selangor), via Padang Besar BCP, to Bangsue (Bangkok, Thailand). The land bridge service permits cross-border movement of containers between Peninsular Malaysia and Thailand by rail, specifically between Port Klang–Bangsue, Map Ta Phut, and Hat Yai. The KTMB-SRT rail track will be part of the SKRL.

Overall Assessment

There are regional disparities between the states in EC2 due to differences in economic fundamentals. The more-developed states are led by the manufacturing sector, especially the electrical and electronics industries, while the less-developed states rely on a combination of manufacturing and agriculture sectors. Under the State Development Blueprint and NCER Blueprint 2.0, several growth nodes have been identified to enhance the respective state economies and address the development gaps. Tourism has been made one of the economic drivers that can help boost the state's GDP.

The state and federal road networks, as well as the expressways, provide good road connectivity in EC2. There is also good connectivity between urban and hinterland areas, which can be reached via state and federal highways. The KTMB railway line and the E1 and E2 form the transportation backbone in the EC2.

Seaports, both the major and secondary ports, serve as the trade gateways for the EC2. However, only the secondary—namely Lumut Port, Port of Port Dickson, and Tanjung Bruas Port—do not have connectivity with the KTMB rail line. These ports can only be accessed via the road network. To achieve seamless connectivity, there have been suggestions to build railway spur lines from Bukit Kayu Hitam in Kedah to Arau in Perlis,[42] ICT to Lumut Port in Perak,[43] Seremban Railway Station to Port Dickson,[44] and Pulau Sebang or Tampin to Tanjung Bruas Port in Melaka.[45]

Industry players that operate in industrial parks can access land bridge services provided by the KTMB in cooperation from the SRT. The land bridge service permits cross-border movement of containers between Peninsular Malaysia and Thailand by railway. The land bridge services between the EC2 and Thailand are through the following routes: (i) Penang Port (NBCT): Hat Yai–Thunsong–Surat Thani; and (ii) Port Klang: Hat Yai–Maptaput–Bangsue.

The existing inland ports—Padang Besar Container Terminal (PBCT-Perlis), Ipoh Cargo Terminal (ICT-Perak), and Nilai Inland Port (NIP-Negeri Sembilan)—and the ones that have been proposed—PIP and BKHIP—will further increase the efficiency of container cargo movement and enhance the industry supply chain within the EC2.

Air connectivity is adequate between the major cities in EC2. Air connectivity with Sumatera and Thailand is through airports in Penang, Selangor, and Melaka. Air Asia services many destinations in Sumatera and Southern Thailand compared to other local carriers. Flights to Sumatera from KLIA are headed to Banda Aceh, Medan, Padang, Palembang, and Pekanbaru. Concerning links with Thailand, Air Asia provides flights to Hat Yai, Krabi, Phuket, and Surat Thani. Low-cost carriers support tourism activities within the EC2 and IMT-GT provinces.

Air connectivity in EC2 between Malaysia, Sumatera, and Thailand are adequate and has supported the tourism industry. The Yala International Airport in Betong will further promote regional cross-border connectivity between Yala and Perak.

In comparison with other BCPs, cross-border trade between the northern states of Malaysia and Southern Thailand is concentrated at Bukit Kayu Hitam and Padang Besar. However, growth nodes identified under the NCER Blueprint 2.0, such as the KRC, Perlis–Kedah–Thailand Strategic Border Zone, and Baling–Pengkalan Hulu–Betong Border Zones, will serve as a catalyst to improve trade activities in BCPs with low volumes of cross-border trade.

---

[42] R. Augustin. 2019. Kedah-Perlis Rail Link Better than ECRL to Boost Trade. *Free Malaysia Today.* 9 January. https://www.freemalaysiatoday.com/category/nation/2019/01/09/kedah-perlis-rail-link-better-than-ecrl-to-boost-trade-expert-says/.

[43] Komen and Pendapat. 2010. Railway Link to Lumut. *Perak Today.* 21 September. https://peraktoday.com.my/2010/09/railway-link-to-lumut/.

[44] *The Star.* 2016. Seremban-PD rail link to be revived. 24 November. https://www.thestar.com.my/news/nation/2016/11/24/serembanpd-rail-link-to-be-revived-massive-project-to-see-cooperation-between-govt-and-private-secto.

[45] Under Melaka's State Structure Plan 2015–2035 (Melaka 2035), a proposal was made to build a railway connecting Tanjung Bruas Port with the inland port to be developed in Taboh Naning (Alor Gajah, Melaka). The Taboh Naning Inland Port will be built by the state government in collaboration with the federal government. This inland port will be connected to Pulau Sebang or Tampin Railway Station. However, the proposal to build the Inland Port Taboh Naning, in Alor Gajah (Melaka) and the railway is still in the planning phase.

By enhancing transportation connectivity and establishing growth centers, both the State Development Blueprint and the NCER Blueprint 2.0 support the goal of the IMT-GT ECs. The blueprints concentrate on transportation infrastructure to improve connectivity between growth nodes and facilitate supply chain flows between primary, secondary, and tertiary industries in the EC2. The logistics services in the EC2 have been enhanced to improve connectivity between existing inland ports and major seaports. The proposed BKHIP and PIP, as well as the expansion of PBCT, are intended to meet the growing need for cargo movement between Malaysia and Thailand as a result of the expected increase in cargo movement between Malaysia and Thailand following the anticipated increase in cross-border trade in the near future.

Reconfiguration of EC2

Malaysia's strategy for EC2 aligns with the development strategy of the NCER to leverage good physical connectivity and regional trade networks with the development of core industry clusters for the region to achieve a world-class economic status by 2025. In reconfiguring EC2, Malaysia added new nodes at Chuping Valley, Kuala Perlis, Kamunting, Lumut, Batu Kawan, Kuah, Tanjung Bruas Port, Port Dickson, and Seremban. These nodes will widen the connectivity with existing nodes to achieve seamless connectivity and serve as growth nodes for the state's transition to a high-income economy and narrow regional disparities in the EC2 (Table 50).

In the case of Thailand, EC2 was extended northward to include Phangnga and Krabi to develop land and sea connectivity along the Andaman Sea coast for tourism and pave the way to connect EC2 with Ranong and Phuket in EC5. This is part of the SEC strategy to connect tourist destinations along the coasts of the Andaman Sea, both by land and by sea.

The reconfigured EC2 involving additional nodes in Malaysia, and additional provinces and nodes in Thailand will enhance the coastal corridor along the Strait of Malacca. The EC2 has been renamed the **Andaman–Strait of Malacca Economic Corridor** (Maps 8 and 9).

Table 50: Economic Corridor 2: Existing and Additional Provinces and Nodes, by Type

Province/State	Node	Type				
		CAP	COM	BCP	MGP	TOUR
MALAYSIA						
Perlis	Wang Kelian			✓		✓
	Padang Besar			✓		✓
	Chuping Valley*		✓			
	Kuala Perlis*		✓			
Perak	Pengkalan Hulu			✓		✓
	Kamunting*		✓			
	Lumut*		✓			
Penang	Penang Port • Butterworth • George Town				✓	✓
	Batu Kawan*		✓			
Selangor	Port Klang				✓	✓
Kedah	Kuah*				✓	✓
	Langkawi					✓
Melaka	Melaka City	✓				✓
	Tanjung Bruas Port (Port of Melaka)*				✓	
Negeri Sembilan	Port Dickson*		✓		✓	✓
	Seremban*	✓	✓			
THAILAND						
Krabi*	Krabi City*	✓	✓			✓
Phangnga*	Phangnga City*	✓	✓			
Trang	Trang City	✓	✓			
	Kantang Port				✓	
Satun	Satun City	✓	✓			
	Wang Prachan			✓		
	Tammalang Port*				✓	✓
	Tarutao Island*					✓

BCP = border crossing point, CAP = capital, COM = commercial, MGP = maritime gateway port, TOUR = tourism.
Note: * denotes additional provinces and nodes.
Source: Study team.

Map 8: Andaman Sea–Strait of Malacca Economic Corridor
(Economic Corridor 2)

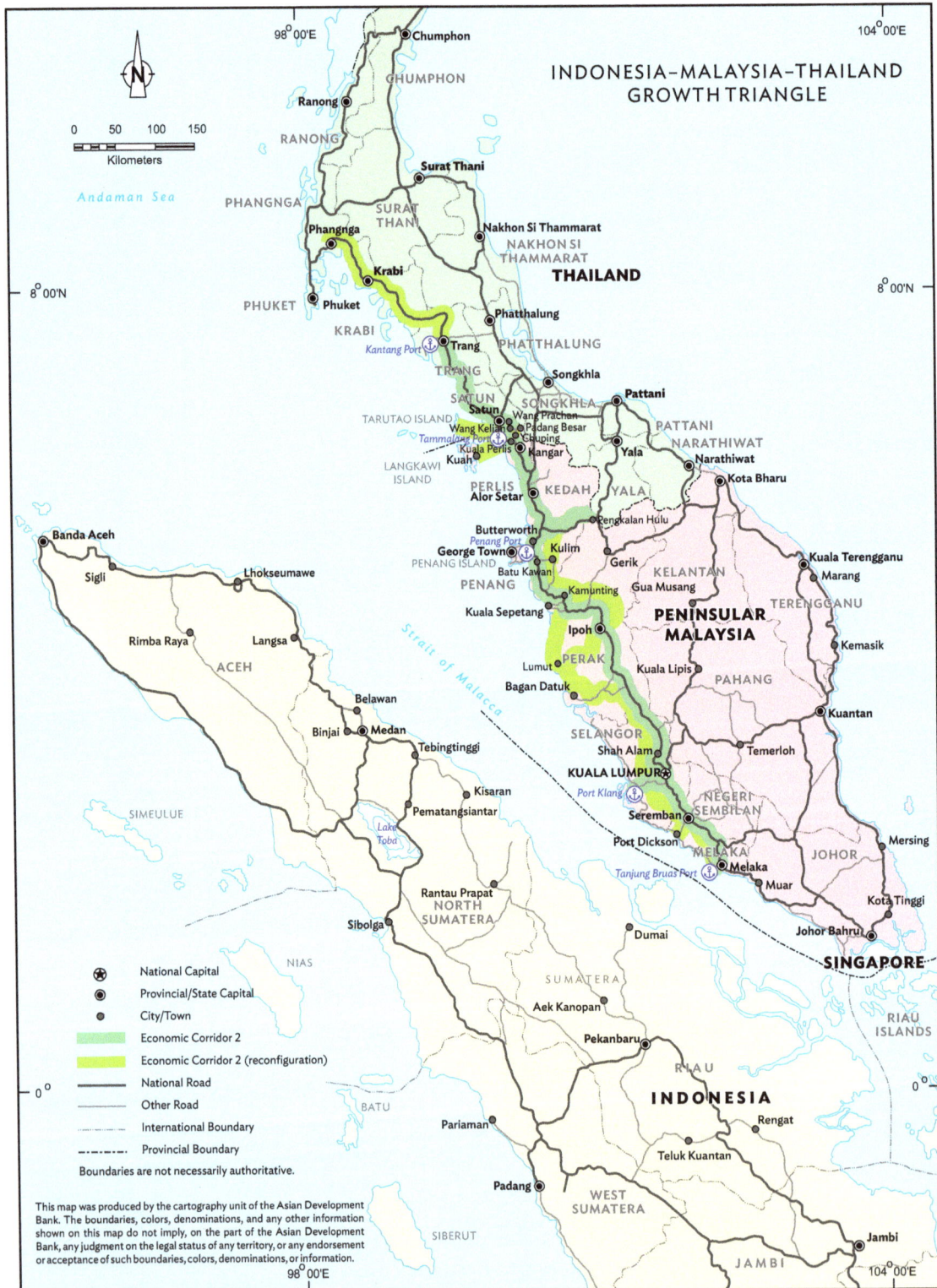

98° 00'E
104° 00'E

Chumphon

INDONESIA–MALAYSIA–THAILAND
GROWTH TRIANGLE

CHUMPHON

Ranong

RANONG

N

0 50 100 150
Kilometers

Surat Thani

Andaman Sea

PHANGNGA

SURAT
THANI

Nakhon Si Thammarat

NAKHON SI
THAMMARAT

Phangnga

Krabi

THAILAND

8° 00'N

Phuket

Phatthalung

8° 00'N

PHUKET

KRABI

Kantang Port   Trang

PHATTHALUNG

TRANG

Songkhla

SATUN

SONGKHLA

Pattani

Satun

Wang Prachan

TARUTAO ISLAND

Wang Kelian   Padang Besar

PATTANI

Tammalang Port   Chuping

NARATHIWAT

Kuala Perlis   Kangar

Yala

Kuah

YALA

Narathiwat

LANGKAWI
ISLAND

PERLIS

Alor Setar

Kota Bharu

Butterworth   Pengkalan Hulu

Penang Port   KEDAH

George Town   Kulim

Kuala Terengganu

Batu Kawan

Gerik

KELANTAN

Marang

PENANG ISLAND

PENANG

Gua Musang

TERENGGANU

Banda Aceh

Kamunting

Sigli

Lhokseumawe

Kuala Sepetang

PENINSULAR
MALAYSIA

Langsa

Rimba Raya

ACEH

Ipoh

Kemasik

PERAK

Lumut

Kuala Lipis

Belawan

Bagan Datuk

PAHANG

Kuantan

Binjai   Medan

Tebingtinggi

SIMEULUE

SELANGOR

Shah Alam

Temerloh

Kisaran

Pematangsiantar

KUALA LUMPUR

NEGERI
SEMBILAN

Lake
Toba

Port Klang

Seremban

Mersing

Port Dickson

MELAKA

JOHOR

Rantau Prapat

NORTH
SUMATERA

Tanjung Bruas Port   Melaka

Muar

Sibolga

Dumai

Kota Tinggi

NIAS

Johor Bahru

SINGAPORE

SUMATERA

RIAU
ISLANDS

Aek Kanopan

0°

0°

Pekanbaru

BATU

R I A U

INDONESIA

Pariaman

Rengat

WEST
SUMATERA

Teluk Kuantan

Padang

Jambi

SIBERUT

JAMBI

98° 00'E

104° 00'E

Legend
- ⊛ National Capital
- ⊚ Provincial/State Capital
- • City/Town
- Economic Corridor 2
- Economic Corridor 2 (reconfiguration)
- National Road
- Other Road
- International Boundary
- Provincial Boundary

Boundaries are not necessarily authoritative.

This map was produced by the cartography unit of the Asian Development Bank. The boundaries, colors, denominations, and any other information shown on this map do not imply, on the part of the Asian Development Bank, any judgment on the legal status of any territory, or any endorsement or acceptance of such boundaries, colors, denominations, or information.

Source: Asian Development Bank.

**Map 9: Andaman Sea–Strait of Malacca Economic Corridor
(Economic Corridor 2) - Malaysia**

INDONESIA–MALAYSIA–THAILAND
GROWTH TRIANGLE

PENINSULAR
MALAYSIA

Strait of Malacca

NORTH
SUMATERA

SUMATERA

INDONESIA

RIAU

RIAU
ISLANDS

SINGAPORE

Legend	
⊛	National Capital
◉	Provincial/State Capital
•	City/Town
	Economic Corridor 2
	Economic Corridor 2 (reconfiguration)
	National Road
	Other Road
	Provincial Boundary
	International Boundary

Boundaries are not necessarily authoritative.

This map was produced by the cartography unit of the Asian Development Bank. The boundaries, colors, denominations, and any other information shown on this map do not imply, on the part of the Asian Development Bank, any judgment on the legal status of any territory, or any endorsement or acceptance of such boundaries, colors, denominations, or information.

Source: Asian Development Bank.

Additional Nodes

Perlis. New nodes added were Chuping Valley and Kuala Perlis. The Chuping Valley Industrial Area (CVIA) is being developed by the state government. Under the CVIA, the PIP will be established as a logistics hub to increase the efficiency of cargo movement between Malaysia and Thailand. The Kuala Perlis Jetty, which is the tourist gateway to Langkawi and Satun, has been expanded to accommodate the increasing number of domestic and international tourists. This will have a large impact on the development of Kuala Perlis. The Kuala Perlis–Langkawi–Satun connectivity has greatly promoted the tourism industry in Perlis and Langkawi.

There are also plans to build a 14 km bridge that links Bukit Putih (Kuala Perlis) and Tammalang (Satun). Once approved by both the governments of Malaysia and Thailand, the bridge would shorten the 187 km journey carrying cargo from Bangkok to Padang Besar or Bukit Kayu Hitam in Kedah. Currently, container trucks take the Satun–Songkhla–Hat Yai–Sadao–Padang Besar or Bukit Kayu Hitam routes. Other than reducing the logistics costs, this bridge is capable of facilitating the tourism industry in Perlis and can have spillover effects on Langkawi. With this new connectivity, Perlis, which is a relatively small state, will have another border entry apart from Padang Besar and Wang Kelian.[46]

Perak. The new nodes added were Kamunting and Lumut, with each under their respective development projects, namely, the Greater Kamunting Conurbation and Manjung Aman Jaya Maritime City. Lumut Port is the main trade gateway for the state of Perak.

Penang. Bandar Batu Kawan is a new node on mainland Penang and it is part of the Batu Kawan Development project. The project aims to develop the less-developed regions of mainland Penang, especially South Seberang Perai. This new node has good road connectivity with the federal road and expressway to Penang Port in Butterworth and Penang International Airport in Bayan Lepas.

Kedah. The Kuah Jetty in Kuah (Langkawi) is the main tourist gateway into Langkawi and has ferry connectivity with Penang Port (George Town), Kuala Perlis (Perlis), and Kuala Kedah (Kedah). Langkawi is among the main tourist destinations for both local and international travelers. In 2007, UNESCO declared the Langkawi archipelago as one of 64 globally recognized geoparks.

Melaka. Tanjung Bruas Port serves as the main trade gateway to Riau Province. The Melaka–Dumai Ro-Ro Ferry Project, which involves Tanjung Bruas, will further facilitate connectivity between the southern EC2 regions of Melaka and Negeri Sembilan, and Sumatera.

Negeri Sembilan. The new nodes are Port Dickson and Seremban. Both cities are under the MVV 2.0, which was launched in 2018 to generate economic growth for the state toward a high-income economy. Seremban, the capital city, is the center of administration and business that facilitates state economic activities by providing services to the general public, business communities, and industry players. The Port of Port Dickson is the trade gateway for Negeri Sembilan. This port serves as a major oil terminal as well as a minor port for general cargo.

---

[46]   *The Sun Daily*. 2017. Perlis Hails Thai Proposal to Build Tammalang Bukit Putih Bridge. 4 October. https://www.thesundaily.my/archive/perlis-hails-thai-proposal-build-tamelang-bukit-putih-bridge-FTARCH489644.

Economic Corridor 4. The Melaka–Dumai Economic Corridor

Overview

EC4 is a maritime corridor linking Riau Province in Sumatera to the state of Melaka in Peninsular Malaysia (Map 10). The underpinning economic rationale for this link is based on the strategic location of Dumai Port and Tanjung Bruas Port located opposite each other in one of the narrowest stretches of the Strait of Malacca, thus having the shortest distance between them across the strait. This maritime corridor has a long tradition of freight and passenger traffic between Sumatera and Malaysia. Tanjung Bruas Port is the maritime gateway for Melaka, while Dumai is the gateway port of Riau Province, one of the richest provinces in Indonesia with abundant palm oil plantations and onshore oil and gas resources. The corridor includes the development of land connectivity to Dumai Port, as well as the development of Tanjung Bruas Port.

EC4 covers only the state of Melaka on the Malaysian side. The state is also part of the EC2. The existing node is Tanjung Bruas Port is part of the Melaka–Dumai Economic Corridors Multimodal Transport Project (Map 11).

The existing EC4 can be extended to Johor, taking into account the state's potential strategic connectivity with South Sumatera, Bangka Belitung, and the Riau Islands. The existing EC4 plus Johor can be referred to as Extended EC4. This corridor interlinks with the proposed EC6 that runs from Southern Thailand to the east coast of Peninsular Malaysia and to Port Klang in the west coast and link to Johor Bahru by road and rail connectivity. Johor Bahru is linked to South Sumatera, Riau Islands, and Bangka Belitung Islands via maritime transport.

Map 10: Melaka–Dumai Economic Corridor
(Economic Corridor 4)

INDONESIA–MALAYSIA–THAILAND
GROWTH TRIANGLE

Chumphon
CHUMPHON
Ranong
RANONG
Andaman Sea
Surat Thani
PHANGNGA
SURAT THANI
Nakhon Si Thammarat
Phangnga
Krabi
NAKHON SI THAMMARAT
THAILAND
PHUKET
Phuket
KRABI
Phatthalung
Trang
PHATTHALUNG
TRANG
Songkhla
SATUN
SONGKHLA
Pattani
Satun
Yala
PATTANI
NARATHIWAT
Kuah
Narathiwat
LANGKAWI ISLAND
Kangar
Kota Bharu
PERLIS
KEDAH
Alor Setar
Butterworth
Kulim
Kuala Terengganu
PENANG ISLAND
George Town
KELANTAN
Gerik
Marang
PENANG
Gua Musang
TERENGGANU
Kuala Sepetang
Ipoh
Kuala Lipis
Kemasik
PERAK
PAHANG
Bagan Datuk
Kuantan
SELANGOR
Shah Alam
Temerloh
PENINSULAR
KUALA LUMPUR
NEGERI
MALAYSIA
SEMBILAN
Seremban
Port Dickson
MELAKA
Mersing
Tanjung
Bruas Port
JOHOR
Muar
Melaka
Dumai Port
Kota Tinggi
Dumai
Johor Bahru
SINGAPORE
Aek Kanopan
Batam
Pekanbaru
Tanjungpinang
RIAU ISLANDS
RIAU
LINGGA
Banda Aceh
Sigli
Lhokseumawe
Rimba Raya
Langsa
ACEH
Belawan
Medan
Binjai
Tebingtinggi
Kisaran
Pematangsiantar
Lake Toba
SIMEULUE
Rantau Prapat
NORTH SUMATERA
Sibolga
NIAS
Rengat
Teluk Kuantan
Pariaman
RIAU
BATU
Padang
WEST SUMATERA
INDONESIA
BANGKA
SIBERUT
Jambi
JAMBI
Pangkalpinang
BANGKA BELITUNG ISLANDS
Belitung
PAGAI
BELITUNG
Palembang
SOUTH SUMATERA
Lahat
Bengkulu
Baturaja
BENGKULU
LAMPUNG
Lampung
Bandar Lampung
ENGGANO
Java Sea
INDIAN OCEAN

Strait of Malacca

Andaman Sea

8°00'N

0°

4°00'S

98°00'E

104°00'E

N

0 50 100 150 200 250
Kilometers

Legend:
- ⊛ National Capital
- ⊙ Provincial/State Capital
- • City/Town
- Economic Corridor 4
- National Road
- Other Road
- Provincial Boundary
- International Boundary

Boundaries are not necessarily authoritative.

This map was produced by the cartography unit of the Asian Development Bank.
The boundaries, colors, denominations, and any other information shown on this
map do not imply, on the part of the Asian Development Bank, any judgment on
the legal status of any territory, or any endorsement or acceptance of such
boundaries, colors, denominations, or information.

Source: Asian Development Bank.

**Map 11: Melaka–Dumai Economic Corridor
(Economic Corridor 4) - Malaysia**

SATUN

Satun

Kuah

Kangar

PERLIS

Alor Setar

KEDAH

Butterworth

George Town

PENANG ISLAND

Kulim

PENANG

SONGKHLA

Pattani

PATTANI

Yala

NARATHIWAT

Narathiwat

YALA

Kota Bharu

INDONESIA–MALAYSIA–THAILAND
GROWTH TRIANGLE

Gerik

KELANTAN

Kuala Terengganu

Marang

Kuala Sepetang

Gua Musang

TERENGGANU

Ipoh

PERAK

Kuala Lipis

**PENINSULAR
MALAYSIA**

Kemasik

Bagan Datuk

PAHANG

Strait of Malacca

Kuantan

SELANGOR

Shah Alam

Temerloh

KUALA LUMPUR

Kisaran

NORTH
SUMATERA

Rantau Prapat

NEGERI
SEMBILAN

Seremban

Port Dickson

MELAKA

Tanjung Bruas Port **Melaka**

Muar

JOHOR

Mersing

Dumai

Kota Tinggi

Johor Bahru

SINGAPORE

SUMATERA

INDONESIA

Aek Kanopan

RIAU

Pekanbaru

RIAU
ISLANDS

	National Capital
	Provincial/State Capital
	City/Town
	Economic Corridor 2
	National Road
	Other Road
	Provincial Boundary
	International Boundary

Boundaries are not necessarily authoritative.

This map was produced by the cartography unit of the Asian Development Bank. The boundaries, colors, denominations, and any other information shown on this map do not imply, on the part of the Asian Development Bank, any judgment on the legal status of any territory, or any endorsement or acceptance of such boundaries, colors, denominations, or information.

Source: Asian Development Bank.

Macroeconomic Indicators

The states of Melaka and Johor recorded higher economic growth rates when compared to the national average, with Johor having a higher GDP compared to Melaka (Table 51). The manufacturing and agriculture sectors drive Melaka and Johor's economic growth (Table 52).

Table 51: Economic Corridor 4: Melaka and Johor Selected Macroeconomic Indicators, 2014–2018

	2014	2018	Average (2014–2018)	Average Share to Malaysia %	CAGR* (2014–2018), % (based in RM)
GDP (at constant 2015 prices, $ million)*					
Melaka	10,264	10,504	9,684	2.9	6.0
Johor	30,866	32,338	29,472	8.8	6.6
Malaysia	336,823	336,823	336,823	–	5.4
GDP per capita (at constant prices 2015, $)*					
Melaka	11,774	11,388	10,770	–	4.5
Johor	8,671	8,625	8,066	–	5.2
Malaysia	10,968	10,968	10,968	–	
Population (million)					
Melaka	0.9	0.9	1	2.9	1.4
Johor	3.6	3.7	4	11.9	1.3
Malaysia	30.7	30.7	31	–	1.3
Population Density (population/square kilometer)					
Melaka	528	544	542	–	0.8
Johor	93	98	96	–	1.3
Malaysia	93	98	96	–	1.3

– = not applicable, CAGR = compound annual growth rate, GDP = gross domestic product, RM = Malaysian ringgit.
* The CAGR was calculated using the local currency (Malaysian ringgit) to avoid erratic fluctuations in foreign exchange rates.
Source: Department of Statistics Malaysia. 2019. *State's Socioeconomic Report (various states)*. Putrajaya: DOS Malaysia.

Table 52: Economic Corridor 4: Melaka and Johor Share of Sector Value-Added to Gross Domestic Product by Economic Activity

State	Agriculture (%)	Mining and Quarrying (%)	Manufacturing (%)	Construction (%)	Services (%)
Melaka	10.8	0.1	38.6	3.5	46.6
Johor	12.5	0.5	29.4	7.1	49.3
Malaysia	**7.3**	**7.6**	**22.4**	**4.9**	**56.7**

Source: Department of Statistics Malaysia. 2019. State's Socioeconomic Report (various states). Putrajaya: DOS Malaysia.

Under the state and regional development blueprints, several strategic growth nodes have been identified to enhance the economies of Melaka and Johor (Table 53). The new nodes in Melaka are Melaka City and MIFT. For Johor, which is not a participating state in the IMT-GT, the new nodes are Johor Bahru City, Tanjung Pelepas Port (Gelang Patah), and Johor Port (Pasir Gudang). These new nodes would further strengthen and widen the connectivity with the existing nodes.

Table 53: Economic Corridor 4: State and Regional Development Blueprint of Melaka and Johor

EC2	State Development Blueprint	Regional Development Blueprint
Melaka	Melaka Strategic Plan 2035 (2020–2035)	• No regional blueprint
Johor	Johor Sustainable Development Plan 2015–2030	• ECERDC: ECER Blueprint 2.0 (2018–2025) • IRDA: The 2nd Comprehensive Development Plan (2014–2025)

EC = economic corridor, ECER = East Coast Economic Region, ECERDC = East Coast Economic Region Development Council, IRDA = Iskandar Regional Development Authority.
Source: Compiled by author from state development blueprint and regional development blueprints.

Existing Nodes

Tanjung Bruas Port serves as the main trade gateway to Riau (Sumatera). The Melaka–Dumai Ro-Ro Ferry Project, which has been planned under the IMT-GT IB 2012–2016 and continued under IB 2017–2021, involve Tanjung Bruas Port in Melaka and Sri Junjungan Port in Riau. Both port authorities will build their respective Ro-Ro terminal facilities.[47]

The Melaka–Dumai Ro-Ro Ferry Project will facilitate cargo shipment between Melaka and Dumai using lorries transported by Ro-Ro ferries. Cargo lorries from Sumatera would be able to travel directly to Malaysia through Melaka. Previously, cargo shipments had to undergo the process of loading and unloading at the ports which could take up to a week, as compared to the Ro-Ro ferry service, which could take around only 5 hours to cross the Strait of Malacca. Maritime trade activities between Malaysia and Sumatera Island will be given a boost due to reduced travel time.

To date, the planned Ro-Ro ferry link between Dumai and Melaka has yet to materialize as there are still outstanding physical infrastructure and regulatory issues that need to be resolved. Cross-border formalities, procedures, and rules governing the movement of road vehicles in IMT-GT remain complicated and lack standardization and harmonization. This includes the customs, immigration, and quarantine (CIQ) rules, regulations, and procedures governing admission of foreign commercial and private vehicles and cargo and passengers on-board the vehicles. Furthermore, there are practical challenges with respect to mutual recognition of vehicle inspection certificates, insurance policies, vehicle registrations, and cross-border vehicle permits. Discussions on the technical specifications of vehicles that will enter or exit ports and cross the border areas are still being deliberated.

Status of Physical Connectivity

Road connectivity

The Tanjung Bruas Port is easily accessible by state and federal roads. Tanjung Bruas Port is the trade gateway to Dumai. The distance between Tanjung Bruas Port and the Port of Sri Junjungan (Dumai) is 177 km. The distance between Tanjung Bruas Port and Melaka City is 18 km. From Melaka City, the road network to Johor Bahru is via the E1 or E2 (Table 54).

---

[47] Ro-Ro ships are vessels designed to carry wheeled cargo, such as cars, trucks, semi-trailer trucks, trailers, and railroad cars, that are driven on and off the ship on their own wheels or using a platform vehicle, such as a self-propelled modular transporter. Ro-Ro vessels have either built-in or shore-based ramps that allow the cargo to be efficiently rolled on and off the vessel when in port.

There are two major ports in Johor that are close to Johor Bahru, namely, the Port of Tanjung Pelepas (Gelang Patah) and Johor Port (Pasir Gudang). Both ports are important trade gateways to international destinations, including Sumatera and Thailand. Apart from cargo terminals, ferry terminals in Tanjung Pelepas Port and Johor Port also provide passenger ferry services to Batam and Tanjungpinang (Riau Islands).

Table 54: Extended Economic Corridor 4: Connectivity Nodes in Melaka and Johor

Start Point	End point	Route	Distance (km)	Traffic Lanes	Road Class
Melaka City, Melaka	Melaka International Ferry Terminal, Banda Hilir	192	5	2	Federal road
Melaka International Ferry Terminal	Tanjung Bruas Port, Melaka	5	13	2	Federal road
Tanjung Bruas Port	Port of Sri Junjungan, Dumai	Maritime links	151 km (82 nm)		Shipping and ferry links
Melaka City, Melaka	Johor Bahru	E1/AH2, 1, J3	220	4	Federal, state road, and expressway
Johor Bahru	Tanjung Pelepas Port	52, 177	31	2–4	Federal road
	Johor Port, Pasir Gudang	1, 35	25	2–4	Federal road
Tanjung Pelepas Port, Stulang	Batam	Maritime links	97 km (52 nm)	Ferry links	Passenger ferry Terminal
Johor Port, Pasir Gudang	Batam		51 km (28 nm)		
	Tanjungpinang, Bintan		99 km (54 nm)		

AH2 = Asian Highway 2, km = kilometer, nm = nautical miles.
Source: Compiled by author.

Rail Connectivity

The KTMB South Line. Melaka and Johor are under the KTMB South Line. The railway track to the south begins at Pulau Sebang or Tampin (Melaka) and ends at Johor Bahru (Johor). The distance between the two railway stations is 172 km, which goes through several cargo terminals and stations (Table 55). The related inland ports along the South Line are the Batu Pahat Container Terminal (BPCT) and Segamat Inland Port (SIP). There are also proposals to build an inland port in Melaka, namely Taboh Naning Inland Port in Alor Gajah under the Melaka SSP 2035.[48]

---

[48]   Plan Malaysia. 2014. *Melaka State Structure Plan (2015–2035)*. Kuala Lumpur. Plan Malaysia.

Table 55: Extended Economic Corridor 4: Central and South Line (Port Klang–Johor Bahru)

Region/State	Start Point	to	End Point	Km	Inland Port
Central Line (Selangor and Kuala Lumpur)					
Kuala Lumpur/ Port Klang	Kuala Lumpur/ Port Klang	→	Seremban	130	Port Klang is the major trade gateway to international market.
South Line					
Negeri Sembilan	Seremban	→	Pulau Sebang/ Tampin	49	Nilai Inland Port provides road and rail links and logistics services to industries in Central Region.
Melaka	Pulau Sebang/ Tampin	→	Batang Melaka	26	Tanjung Bruas Port is a major trade gateway to Dumai, Taboh Naning Inland Port; proposed under the Melaka Structure Plan (2015–2035) for connectivity with Tanjung Bruas Port.
			Seremban–Batang Melaka	**75**	
Negeri Sembilan/ Johor	Gemas	→	Segamat	15	Batu Pahat Container Terminal Barge feeder terminal, jointly developed by the People's Republic of China's Orient Overseas Container Line, to link Pasir Gudang industrial zone (in the south) to Port Klang.
	Segamat	→	Johor	172	Segamat Inland Port offers feeder rail link to Port Klang to shippers in the South central region.
Johor/Singapore	Johor Bahru	→	Woodlands, Singapore	27	Kempas Baru Station is a junction for the Pasir Gudang (Johor Port) and Tanjong Pelepas (Gelang Patah) freight line. Tanjung Pelepas Port and Johor Port (Pasir Gudang); major trade gateways to international markets.
			Gemas-Woodlands	**214**	

Source: Compiled by author from KTMB's various publication sources. Retrieved from http://www.ktmb.com.my/index.html.

Johor Bahru–Singapore Rapid Transit System. The proposed Johor Bahru–Singapore Rapid Transit System (RTS) is a cross-border rapid transit system that would connect Woodlands, Singapore and Johor Bahru, Johor, crossing the Strait of Johor. The RTS will have two stations, with the Singapore terminal located at Woodlands north station and the Malaysia terminal at Bukit Chagar station. Both stations will have co-located Singaporean and Malaysian CIQ facilities. The RTS Link is expected to replace the railway line and shuttle train services between Johor Bahru Sentral and Woodlands Train Checkpoint. The RTS Link will significantly ease Causeway congestion, and facilitate business and tourism. The RTS Link will have a capacity of 10,000 passengers.[49]

Maritime Connectivity

Tanjung Bruas Port. The Tanjung Bruas Port commenced operations in the early 1980s to provide port facilities and services as well as trade gateways to industrial players in the EC4. To date, there are no trading links between Tanjung Bruas Port and Dumai. However, there are potential trade links under the Melaka–Dumai Ro-Ro Project under discussion. Tanjung Bruas has maritime trade links with other ports in Palembang (South Sumatera) and Lhokseumawe (Aceh).

---

[49]   MRT Corp. Rapid Transit System Link Project Between Johor Bahru and Singapore. https://www.mymrt.com.my/public/rts-link/.

The Melaka International Ferry Terminal. The MIFT in Banda Hilir also serves as a port-of-call for cruise liners that traverse through the Strait of Malacca. In 2018, about 13,500 cruise ship passengers arrived at this port-of-call, which is the fourth most important port-of-call in the country.[50] The terminal also provides passenger ferry service between Melaka and Dumai (Port of Bandar Sri Laksamana, Bengkalis) with a journey time of approximately 2 hours for a distance of 100 km. The importance of the terminal to Sumatera is evident in the large number of Indonesian passengers (63,796 tourists, or 98% of total international visitors) that arrived at the Terminal in 2018. Many tourists from Dumai have made Melaka a health tourism destination.[51]

Tanjung Pelepas Port. The Tanjung Pelepas Port is the premier transshipment port in Malaysia. Protected by a deep-water bay, it allows PTP to accommodate the biggest cargo vessels. With more than 30 shipping lines and operators calling Tanjung Pelepas Port, this port is connected to over 300 ports-of-call globally. The Tanjung Pelepas Port has trading ties with the Port of Belawan (North Sumatera).

The Tanjung Pelepas Free Zone is integrated with the Tanjung Pelepas Port and makes it ideal for manufacturing activities and commercial activities such as value adding activities, cargo consolidation, international procurement centers, and regional distribution operations.

The Tanjung Pelepas Port is easily accessible by roads and railways that connect it with important economic nodes in the EC4. The port is also linked to Thailand by rail land bridge from Johor Bahru to Bangsue, Surat Thani, and Hat Yai. The ferry terminal at Tanjung Pelepas Port Ferry provides passenger ferry services to Batam (Riau Islands) and is the main gateway between the Riau Islands and Johor.

Johor Port Pasir Gudang. Built in 1977, Johor Port is a multipurpose port that handles all kinds of cargo. Johor Port has been handling liquid bulk cargoes since it began operating. Johor Port has facilities for both edible (primarily soya bean oil and palm oil) and nonedible liquids (mainly petroleum products). The port has the world's largest palm oil storage facility in its Free Trade Zone. Johor Port is also one of the largest discharging points for rice and cocoa in Malaysia, as well as being one of the biggest terminals in Malaysia for fertilizer and cement.

The Johor Port Free Zone area covers about two-thirds of the port area, providing companies with facilities to carry out industrial and commercial activities such as intermodal cargo conversion—break bulking, containerization, liquid to containers and drums; packaging and labeling; processing, manufacturing, and assembly; and import and reexport activities.

There are well-connected road and railway networks connecting Johor Port. The Johor Port is linked to Thailand by a rail land bridge from Johor Bahru to Bangsue, Surat Thani and Hat Yai. The port has trading links with ports in Sumatera, Palembang, and Belawan. Meanwhile, the Johor Port Ferry Terminal provides passenger ferry services to Batam and Tanjungpinang (Bintan Island) and is the alternative entry for residents of Riau Island into Johor.

---

[50]   Ministry of Tourism, Arts and Culture. 2020. *Statistics of Ship Calls and Cruise Passenger Arrivals to Malaysia*. Putrajaya. MOTAC Malaysia.

[51]   Tourism data were compiled from Tourism Melaka. 2020. *Melaka Tourism Basic Data*. Melaka: Tourism Melaka.

Air Links

The Melaka International Airport services flights into Pekanbaru (Riau). There are no flights to Sumatera and Southern Thailand from Senai International Airport (Johor). For air links within the ECs 1, 2, and 6, Senai International Airport provides more flight destinations than Melaka International Airport (Table 56).

Table 56: Economic Corridor 4: Melaka and Senai International Airport - Flight Routes

Airports	Airlines	Destinations to Sumatera and Southern Thailand	Destinations within ECs in Malaysia	Other International Destinations
Melaka International Airport, Batu Berendam, Melaka	Air Asia	No flight	Penang	–
	Malindo Air	Sumatera: Pekanbaru	Penang	–
Senai International Airport, Johor Bahru	Air Asia		Kuala Lumpur, Penang, Alor Setar, Langkawi, Ipoh	Bangkok, Jakarta, Surabaya, Ho Chi Minh City, Guangzhou
	MAS	No flights available	Kuala Lumpur	–
	Firefly		Subang, Kota Bharu	–
	Malindo Air		Kuala Lumpur, Subang, Ipoh	Guangzhou, Haikou
	Jin Air*		–	Seoul-Incheon

– = not applicable. EC = economic corridor, MAS = Malaysia Airlines.
* International airline
Source: Compiled by author from the websites of relevant domestic and international airlines.

Trade

As of 2021, there was no trade link between Tanjung Bruas Port and Dumai, pending the implementation of the Melaka–Dumai Ro-Ro Ferry Project. Tanjung Bruas Port however has trade links with other ports in Sumatera, particularly Palembang (South Sumatera) and Lhokseumawe (Aceh). Commodities imported from Palembang are gypsum and coal; from Aceh, ammonia gas.

Tourism

The Melaka state government does not have a tourism blueprint in place. However, Johor has the Johor Tourism Master Plan 2014–2023. Melaka's tourism development plan is, however, outlined by Plan Malaysia under the Melaka State Structure Plan 2035. Specifically for Johor, the tourism industry development plan has also been integrated into the ECER Blueprint 2.0 and the Iskandar Malaysia Tourism Blueprint Agenda.

The current trend shows that the archaeotourism, ecotourism, heritage tourism, and geotourism sectors have been given priority by each state government to advance their respective tourism industries. All these tourism sectors are aligned with the highlighted sectors under the National Ecotourism Plan 2016–2025 and the National Tourism Policy 2020–2030.

The tourism industry is also clustered according to each respective comparative advantage in each region, so that it can have a greater impact on the state economy. Table 57 provides examples of regional ecotourism clusters for Melaka and Negeri Sembilan, as highlighted in the National Ecotourism Plan 2016–2025.[52]

Table 57: Economic Corridor 4: Regional Ecotourism Cluster

State	Regional Ecotourism Cluster
Melaka	• Melaka Urban Ecotourism Cluster (Melaka Historical City–Ayer Keroh) • Tanjung Keling–Pengkalan Balak–Sungai Linggi–Tanjung Tuan • Jasin–Selandar–Tebong–Asahan
Johor	• RAMSAR Johor–Gunung Pulai–Sungai Johor • Kota Tinggi–Sungai Johor–Desaru–Sedili • Mersing–Sultan Iskandar Marine Park • Kluang–Endau Rompin–Segamat • Tangkak–Sagil–Gunung Ledang • Batu Pahat–Parit Jawa–Muar

Source: Ministry of Tourism and Culture Malaysia. 2016. National Ecotourism Plan 2016-2025: Executive Summary. Putrajaya: MOTAC.

Melaka has been designated as a historic city in 1989 and World Heritage City by UNESCO in 2008. Such recognition has positioned Melaka as one of the top tourist destinations in the world. This sector has opened up various work and business opportunities to the people of Melaka. Under the Melaka SSP 2035, the tourism industry has been clustered according to zones and niche areas. The main objective of the Johor Tourism Master Plan (2014–2023) is to increase the role and potential of Johor as the main tourist destination in Malaysia (Table 58).

---

[52]   For detailed tourism spatial development planning, refer to Melaka State Structure Plan 2035 and Johor State Structure Plan 2030.

Table 58: Melaka and Johor Tourism Zones and Focus Areas

Tourism Cluster	Tourism Product
Melaka	
Main Tourism	Melaka City and Melaka Gateway
Family Tourism	Ayer Keroh and Melaka City
Beach Tourism	Along Melaka's coastline, particularly Pantai Kundur, Tanjung Kling, and Tanjung Bidara
Agrotourism	Sungai Chin-Chin, Sungai Rambai–Serkam-Umbai
Heritage and Culture	Simpang Ampat–Alor Gajah–Masjid Tanah
Ecotourism and Agrotourism	Jasin–Gunung Ledang–Asahan–Selandar–Bukit Senggeh
Johor	
Family Fun	LEGOLand
Urban Heritage and Lifestyle	Danga Bay, Johor Bahru City Center
Leisure Shopping	Johor Premium Outlet
Mangrove and Rural Gateway	Tanjung Piai–Pulau Kukup–Sungai Pulai National Park
Coastal Retreat	Desaru
Marine and Island Escapade	Mersing Islands
Eco Adventure Challenge	Endau Rompin National Park
Cradle of Johor Heritage	Muar Royal Town and Batu Pahat
Mystical Nature	Gunung Ledang National Park
Agri Delights	Zenxin Organic Farm, UK Farm, Koref Eco Farm Resort
Orchard Route	Orchard Farms

Sources: Plan Malaysia. 2015. *Melaka State Structure Plan 2035.* Putrajaya: Plan Malaysia; *Johor State Economic Planning Unit. 2014. Johor Tourism Master Plan 2014–2023. Johore Bahru. Johor SEPU.*

The tourism industry trend is reflected in the number of guests staying in hotels in the state that they visit. Johor received about 7 million hotel guests each year for 2014–2018, while Melaka received about 5 million hotel guests. Local tourists dominated the hotel guest pattern (Table 59).

Table 59: Economic Corridor 4: Hotel Guests by States, 2014 and 2018
(million)

	2014	2015	2016	2017	2018	Average (2014–2018)	Average Share to State, %	CAGR (2014–2018), %
Melaka	4.4	4.6	4.6	4.8	4.9	4.7	100	2.6
Foreign	1.8	1.8	1.8	1.7	1.6	1.7	37	(3.0)
Domestic	2.7	2.8	2.8	3.1	3.4	2.9	63	5.9
Johor	6.4	7.0	7.0	7.4	7.6	7.1	100	4.3
Foreign	2.4	2.6	2.6	2.6	2.6	2.6	36	2.1
Domestic	4.0	4.4	4.4	4.8	5.0	4.5	64	5.6
Malaysia	71.7	71.5	72.3	77.3	82.4	75.0	100	3.6
Foreign	26.3	25.6	25.9	28.0	30.0	27.2	36	3.4
Domestic	45.4	45.9	46.4	49.2	52.4	47.9	64	3.7

( ) = negative, CAGR = compound annual growth rate.
Source: My Tourism Data Portal. http://mytourismdata.tourism.gov.my/ (accessed 1 June 2021).

Industrial Activities

As of end December 2018, there were 21 industrial parks in Melaka developed by the state government and the private sector to attract investments. Among these, there are specialized high-tech parks such as Melaka World Solar Valley and Composite Technology City. There are industrial parks with free trade zone (FTZ) status, such as the FTZ Batu Berendam (Table 60).

Johor has established 55 industrial parks, which is the highest number in Malaysia. The industrial parks in Johor are concentrated in the southern region of the state, specifically in Iskandar Malaysia. Iskandar Malaysia is IRDA's southern development corridor. Investment in Johor is currently concentrated in the petroleum and gas industry, such as the Pengerang Integrated Petroleum Complex and Tanjung Bin Petrochemical Maritime Industry Center. These industrial parks are supported by Tanjung Pelepas Port (Gelang Patah) and Johor Port (Pasir Gudang), which is a trade gateway for manufacturers and traders operating in the industrial parks.

Industrial parks in Melaka and Johor generally have good connectivity to their respective seaports through the road and railway networks. The E1–E2 and KTMB railway South and Central Line form the transport backbone of the EC4 Extended. Tanjung Pelepas Port, Johor Port, and Tanjung Bruas Port are the main trade gateways for industry players within the EC4. Manufacturers in the industrial parks also have direct access to the markets in Southern Thailand through the road transport network, namely via AH2 and through the Bukit Kayu Hitam BCP. AH2 is joined with E1 and E2 in Malaysia.

Industry players operating within the industrial parks will have ready access to the land bridge service provided by the KTMB in collaboration with SRT. The land bridge service permits cross-border movement of containers between Malaysia and Thailand by rail. The containers are sealed once for the entire trip and the cargo clears both Malaysian and Thai customs at the point of origin. The benefit of using this land bridge service is that logistics costs are reduced and transportation time is significantly shortened. The EC4 and Southern Thailand are connected by land via the following routes:[53] (i) Johor Port: Hat Yai–Surat Thani–Bangsue; and (ii) Tanjung Pelepas Port: Hat Yai–Surat Thani–Bangsue.

The KTMB and SRT land bridge services are part of the proposed Trans-Asian Railway Network and Singapore–Kunming Rail Link (SKRL). The proposed regional link will strengthen and expand trade between Malaysia and Thailand, as well as open up new markets in Southeast Asia and the PRC.[54]

Manufacturers and traders in industrial parks can have access to inland port services in the EC4 and EC2. For industry players in Johor, they can access the SIP and BPCT for the distribution and export of their products to their selected market destinations. Meanwhile, the NIP in Negeri Sembilan provides logistics services to industry players in Melaka.

The SIP, which commenced operations in 1998, is located in the southern part of the Peninsular Malaysia. It is a mid-range inland port between Tanjung Pelepas Port and Port Klang. The SIP offers facilities and services to manufacturers in the southern region of Johor and has been developed as a national load center and transshipment hub (footnote 20).

---

[53]   The information on land bridge was compiled from Keretapi Tanah Melayu Berhad found at https://www.ktmb.com.my/Kargo.html.

[54]   The information on Trans-Asian Railway Network and Singapore-Kunming Rail Link (SKRL) were compiled from UNESCAP found at https://www.unescap.org/our-work/transport/trans-asian-railway-network.

Table 60: Economic Corridor 4: Industrial Parks in Melaka and Johor

(as of end-December 2018)

Melaka	Johor		
1. Alor Gajah Industrial Estate 2. Ayer Keroh Business Industrial Park 3. Ayer Keroh Industrial Estates 4. Bukit Rambai Industrial Park 5. Cheng Technology Park 6. Elkay Industrial Park 7. HICOM Pegoh Industrial Park 8. Jasin Industrial Park 9. Krubong Industrial Park 10. Masjid Tanah Industrial Estate 11. Merlimau Industrial Estate 12. Rembia Industrial Estate 13. Smart Industrial Center, Bukit Rambai 14. Taman Tasik Utama Industrial Park 15. Tangga Batu Industrial Estate 16. Telok Gong Industrial Estate 17. Telok Mas Industrial Estate **Special Economic Zone** 18. Batu Berendam Free Trade Zone **Specialized Park** 19. Melaka Halal hub, Serkam 20. Composite Technology City 21. Melaka World Solar Valley	1. Alam Jaya Industrial Park 2. Bandar Penawar Industrial Park 3. Batu Pahat Industrial Area 4. Cemerlang Industrial Area, Johor Bahru 5. Desa Cemerlang Industrial Area 6. Desa Cemerlang Industrial Area 7. Eco Business Park I 8. Eco Business Park II 9. Eco Business Park III 10. Frontier Industrial Park 11. Harvestgreen @ Sime Darby Business park 12. I-Park@Tanjung Pelepas 13. I-Park@Indahpura 14. I-Park@Senai Airport City 15. I-Park@SILC Iskandar Puteri 16. Indahpura Industrial Park 17. Johor Technology Park 18. Kempas Industrial Area 19. Kluang Industrial Park	20. Kota Tinggi Industrial Park 21. Kulai Industrial Park 22. Kulai Iskandar Data Exchange 23. Masai Industrial Area Pasir Gudang 24. MEDINI 25. Mersing Industrial Park 26. Nusa Cemerlang Industrial Park 27. Nusajaya Tech Park 28. Pasir Gudang Industrial Area 29. Pekan Nenas Industrial Park 30. Pontian Industrial Area 31. Segamat Industrial Area II 32. Segamat Inland Port Industrial Park 33. Senai Airport City Industrial Area 34. Senai Industrial Estate 1, 2, 3 and 4 35. Setia Business Park I 36. Setia Business Park II 37. Sime Darby Business Park, Bandar Universiti Pagoh 38. Sime Darby Industrial Park, Pasir Gudang 39. Simpang Renggam Industrial Park 40. Southern Industrial and Logistics Cluster 41. Sri Gading Industrial Area 42. Tangkak Industrial Area, Tangkak	43. Tanjung Langsat Industrial Complex 44. Tanjung Langsat Port Area 45. Tanjung Piai Maritime Industrial Park 46. Tebrau Industrial Area 47. Wawasan industrial Area, Batu Pahat **Special Economic Zone** 48. Senai Airport Free Zone Industrial Area 49. Johor Port Free Zone 50. Port of Tanjung Pelepas Free Zone **Specialized Park** 51. Palm Oil Industrial Cluster, Tanjung Langsat 52. Pengerang Integrated Petroleum Complex 53. Tanjung Bin Petrochemical Maritime industry Center 54. Iskandar Halal Park 55. Muar Furniture Park

Source: Malaysian Investment Development Authority. 2018. Industrial Park in Malaysia. Kuala Lumpur: MIDA

The BPCT, which opened in 2000, is located some 1 km away from the Batu Pahat river mouth.[55] The inland port offers barge feeders connecting Batu Pahat with Northport (Port Klang) in the central region and Batu Pahat[56] with the Pasir Gudang sector in the southern region. The terminal, which serves industry players within the Batu Pahat industrial hinterland, provides huge savings and links up with main line operators calling at Port Klang. Shippers derive savings from haulage and clearance by using the one-stop service center at the terminal.

The NIP is considered as a short-range inland port for Port Klang. The NIP offers a range of value-added services, facilities, and spaces to support the growing container volumes at Port Klang in the central region (Melaka and Negeri Sembilan).

• Under Melaka's SSP 2015–2035 (Melaka 2035), a proposal was made to build a railway connecting Tanjung Bruas Port with the inland port to be developed in Taboh Naning (Alor Gajah, Melaka). The Taboh Naning Inland Port will be built by the state government in collaboration with the federal government. This inland port will be connected to Pulau Sebang or Tampin Railway Station. However, the proposal to build the Taboh Naning Inland Port, in Alor Gajah (Melaka), and the railway is still in the planning phase.[57] If the spur line railway and inland port projects are successfully implemented, this will increase the role of the Tanjung Bruas Port as the main trade gateway in Melaka and reduce logistics costs for the industry players in Melaka that operate in industrial parks.

Overall Assessment

Under the State Development Blueprint, several growth nodes have been identified to enhance the respective state economies and overcome the problem of development gaps. Tourism is one of the economic drivers that can help boost the state's GDP.

The Johor Bahru–Singapore RTS is a cross-border rapid transit system that would connect the Woodlands (Singapore) and Johor Bahru (Johor), crossing the Strait of Johor. The RTS Link will significantly ease causeway congestion and facilitate business and tourism. The RTS Link will have a capacity of 10,000 passengers. Residents from Batam and Riau Islands can use this RTS as an interchange node between Johor and Melaka for tourism or business purposes.

The MIFT in Banda Hilir is the main gateway to Riau Province. The ferry passenger service between Melaka and Dumai takes approximately 2 hours. Air service from Melaka to Pekanbaru takes 45 minutes. The importance of the terminal to the people of Sumatera is clearly demonstrated by the arrival of Indonesian passengers, who accounted for 98% of all international passengers who embarked at the terminal (65,309 passengers) in 2018. A large number of tourists from Dumai have made Melaka a health tourism destination. The terminal is also a port-of-call for cruise tourism in the Strait of Malacca. In 2018, the number of cruise passengers arriving at this port-of-call was 13,455 people. It is the fourth most important port-of-call in the country.

[55] P.T. Bangsberg. 2000. OOCL to expand Malaysia operations, add barge service. *The Journal of Commerce online.* 3 October. https://www.joc.com/maritime-news/oocl-expand-malaysia-operations-add-barge-service_20001003.html.

[56] Despite being a small town, Batu Pahat consists of one of the largest transacted volumes of textile and garments movements in Malaysia involving imports of raw materials and exporting of finish products. Apart from that, electrical goods such as television, DVD players, notebooks, and computer parts also play a major role contributing to major container volumes. Many haulage companies have established their inland transit depot around this area too to cater to long haul movements to and from Pasir Gudang and Port of Tanjung Pelepas.

[57] The information on Taboh Naning Inland were compiled from Plan Malaysia. 2014. *Melaka State Structure Plan (2015–2035).* Kuala Lumpur: Plan Malaysia.

Johor's relationship with the Riau Islands, particularly Batam, is through the ferry link between Johor Bahru International Ferry Terminal and Pasir Gudang Ferry Terminal and Batam Centre Ferry Terminal in Batam. Apart from Batam, there is also a ferry link between Johor Bahru International Ferry Terminal and Tanjungpinang Ferry Terminal, Bintan Island. Passenger arrivals from Batam at both the ferry terminal port, which is the main entrance from Batam, and Bintan Island, averaged approximately 576,000 people each year for the period 2014–2018.

Air connectivity within the Extended EC4 only exists between Melaka and Pekanbaru from Melaka International Airport. There are no flights to Sumatera and Southern Thailand from Senai International Airport in Johor since flight destinations to Sumatera and Southern Thailand have been catered by KLIA in EC2. Maritime links are well-connected between the ports of the EC4 Extended and Sumatera. Between EC4 Extended and Southern Thailand, the road and rail networks are also well-connected.

Reconfiguration of EC4

As part of its development strategy for Sumatera Island, Indonesia has included (i) the outermost islands of Riau Province (Rupat Island), (ii) Sri Junjungan Port, and (iii) West Sumatera (including its capital Padang) as part of EC4. The inclusion of these nodes or provinces is a means to promote a more balanced distribution of the benefits of growth by promoting connectivity between Riau and West Sumatera to enhance value linkages and expand trade opportunities along Sumatera's eastern coast (Table 61).

In Malaysia, recent developments have opened other opportunities for Melaka to develop economic links between the southern part of Peninsular Malaysia and Sumatera. These developments include the increasing popularity of cruise tourism and medical tourism and the proposed Johor Bahru–Singapore RTS that would connect the Riau Islands and Johor Bahru (Johor) via Singapore. Taking these into account, EC4 will include Johor in EC4, with Tanjung Pelepas Port (Gelang Patah) and Johor Port (Pasir Gudang) as key nodes. Melaka City and the Melaka International Ferry Terminal were included as additional nodes in Melaka.

The EC4 has been renamed the **Central Sumatera–Southern Malaysia Economic Corridor** (Maps 12 and 13).

Melaka City, the capital of Melaka, is a major destination for local and international tourists. The city is an important tourism node in the state of Melaka. In 2018, 17 million tourists visited Melaka, demonstrating the importance of the tourism industry. Singaporeans made up the majority of the international visitors.[58]

The MIFT in Banda Hilir is a passenger terminal ferry and is the main gateway to Riau Province. A large number of tourists from Dumai has made Melaka a health tourism destination. The terminal is also a port-of-call for cruise liners along the Strait of Malacca. In 2018, the Terminal was the fourth most important port-of-call in the country.[59]

---

[58] Tourism data were provided by Tourism Melaka. *Tourist Arrivals and Tourist Receipt* (2000–2018).

[59] Statistics of ship calls and cruise passenger arrivals to Malaysia were provided by Ministry of Tourism, Arts and Culture Malaysia, 2020. Putrajaya: MOTAC.

Table 61: Economic Corridor 4: Existing and Additional Provinces and Nodes, by Type

Province/State	Node/Type	CAP	COM	MGP	TOUR
INDONESIA					
Riau	Dumai Port			✓	
	Dumai City		✓		
	Sri Junjungan Port*			✓	
	Rupat Island*				✓
	Pekanbaru	✓	✓		
West Sumatera*	Padang*	✓	✓		
MALAYSIA					
Melaka	Tanjung Bruas Port (Port of Melaka)			✓	
	Melaka International Ferry Terminal*			✓	✓
	Melaka City*	✓	✓		✓
Johor*	Johor Bahru*	✓	✓		
	Tanjung Pelepas Port, Gelang Patah*			✓	
	Johor Port, Pasir Gudang*			✓	

CAP = capital, COM = commercial, MGP = maritime gateway port, TOUR = tourism.
Note: * denotes additional provinces and nodes.
Source: Study team.

Johor Bahru is the capital of the state of Johor. It is a growth center under the Iskandar Malaysia corridor designed by IRDA. The Iskandar Malaysia project covers the following Flagship Zone: (i) Johor Bahru City Center, (ii) Iskandar Puteri, (iii) Tanjung Pelepas, (iv) Senai–Skudai, and (v) Pasir Gudang–Tanjung Langsat. Johor Bahru will be the main entrance from the Riau Islands (Batam) and South Sumatera via Singapore. The proposed RTS is a cross-border rapid transit system that would connect Woodlands (Singapore) and Johor Bahru (Johor). It will be the main entry-exit gateway for the residents in Batam (Riau Islands) via Singapore.

Johor Bahru has road and rail connectivity with the Tanjung Pelepas Port (Gelang Patah) and Johor Port (Pasir Gudang). Both ports are the main trade gateway for manufacturers operating in Johor. The ferry terminal at Tanjung Pelepas Port and Johor Port will connect the population of Riau Islands (Batam) to Johor. The Tanjung Pelepas Port is the premier transshipment port in Malaysia. Protected by a deep-water bay, it allows the port to accommodate the biggest cargo vessels. Tanjung Pelepas Port is connected to over 300 ports-of-call globally.

Johor Port is a multipurpose port to handle all kinds of cargo. Johor Port handles liquid bulk cargoes since it began operating. Johor Port has facilities for both edible (primarily soya bean oil and palm oil) and nonedible liquids (mainly petroleum products). The port has the world's largest palm oil storage facility in its FTZ. Johor Port is also one of the largest discharging points for rice and cocoa in Malaysia as well as being one of the biggest terminals in Malaysia for fertilizer and cement.

Map 12: Central Sumatera–Southern Malaysia Economic Corridor
(Reconfigured Economic Corridor 4)

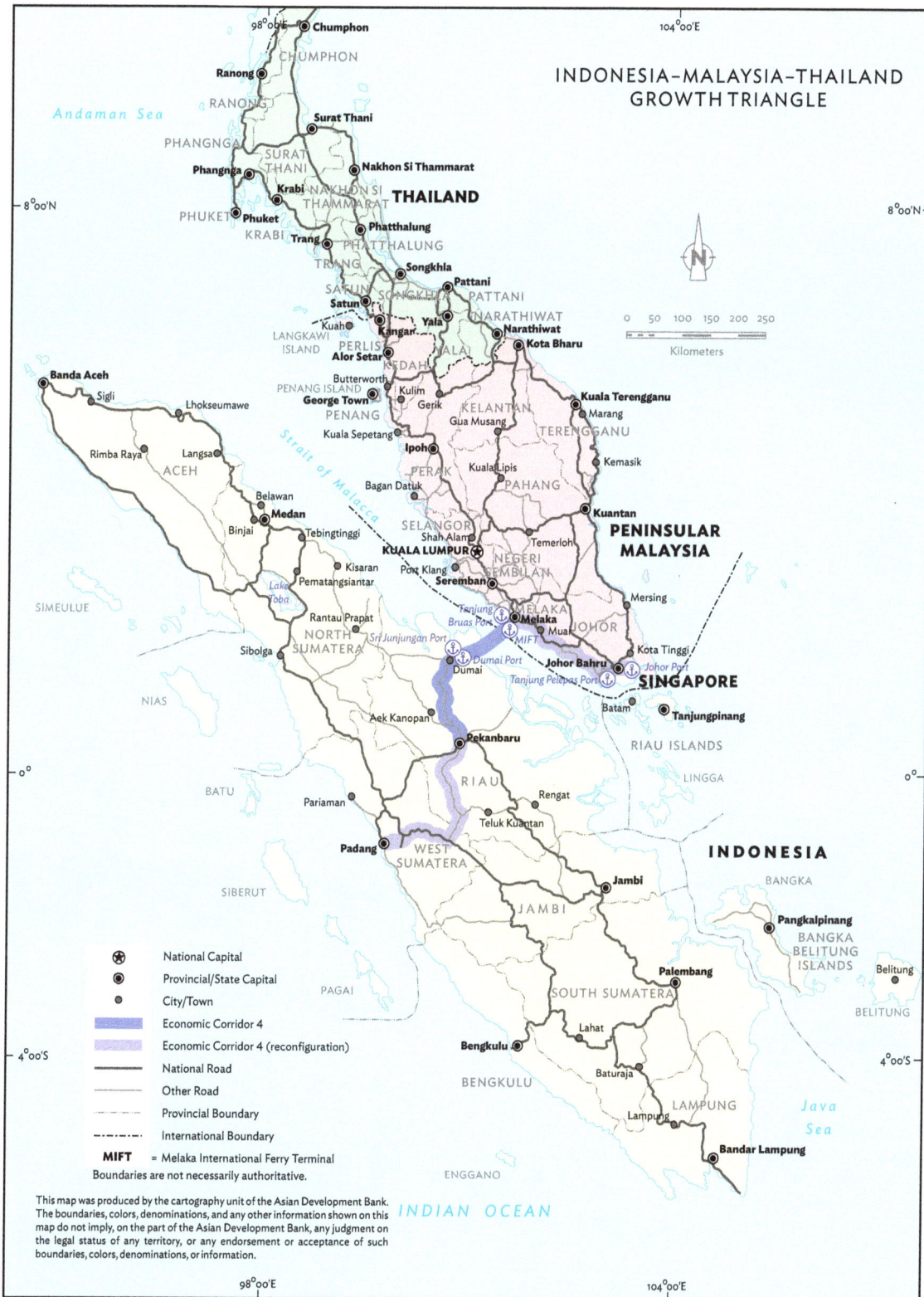

Source: Asian Development Bank.

**Map 13: Central Sumatera–Southern Malaysia Economic Corridor
(Reconfigured Economic Corridor 4) - Malaysia**

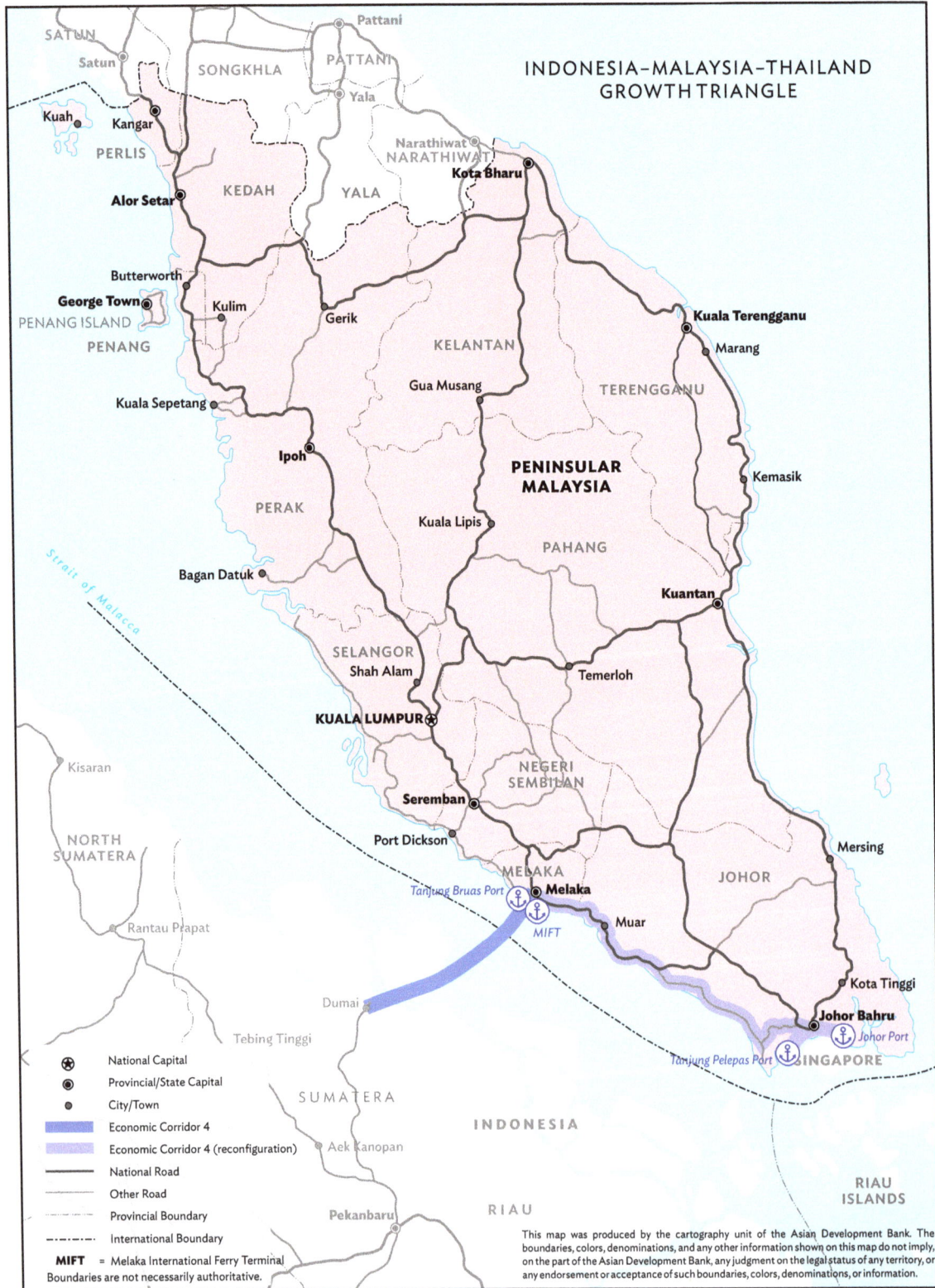

Source: Asian Development Bank.

Economic Corridor 5. The Ranong–Phuket–Aceh Economic Corridor

Overview

EC5 is mainly a maritime corridor linking ports in the northern part of Sumatera (mainly Ulee Lheue and Malahayati in Aceh Province) with Southern Thailand along its western coast facing the Andaman Sea, with the aim of exploiting tourism potentials (Map 14). In Sumatera, Aceh Province is part of the corridor and Banda Aceh, the capital, and Sabang (located in the adjacent We Island) are the gateway and tourism nodes, respectively.

Reconfiguration of Economic Corridor 5

Thailand has included the provinces of Phangnga and Krabi in the reconfigured EC5. The inclusion of Phangnga and Krabi in EC5 will support Thailand's strategy for the SEC to develop an inland tourism network between the coasts along the Gulf of Thailand and the Andaman Sea. The network will link high-potential tourist destinations, namely Phuket, Phangnga, Krabi, Surat Thani (Ko Samui, Ko Pha-ngan, Ko Toa), Chumphon, and Nakhon Si Thammarat (Sichon and Khanom beaches). This collective area will also integrate provincial production networks for rubber latex, rubber wood, and halal food supply chains in EC5 and EC6.

Malaysia is not included in the existing EC5. However, Malaysia has included Langkawi Island (Kedah) in the reconfigured EC5 to exploit the potential of the cruise tourism industry between Phuket and Aceh. Langkawi is on the international cruise liner route along the Strait of Malacca (Table 62). Langkawi island could serve as a new link between Sabang and Phuket, creating the Sabang–Phuket–Langkawi (SAPULA) Tourism Belt or Marine Tourism Triangle. Langkawi's economy is based on tourism, which is an important source of income for the state. The island has had a duty-free status since 1987 and is one of the most popular tourist destinations among local and international tourists.

Within Langkawi, the important nodes are Kuah and Teluk Ewa Port. Kuah is the main commercial center of Langkawi. The Kuah Jetty in Kuah is the main tourist gateway into Langkawi and has ferry connectivity with Penang Port (George Town), Kuala Perlis (Perlis), and Kuala Kedah (Kedah). Langkawi is among the main tourist destinations for both local and international travelers.

The Teluk Ewa Port is a trading and minor port in Langkawi. There has been a suggestion to expand Teluk Ewa Port as a major port. This port would enable Langkawi to connect to and shorten the trade passageway to Northeast Asia countries, which currently passes through Singapore. From this aspect, it can also potentially shorten cargo movement, through multimodal transport, to Songkhla Port in Southern Thailand. This will make Langkawi a trading hub in the Asian region.

No additional nodes in Sumatera have been included in the reconfigured EC5. However, Aceh should be able to expand tourism opportunities with Langkawi, in addition to Phuket, to revitalize the corridor. The collaboration between SAPULA for cruise tourism has been initiated under the IMT-GT framework.

Map 14: Ranong–Phuket–Aceh Economic Corridor
(Economic Corridor 5)

INDONESIA–MALAYSIA–THAILAND
GROWTH TRIANGLE

Chumphon

CHUMPHON

Ranong
Ranong Port
RANONG

Andaman Sea

PHANGNGA

Surat Thani

SURAT
THANI

Nakhon Si Thammarat

Phangnga

Krabi   NAKHON SI
THAMMARAT   THAILAND

8°oo'N

PHUKET   Phuket Port   Phuket
Phuket Port

KRABI

Trang   Phatthalung

TRANG   PHATTHALUNG

Songkhla

SATUN SONGKHLA   Pattani

Satun   PATTANI

SABANG
ISLAND

Sabang Port   Kangar   Yala   NARATHIWAT

Balohan Port
Malahayati Port   Alor Setar   PERLIS   Narathiwat

Ulee Lheue Port   Banda Aceh   KEDAH   Kota Bharu

Sigli   Butterworth   Kulim   Kuala Terengganu

Lhokseumawe   PENANG ISLAND   Gerik   KELANTAN   Marang

LANGKAWI
ISLAND

George Town   Kuala Sepetang   Gua Musang   TERENGGANU

PENANG

Langsa   Ipoh   Kuala Lipis   Kemasik

Rimba Raya   ACEH   PERAK   PAHANG

Belawan   Bagan Datuk

Binjai   Medan   Kuantan

Tebingtinggi   SELANGOR   Temerloh   PENINSULAR
MALAYSIA

Kisaran   Shah Alam
Pematangsiantar   KUALA LUMPUR ✪   NEGERI
SEMBILAN

Lake
Toba   Seremban   Mersing

SIMEULUE   Rantau Prapat   Port Dickson   MELAKA

NORTH
SUMATERA   Melaka   JOHOR

Sibolga   Dumai   Muar   Kota Tinggi

Johor Bahru   SINGAPORE

NIAS   Aek Kanopan

Pekanbaru

RIAU ISLANDS   Tanjungpinang

0°   RIAU   LINGGA   0°

BATU   Rengat

Pariaman   Teluk Kuantan   INDONESIA

Padang   WEST
SUMATERA   Jambi   BANGKA

SIBERUT   JAMBI   Pangkalpinang   BANGKA
BELITUNG
ISLANDS   Belitung

PAGAI   BELITUNG

National Capital   SOUTH SUMATERA   Palembang

Provincial/State Capital

City/Town   Lahat

4°oo'S   Economic Corridor 5   Bengkulu   Baturaja   Java
Sea   4°oo'S

National Road   BENGKULU   LAMPUNG

Other Road   Lampung

Provincial Boundary   Bandar Lampung

International Boundary   ENGGANO

Boundaries are not necessarily authoritative.   INDIAN OCEAN

This map was produced by the cartography unit of the Asian Development Bank.
The boundaries, colors, denominations, and any other information shown on this
map do not imply, on the part of the Asian Development Bank, any judgment on
the legal status of any territory, or any endorsement or acceptance of such
boundaries, colors, denominations, or information.

98°oo'E   104°oo'E

0   50 100 150 200 250
Kilometers

Strait of Malacca

Source: Asian Development Bank.

Table 62: Economic Corridor 5: Existing and Additional Provinces and Nodes, by Type

Province/State	Node	Type			
		CAP	COM	MGP	TOUR
INDONESIA					
Aceh	Banda Aceh	✓			
	Sabang City		✓		
	Ulee Lheue Port			✓	
	Malahayati Port			✓	
	Sabang Port		✓	✓	✓
	Balohan Port			✓	
MALAYSIA					
Kedah	Langkawi*				✓
	Teluk Ewa Port*			✓	
THAILAND					
Ranong	Ranong City	✓	✓		✓
	Ranong Port			✓	
Phuket	Phuket City	✓	✓		✓
	Phuket Port			✓	
Krabi*	Krabi City*	✓	✓		✓
Phangnga*	Phangnga City*	✓			

CAP = capital, COM = commercial, MGP = maritime gateway port, TOUR = tourism.
Note: * denotes additional provinces and nodes.
Source: Study team.

The existing EC5 has been renamed the **Southwestern Thailand–Northern Sumatera–Northwestern Malaysia Economic Corridor** (Maps 15 and 16).

Map 15: Southwestern Thailand–Northern Sumatera–Northwestern Malaysia Economic Corridor (Reconfigured Economic Corridor 5)

Source: Asian Development Bank.

Map 16: Southwestern Thailand–Northern Sumatera–Northwestern Malaysia Economic Corridor (Reconfigured Economic Corridor 5) - Malaysia

Source: Asian Development Bank.

Socioeconomic Profile

Langkawi consists of a cluster of 99 small and large islands. Langkawi is the largest island with an area of 526 square kilometers (km^2), accounting for 5% of the total area of Kedah. Langkawi is one of the 12 districts in Kedah and has 6 subdistricts: Ayer Hangat, Bohor, Kedawang, Kuah, Padang Matsirat, and Ulu Melaka. The total population of Langkawi was approximately 110,000 inhabitants in 2018 with a population density of 209 per km^2. The tourism industry drives Langkawi's economy, which contributes significantly to Kedah State's GDP. The island, which has been duty free since 1987, is one of the most popular tourist destinations among local and international tourists. The income from the tourism sector was $0.4 billion in 2018, contributing 8% to the nominal GDP in Kedah (Table 63).

Table 63: Langkawi: Selected Socioeconomic Indicators, 2018

Selected Macroeconomic Indicators	2018
Population ('000)	109.8
Land Area (square kilometer)	526.0
Population Density (population/square kilometer)	209.0
Revenue from Tourism ($ billion)*	0.4 (2018) 1.6 (2014)
Monthly Household Gross Income (median, $)	1,232.0
Incidence of Poverty, %	3.8

* Revenue from Tourism in Langkawi was abstracted from Langkawi Annual Report 2014 and 2018.
Source: Department of Statistics Malaysia. 2020. *My Local Stats Kedah 2019: Langkawi.* Putrajaya: DOS Malaysia.

The agriculture sector, in addition to tourism, contributes to Langkawi's economy. Rubber plantations and paddy fields are the principal crops, accounting for over 80% of total agricultural land. Mixed agriculture is in second with 15.0%, followed by aquaculture and livestock with 2%.[60]

Development Strategy for Langkawi

Cruise tourism is among the key focus areas of Malaysia's tourism development plans. Under the Economic Transformation Programme, efforts to grow this segment have resulted in the establishment of the Malaysia Cruise Council, a policymaking advisory committee comprising representatives from both the public and private sectors, including the Ministry of Tourism. Arts and Culture, the Ministry of Transport, and local port authorities. Plans are also underway for the development of a Straits Riviera in Malaysia, comprising six primary ports, i.e., Langkawi, Penang, Port Klang, Kota Kinabalu, Melaka, Kuching, and other secondary ports.[61]

A memorandum of understanding on Marine Tourism Triangle Cooperation was signed in April 2017 that will establish a cruise route between Langkawi in Malaysia, Phuket in Thailand, and Sabang in Aceh Province. The agreement, which was made in Bangkok during the World Travel and Tourism Council 2017 Global Summit, aims to help develop the Triangular Sailing Passage between Langkawi, Phuket, and Sabang.[62]

---

[60] Plan Malaysia. 2020. *Rancangan Tempatan Daerah Langkawi 2030.* Kuala Lumpur. Plan Malaysia.

[61] PEMANDU Malaysia. 2010. *Economic Transformation Programme: A Roadmap for Malaysia.* Putrajaya. Performance Management and Delivery Unit (PEMANDU), Prime Minister Office.

[62] The *Jakarta Post*. 2017. Malaysia, Indonesia to cooperate in Marine Tourism Triangle. 28 April. https://www.thejakartapost.com/travel/2017/04/28/malaysia-indonesia-to-cooperate-in-marine-tourism-triangle.html.

This memorandum of understanding is also in line with the vision of the Langkawi Tourism Blueprint (2016–2020) to showcase Langkawi as a world-class tourism destination with cruise tourism as one of the market segments to be promoted.

Status of Physical Connectivity

Land. Kuah is Langkawi's largest town and commercial center. Kuah Jetty, as well as the airport and seaports, are all easily accessible by road from Kuah. The roads in Langkawi are mainly federal roads and are well-connected (Table 64).

Table 64: Economic Corridor 5: Start and End Points in Langkawi

Start Point	End point	Route	Distance (km)	Traffic Lanes	Road Class
Kuah	Kuah Jetty, Kuah	110	4	2–4	Federal road
	Langkawi International Airport, Padang Mat Sirat	112	15	2–4	Federal road
	Langkawi Port (Tanjong Lembong Port), Kedawang	167	10	2–4	Federal road
	Star Cruise Jetty, Kedawang	112, 167, 117	21	2–4	Federal road
	Teluk Ewa Port, Air Hangat	112, 111	22	2–4	Federal road

km = kilometer.
Source: Compiled by author.

Maritime links. Langkawi can be accessed by ferry from Penang (Penang Port), Perlis (Kuala Perlis), and mainland Kedah (Kuala Kedah). The island can also be accessed from Thailand via Ko Lipe and Satun (Tammalang Pier). Key entry points for passengers to Langkawi are through Kuah Jetty, the Port of Langkawi (Tanjong Lembong Port), Telaga Harbor Jetty and Star Cruise Jetty. The Port of Langkawi operates a Ro-Ro ferry service (cars and passengers) between Kuala Kedah and Kuala Perlis. Teluk Ewa Port (Ayer Hangat) is a minor trading port in Langkawi.

The Kuah Jetty (Langkawi) has maritime connectivity with mainland Kedah, Perlis, and Penang via ferry service to Kuala Kedah Jetty (Kedah), Kuala Perlis Jetty (Perlis), and the Port of Swettenham (Penang), respectively. There are also passenger ferry services between Langkawi and Southern Thailand via Kuah Jetty with Ko Lipe and/or Phuket, and Tammalang Pier (Satun). The Star Cruise Jetty is a port-of-call in Langkawi for cruise liners passing through the Strait of Malacca. The Port of Langkawi provides Ro-Ro ferry services (cars and passengers) to Kuala Perlis Jetty and Kuala Kedah Jetty, and vice versa (Map 17).

Langkawi Island has a ferry link to Phuket via Koh Lipe. However, to date, there are no maritime connectivity and trade links between Langkawi and Sabang in Aceh. The Phuket to Langkawi ferry departs from Phuket's Rassada Pier and travels to Ko Lipe, and subsequently to Telaga Harbor Marina, Langkawi. Immigration controls in Thailand are in Ko Lipe, while in Malaysia they are located in Telaga Harbor Marina (Pantai Kok, Langkawi). The travel time from Phuket to Koh Lipe takes 4 hours, while Ko Lipe to Langkawi takes 1 hour and 30 minutes. The trip between Langkawi and Satun (Tammalang) by ferry takes only 1 hour and 15 minutes on high-speed boats.

Map 17: Maritime Links Between Langkawi and Perlis, Penang, Kedah, and Satun

NAKHON SI THAMMARAT

Phatthalung

THAILAND

Trang

PHATTHALUNG

TRANG

SATUN

Songkhla

Pattani

PATTANI

Ko Lipe Port

Satun

SONGKHLA

Yala

NARATHIWAT

Tammalang Port

Kangar

Kuala Perlis Passenger Jetty Terminal

Narathiwat

Kuah Passenger Jetty Terminal

Kuah

Kota Bharu

LANGKAWI ISLAND

PERLIS

YALA

Kuala Kedah Passenger Jetty Terminal

Alor Setar

KEDAH

Betong

Penang Port

Butterworth

George Town

Kulim

Gerik

PENANG ISLAND

KELANTAN

PENANG

Gua Musang

Kuala Sepetang

Ipoh

PENINSULAR MALAYSIA

● Provincial/State Capital
● City/Town
—— National Road
—— Other Road
- - - Provincial Boundary
-·-·- International Boundary

Boundaries are not necessarily authoritative.

PERAK

Kuala Lipis

PAHANG

Bagan Datuk

This map was produced by the cartography unit of the Asian Development Bank. The boundaries, colors, denominations, and any other information shown on this map do not imply, on the part of the Asian Development Bank, any judgment on the legal status of any territory, or any endorsement or acceptance of such boundaries, colors, denominations, or information.

Source: Asian Development Bank.

Teluk Ewa Port is a minor port in Langkawi. The port is located on the northern coast of Pulau Langkawi. The jetty was built in November 1982 and commenced operations in September 1984. The port is designed to handle petroleum products, coal, and general cargo. The major exports include cement and clinker. Teluk Ewa Port has links with the Port of Palembang (South Sumatera) by importing coal from the port. For Southern Thailand, Teluk Ewa Port imports iron ore from the Port of Krabi (Satun).[63]

There have been proposals to expand Teluk Ewa Port. The waters at Teluk Ewa have a natural depth of 18–30 meters, making it suitable for large trading vessels to pass through or dock at the port. This port would enable Langkawi to connect to and shorten the trade passageway to Northeast Asia countries, which currently passes through Singapore. The port would ease the journey for the cargo vessels, estimating that it would take only between 3–4 hours, via multimodal transport, to reach Songkhla Port in Southern Thailand. This will establish Langkawi as a trading hub in the Asian region.[64]

Air Links

The Langkawi International Airport, located at Padang Mat Sirat, supports the tourism industry in Langkawi. The airport serves as a hub for domestic flights from Penang, Kuala Lumpur, Subang, and Senai (Johor Bahru). Flights departing Langkawi International Airport to Medan are provided by international airlines, such as Sriwijaya Air and Lion Air. Due to the proximity between Langkawi and Phuket, there are no flights to Phuket from Langkawi International Airport (Table 65).

Table 65: Langkawi International Airport: Flight Routes within IMT-GT

Airport	Airlines	Destinations within Malaysia	Destination to Sumatera
Langkawi International Airport, Langkawi, Kedah	Air Asia	Kuala Lumpur, Penang, Johor Bahru	–
	MAS	Kuala Lumpur	–
	Firefly	Subang, Penang	–
	Malindo Air	Kuala Lumpur, Subang	–
	Sriwijaya Air (Indonesia)*	–	Medan
	Lion Air (Indonesia)*	–	Medan

– = not applicable, * = International carriers, MAS = Malaysia Airlines.
Source: Compiled by author from the websites of relevant domestic and international airlines.

Tourism

The Langkawi Development Authority (LADA), established in 1990, plans the development of the tourism industry in Langkawi. The Langkawi Tourism Blueprint 2011–2015 and 2016–2020 determine the development path of the tourism industry in Langkawi. The blueprints aim to make the island one of the world's top 10 islands and ecotourism destinations. Its strategic position on the cruise liner routes in the Andaman Sea and Strait of Malacca will make it an important port-of-call and a cruise tourist destination. Langkawi Island is also

---

[63] The information about Teluk Ewa Port was abridged from Penang Port Commission, Teluk Ewa Port found at https://www.penangport.gov.my/en/port-installation/teluk-ewa-jetty.

[64] *Daily Express.* 2017. Teluk Ewa has Potential to Become Langkawi's Trading Port. 31 October. http://dailyexpress.com.my/news.cfm?NewsID=120755.

part of the Straits Riviera route proposed by the Government of Malaysia in addition to the ports-of-call in Penang, Sepang (Selangor), Melaka, Tanjung Pelepas (Johor), and Kota Kinabalu.[65]

Langkawi was accorded the UNESCO Global Geopark status in June 2007. The Langkawi Geopark comprises Machincang Cambrian Geoforest Park, Kilim Karst Geoforest Park, and *Dayang Bunting* Marble Geoforest Park. All three of these Geoforest Parks are also local and international tourist destinations. This has also strengthened the ecotourism industry in Langkawi (Table 66).

Table 66: Langkawi: Selected Key Tourism Products

Tourism Sector	Tourism Product
Geopark	Machincang Cambrian Geoforest Park, Kilim Karst Geoforest Park, and Dayang Bunting Marble Geoforest Park
Nature Tourism	Pulau Payar Marine Park, Cenang Beach, Telaga Tujuh Waterfall, Dayang Bunting Island
Cultural Heritage	Mahsuri's Tomb (Padang Matsirat)
Manufactured	Gunung Machinchang Cable Car, Galeria Perdana, Langkawi Eagle Suare, Langkawi Underwater World, Langkawi Crystal, Telaga Harbor Park

Source: Compiled by author.

For 2016–2018, tourist arrivals from Ko Lipe were on average almost 21,000 people each year, accounting for 1% of the total tourist arrivals at Kuah Jetty Terminal. Meanwhile, tourist arrivals from Satun (Tammalang Pier) were 78,000 every year, accounting for 3% of the total passengers arriving at Kuah Jetty Terminal. Factors such as distance and transportation costs determine the difference in total arrivals between Satun and Ko Lipe (Table 67).

Although Phuket's contribution to the total tourism arrivals in Langkawi was small, tourist arrivals from Phuket showed an increasing trend with a high growth rate of 76% for 2016–2018, compared to arrivals from Satun (–3%) and domestic tourists (–17%), which showed a downward trend. This demonstrates great potential for strengthening cross-border tourism between Phuket and Langkawi.

---

[65]   The information on Straits Riviera route was abridged from *Travel Weekly Asia*. Straits Riviera: Malaysia's cruise playground of the East? found at https://www.travelweekly-asia.com/Destination-Travel/Straits-Riviera-Malaysia-s-cruise-playground-of-the-East.

Table 67: Kuah Jetty Terminal: Arrivals and Departures, 2016–2018

('000 passengers)

Arrivals and Departures		2016	2017	2018	Average (2016–2018)	Share to Total Passengers (%)	CAGR (2016–2018), %
Arrivals	Domestic	2,077	2,002	1,941	2,007	95	(3)
	Satun	97	70	68	78	4	(17)
	Ko Lipe	8	28	26	21	1	76
	Subtotal	2,182	2,099	2,035	2,106	100	(3)
Departures	Domestic	2,083	1,997	1,947	2,009	95	(3)
	Satun	110	75	74	86	4	(18)
	Ko Lipe	8	26	24	19	1	70
	Subtotal	2,201	2,098	2,044	2,115	100	(4)
Total (arrival and departure)	Domestic	4,159	3,999	3,888	4,016	95	(3)
	Satun	208	145	141	165	4	(17)
	Ko Lipe	17	54	49	40	1	73
	Total	4,384	4,198	4,079	4,220	100	(4)

( ) = negative, CAGR = compound annual growth rate.
Source: Maritime Department of Malaysia. 2019. *Statistik Pengendalian Feri dan Penumpang Di Terminal Feri Kuah.* https://www.marine.gov.my/jlm/halaman/pelabuhan-8 (accessed 1 May 2020).

The influx of tourists from Phuket is expected to increase with the availability of air services from Phuket International Airport to Langkawi provided by Malindo Air (Malaysia). However, there are no available flights to Aceh or Southern Thailand from Langkawi International Airport. The number of foreign tourists visiting Kedah (including Langkawi) from 2014–2017 was on average 1.3 million people annually, compared to local tourists of 2.4 million people annually (Table 68).[66] Of the total foreign tourists, Langkawi Island is the host to 96% of foreign travelers to Kedah compared to mainland Kedah, with only 5%. In other words, Langkawi offers more attractive tourism products to international tourists than mainland Kedah, especially in ecotourism.

Table 68: Tourist Arrivals in Mainland Kedah and Langkawi, 2014–2017

Year	Domestic Tourists (million)			Foreign Tourists (million)			Total Tourists (Domestic and Foreign)
	Mainland Kedah	Langkawi Island	Subtotal	Mainland Kedah	Langkawi Island	Subtotal	
2014	1.1	1.0	2.1	0.05	1.2	1.2	3.3
2015	1.0	1.3	2.3	0.05	1.2	1.2	3.5
2016	1.0	1.4	2.5	0.05	1.2	1.3	3.8
2017	1.0	1.6	2.6	0.05	1.4	1.4	4.0
Average (2014–2017)	1.0	1.3	2.4	0.05	1.2	1.3	3.6
Average Share to Total Tourist, %	28	37	65	1	34	35	100

Source: Tourism Malaysia Kedah. 2018. Number of Tourists to Kedah (2014-2017). https://www.data.gov.my/data/ms_MY/dataset/kemasukan-pelancong-ke-negeri-kedah-2014-2017 (accessed 1 May 2020).

---

[66] Data on tourist arrivals published by Tourism Malaysia Kedah and LADA are different. The reason behind this is that LADA does not publish the breakdown of tourism data by area, i.e., mainland Kedah and Langkawi. However, this does not affect the analysis of the tourism industry in Langkawi.

Apart from ecotourism, cruise and yacht tourism have the potential to be developed in Langkawi in the future, even though the sector contribution from cruise and yacht tourism is small. For 2014–2017, about 143,000 tourists from cruises arrive in Langkawi every year, which accounted for 4% of the total number of tourists arriving on Langkawi Island (Table 69).

Table 69: Langkawi Island Visitors' Arrival by Mode of Entry, 2014–2019

('000 visitors)

| Year | Jetty Terminal | | | | Airport | | Langkawi Port | Total |
	Domestic	Foreign	Cruise	Yacht	Domestic	Foreign	Car Passenger Ferry	
2014	2,178	132	159	6	1,019	86	21	3,601
2015	2,067	155	197	6	1,055	86	58	3,624
2016	2,078	136	58	5	1,172	120	67	3,635
2017	1,920	126	157	5	1,206	139	125	3,679
2018	–	–	–	–	–	–	–	3,629
2019	–	–	–	–	–	–	–	3,924
Average (2014–2017)	2,061	137	143	5	1,113	108	68	3,635
Average Share to Total Mode of Entry, %	57	4	4	0	31	3	2	100

– = not available

Source: Langkawi Development Authority (LADA). https://www.lada.gov.my/statistik/ (accessed 1 June 2020).

Meanwhile, tourists from the yacht sector accounted for less than 1%, or about 5,000 tourists per year for 2014–2017. This implies that local tourists were dominant, accounting for 87% of the total tourists arriving at various entry modes in Langkawi, namely Kuah Jetty, Telaga Harbor Jetty, Tanjung Lembong Port (Langkawi Port), Star Cruise Jetty, and Langkawi International Airport.

Table 70 shows the number of ship calls and cruise passengers arriving at the port-of-call in Malaysia. The Star Cruise Jetty, Langkawi (Kedah), is the third most important port-of-call, following BCC (Port Klang) and Swettenham Pier Cruise (Penang). The number of passengers arriving at Star Cruise Jetty was an average of 123,000 per year, with a total of 85 ship calls per year for the period 2016–2018.

Table 70: Malaysia: Ship Calls and Cruise Passenger Arrivals, 2016–2018

Port-of-Call	State	Passengers (Number)				Ship Calls (Number)			
		2016	2017	2018	Average 2016–2018	2016	2017	2018	Average 2016–2018
Boustead Cruise Centre, Port Klang	Selangor	251,499	305,420	364,511	307,143	142	165	249	185
Swettenham Pier Cruise, Penang Port	Penang	213,566	426,140	341,028	326,911	136	267	185	196
Star Cruise Jetty	Langkawi, Kedah	126,786	110,946	131,160	122,964	77	86	91	85
Melaka Marina (Melaka International Ferry Terminal)	Melaka	56,476	50,680	13,455	40,204	45	49	43	46
Lumut Port	Perak	349	387	190	309	1	2	1	1
Johor Port, Pasir Gudang	Johor	0	0	0	0	0	0	0	0
Pulau Redang port	Terengganu	4,589	0	19,783	12,186	3	0	7	5
Tioman Port	Pahang	4,589	0	0	4,589	3	0	0	3
Kota Kinabalu Port	Sabah	20,459	27,541	55,775	34,592	19	20	25	21
Labuan Port	Sabah	0	0	0	0	0	0	0	0
Sandakan	Sabah	0	0	2,577	2,577	0	0	4	4
Kuching Port	Sarawak	3,149	2,313	3,238	2,900	7	5	7	6
Bintulu Port	Sarawak	601	640	1,020	754	2	2	2	2
Sum of Above		682,063	924,067	932,737	846,289	435	596	614	548

Source: Ministry of Tourism, Arts and Culture.2020. *Ship Calls and Cruise Passenger Arrivals, 2016–2018*. Putrajaya: MOTAC Malaysia.

Cruise lines visiting Langkawi in 2019 included AIDA Cruises, Costa Cruises, Cruise & Maritime, Cunard, Dream Cruises, Hapag Lloyd, Holland America, Marella Cruises, NCL, Oceania Cruises, P&O Australia, P&O Cruises, Phoenix Reisen, Princess Cruises, Regent Seven Seas, Royal Caribbean, Seabourn, Silversea, Star Clippers, Star Cruises, TUI Cruises and Windstar Cruises.[67]

- Princes Cruise Line and Norwegian Cruise Line are used as examples of the cruise routes through the port-of-call at Star Cruise Jetty (Langkawi). Princes Cruise Liner's excursions take 29 days, starting from Singapore, with a layover at Port Klang, Langkawi, Phuket, and then ending in Rome (Italy). Whereas, the Norwegian Cruise Line begins in Bangkok and ends in Singapore with an excursion of 12 days. The route shows a strong cruise route link with Phuket. However, there is no cruise link available between Langkawi and Sabang (Aceh). With the inclusion of Langkawi, a SAPULA tourism corridor can be established.

Other than the main entry via Kuah Jetty, Langkawi International Airport is also a main gateway used by tourists. For 2014–2018, the number of passengers (inbound and outbound) is on average 2.5 million tourists each year or making up 4% of the total passengers that is transported by all airports in the Peninsular Malaysia (Table 71).

---

[67] The information on Langkawi, Malaysia Cruise Ships Schedule 2019 was compiled from http://crew-center.com/langkawi-malaysia-·cruise-ships-schedule-2020.

Table 71: Total Passengers Handled by Airports (Inbound and Outbound), Excluding Transit Passengers, 2015–2018 (million travelers)

Airport	2014	2015	2016	2017	2018	Average (2014–2018)	Average Share to All Airports, %	CAGR, (2014–2018), %
Langkawi International Airport, Langkawi, Kedah	2.2	2.3	2.7	2.8	2.7	2.5	4	5.3
All airports in Peninsular Malaysia	65.7	67.1	71.7	78.7	79.9	72.6	–	5.0

– = not applicable, CAGR = compound annual growth rate.
Source: Ministry of Transport. 2019. Transport Statistic Malaysia 2018. Putrajaya: MOT Malaysia.

Overall Assessment

The town of Kuah is easily accessible by state and federal roads. Kuah Jetty is the main gateway into Langkawi for visitors from Penang, mainland Kedah, and Perlis, as well as from Satun and Phuket in Thailand. Other than maritime sea-links, Langkawi International Airport is also the second most important gateway in Langkawi. There are air links between Langkawi and Penang, Kuala Lumpur, Subang, Johor Bahru, Medan, and Singapore.

The economy of Langkawi is mainly based on the tourism industry. The island is famous for its shopping tourism following the establishment of its status as a duty-free island in 1987. Today, Kuah is the main commercial center since Langkawi was designated as a UNESCO Global Geopark in June 2007, which has promoted the island as an attractive tourist destination, especially for international tourists. Other tourism sectors, such as archaeotourism, heritage tourism, and cruise tourism, were prioritized under the Langkawi Tourism Blueprint (2016–2020).

Cross-border tourism between Langkawi and Southern Thailand has been established by the maritime links between Langkawi and Phuket (Ko Lipe) and Satun (Tammalang Pier). To date, there have been no maritime links between Langkawi and Sabang.

Langkawi has the potential to become a hub for cruise tourism because it is located along the routes travelers take through the Strait of Malacca and the Andaman Sea. Langkawi Island is also part of the Straits Riviera route proposed by the Government of Malaysia in addition to the ports of call in Penang, Sepang (Selangor), Melaka, Tanjung Pelepas (Johor), and Kota Kinabalu. The Star Cruise Jetty, Langkawi (Kedah), is the third most important port-of-call, following BCC (Port Klang) and Swettenham Pier Cruise (Penang). The cruise industry is being considered by the government as one of the national key economic areas. The Malaysia Cruise Council was formed in 2012 to chart the development path of cruise tourism in the country, including Langkawi.[68]

---

[68]   The Malaysia Cruise Council (MCC), a policymaking advisory committee comprising representatives from both public and private sectors, including the Ministry of Tourism and Culture, Ministry of Transport, and local port authorities.

Teluk Ewa Port is a Langkawi trading port that handles petroleum products, coal, and general cargo. The major exports include cement and clinker. Teluk Ewa Port has links with the Port of Palembang (South Sumatera) by importing coal from the port. For Southern Thailand, Teluk Ewa Port imports iron ore from the Port of Krabi (Satun). There has been a proposal for the expansion of Teluk Ewa Port, making it suitable for large trading vessels to pass through or to dock at the port. The expansion of the port would enable Langkawi to connect to and shorten the trade route to Northeast Asia countries, which currently passes through Singapore. This port can also facilitate the movement of cargo via multimodal transport to Songkhla Port in Southern Thailand. This would ultimately establish Langkawi as an important trading hub in the Asian region.

CHAPTER

4

PROPOSED ROUTE FOR
ECONOMIC CORRIDOR 6

Overview

EC6 is a new corridor proposed by Thailand during the 24th IMT-GT Ministerial Meeting held on 1 October 2018 in Melaka, Malaysia. The proposed EC6 is envisaged to open new trade routes between Southern Thailand and Malaysia through the East Coast Rail Link (ECRL). The ECRL, which is part of the PRC's Belt and Road Initiative (BRI), will connect the east and west coasts of Peninsular Malaysia. The proposed corridor is perceived to be a game changer for IMT-GT as it creates opportunities for expanded trade with the PRC and Europe. Malaysia is currently undertaking rapid and massive development of its eastern coast to create catalytic growth centers that could leverage on infrastructure expansion in the next decade.

In configuring the EC6 route, the study took into account: (i) the development strategy of the countries the areas to be traversed by the route, (ii) the existing connectivity between provinces or states and nodes along the route, and (iii) economic opportunities and potential value chain linkages.

Development Strategies

Malaysia's strategy for EC6 is aligned with the development objectives of the ECER Blueprint 2.0. To develop the ECER states, the Blueprint identified seven priority development areas: (i) tourism; (ii) oil, gas, and petrochemicals; (iii) manufacturing; (iv) agribusiness; (v) human capital development; (vi) logistics and (vii) services. These clusters will be supported by developments in transportation, infrastructure, property development, and protection of the environment to make the region an ideal destination for business, investments, and quality living. The development of the eastern region will be boosted with the construction of the ECRL, which will provide the peninsula's eastern coast with a more efficient means of access to the west coast along the Strait of Malacca.

Indonesia's strategy for EC6 is to link Riau Islands and Bangka Belitung Islands with rapid developments in Malaysia. Riau Islands and Bangka Belitung Islands are strategic nodes in Sumatera's growth corridor (Batam, Pangkalpinang, and Tanjungpinang) and equalization corridor (*koridor pemerataan*) (Natuna and Tanjung Pandan). Riau Islands is one of Indonesia's southernmost prosperous provinces. It is the fourth-largest province after East Kalimantan, Jakarta, and Riau. Bangka Belitung Islands is known to have the largest tin deposit in the world, but while its economy is growing, the distribution of the benefits of growth has lagged. The SEZs in these territories are spurring industrial development that benefit from their strategic locations—in the case of Riau Islands, to Singapore and Malaysia; and in the case of Bangka Belitung Islands, to South Sumatera

Thailand's strategy for EC6 is to integrate provincial production networks in the three provinces—Narathiwat, Pattani, and Yala—with halal and other food supply chains in Songkhla and nearby areas (EC1). Because of security issues in these provinces that limit outside investments, agricultural produce is transported to nearby factories or exported directly through the Thai–Malaysian borders. Enhancing the domestic value chain will boost the productivity and economic resiliency of provinces in Southern Thailand. The three provinces can also leverage their shared culture and history to expand opportunities for tourism.

The Proposed Route for Economic Corridor 6

The proposed EC6 route involves 17 provinces and states, covering almost the entire area of the IMT-GT triangle. It covers three provinces in Southern Thailand, eight states in Malaysia in two alternative routes, and the six provinces in Sumatera—four provinces in mainland Sumatera, and two archipelagic provinces in the southeastern part (Map 18).

Key Nodes in Malaysia

EC6 encompasses eight states—the ECER states (Kelantan, Terengganu, and Pahang) and the west coast states of Perak, Selangor, Negeri Sembilan, Melaka, and Johor. The following section discusses key nodes in the ECER states. The key nodes in other states have already been reviewed in the sections on EC2 and EC4 in Chapter 3.

The capitals of the ECER states that are involved in the EC6 are Kota Bharu (Kelantan), Kuala Terengganu (Terengganu), and Kuantan (Pahang). These state capitals are important tourism nodes, as well as commercial and administrative centers (Table 72).

The Tok Bali Port in Kelantan is a minor port and fishing port. Under the ECER Blueprint 2.0, this port will be expanded to serve as a feeder port for Kuantan Port. The port has also been identified as a regional distribution hub for the movement of goods for cross-border trade with Southern Thailand, Cambodia, the Lao People's Democratic Republic (Lao PDR), and Viet Nam. It also serves as a halal export hub, focusing on halal production and distribution with its linkage to Pasir Mas Halal Park.

The important seaports in the EC6 are Kemaman Port and Kuantan Port. Both these seaports are key trade gateways to the Mekong countries (Cambodia, the Lao PDR and Viet Nam), northeast Asia, and the Pacific Rim.

- The Kemaman Port is one of the deepest seaports in Malaysia and a fast-emerging port acting as a new gateway to the Asia and Pacific region. The port also serves as a feeder port for Kuantan Port, while serving the logistics requirements of the nearby Kemaman Heavy Industrial Park.

- Kuantan Port, which is strategically located in the heartland of the petrochemical industry, has been developed into a major container terminal for the east coast region. The port will be a catalyst for the rapid expansion of industrial and manufacturing activities in the East Coast Industrial Corridor.

Under the ECER Blueprint 2.0, the state of Kelantan will be positioned as the cross-border gateway and a strategic logistics center for northeastern Malaysia, leveraging on its proximity to Southern Thailand (Narathiwat), Cambodia, the Lao PDR, and Viet Nam. In relation to this, the border towns that are involved include Pengkalan Kubor, Rantau Panjang, and Bukit Bunga. There are cross-border trade activities through the border gateways in Pengkalan Kubor–Tak Bai (Narathiwat), Rantau Panjang–Su-ngai Kolok (Narathiwat), and Bukit Bunga–Ban Buketa (Narathiwat). These three border towns are popular tourist destinations for both local and international tourists. Rantau Panjang and Pengkalan Kubor, which are close to their respective immigration, customs, and quarantine complexes, were given duty-free zone status in 2002 and 1989, respectively. These duty-free zones are also popular tourist destinations.

Map 18: Southeastern Thailand–Eastern Malaysia–Southern Sumatera Economic Corridor
(Proposed Route for Economic Corridor 6)

98°00'E   Chumphon

INDONESIA–MALAYSIA–THAILAND
GROWTH TRIANGLE

104°00'E

CHUMPHON

Ranong

RANONG

Andaman Sea

Surat Thani

PHANGNGA

SURAT
THANI

Nakhon Si Thammarat

Phangnga

NAKHON SI
THAMMARAT

THAILAND

Krabi

8°00'N

PHUKET   Phuket

KRABI   Trang

Phatthalung

TRANG

PHATTHALUNG

SATUN   SONGKHLA   Songkhla

Satun   Kuah   Kangar   Yala

Pattani

PATTANI

NARATHIWAT

Narathiwat

Kota Bharu

8°00'N

LANGKAWI
ISLAND

PERLIS   Alor Setar

KEDAH   Bukit Bunga

YALA

Banda Aceh

Butterworth   Kulim

Gerik

KELANTAN

TERENGGANU

Kuala Terengganu

Marang

Sigli   Lhokseumawe

George Town

PENANG ISLAND   Kuala Sepetang

PENANG

Gua Musang

Langsa

Rimba Raya

ACEH

Ipoh

Kuala Lipis

Kemasik

Strait of Malacca

Lumut Port   PERAK

Bagan Datuk

PAHANG

Belawan   Medan

Binjai   Tebingtinggi

SELANGOR   Shah Alam

KUALA LUMPUR

Kuantan

Kisaran   Pematangsiantar

Lake Toba

Port Klang   NEGERI
SEMBILAN

Temerloh

PENINSULAR
MALAYSIA

SIMEULUE

Seremban

Port Dickson

MELAKA   Mersing

Sibolga

NORTH
SUMATERA

Rantau Prapat

Melaka   Muar

JOHOR

Kota Tinggi   Johor Port

NIAS

Dumai

Aek Kanopan

Johor Bahru

Tanjung Pelepas Port   SINGAPORE

Batam   Tanjungpinang

0°

Pekanbaru

RIAU ISLANDS

LINGGA

0°

BATU

Pariaman

RIAU

Rengat

Teluk Kuantan

SIBERUT

Padang

WEST
SUMATERA

INDONESIA

BANGKA

Jambi

Pangkalpinang

BANGKA
BELITUNG
ISLANDS

PAGAI

JAMBI

Tanjung Pandan

BELITUNG

SOUTH SUMATERA   Palembang

4°00'S

Bengkulu

Lahat

4°00'S

BENGKULU

Baturaja

*Java
Sea*

LAMPUNG

Lampung

ENGGANO

Bandar Lampung

INDIAN OCEAN

98°00'E

104°00'E

Legend:

⊛ National Capital
◎ Provincial/State Capital
• City/Town
▬ Economic Corridor 6 (proposed)
—— National Road
—— Other Road
—·— Provincial Boundary
—··— International Boundary

Boundaries are not necessarily authoritative.

0   50 100 150 200 250
Kilometers

This map was produced by the cartography unit of the Asian Development Bank. The boundaries, colors, denominations, and any other information shown on this map do not imply, on the part of the Asian Development Bank, any judgment on the legal status of any territory, or any endorsement or acceptance of such boundaries, colors, denominations, or information.

Source: Asian Development Bank.

Table 72: Provinces, States, and Nodes in the Proposed Economic Corridor 6, by Type

Province/State	Node	Type CAP	COM	BCP	MGP	TOUR
INDONESIA						
South Sumatera	Palembang	✓	✓			✓
Jambi	Jambi	✓	✓			
Lampung	Bandar Lampung	✓	✓		✓	
Bengkulu	Bengkulu	✓	✓		✓	
Riau Islands	Batam		✓		✓	
	Tanjungpinang	✓			✓	
Bangka Belitung Islands	Tanjung Pandan		✓			✓
	Pangkalpinang	✓				
MALAYSIA						
Kelantan	Rantau Panjang			✓		✓
	Bukit Bunga			✓		✓
	Pengkalan Kubor			✓		✓
	Kota Bharu	✓				
	Tok Bali Port		✓		✓	
Terengganu	Kuala Terengganu	✓				
	Kemaman Port		✓			
Pahang	Kuantan	✓	✓	✓		
	Kuantan Port		✓			
Perak	Ipoh	✓				
	Lumut Port				✓	
Selangor	Port Klang				✓	
Melaka	Melaka City	✓				
	Tanjung Bruas Port				✓	
	Melaka International Ferry Terminal				✓	
Johor	Johor Bahru	✓				
	Tanjung Pelepas Port, Gelang Patah				✓	
	Johor Port, Pasir Gudang				✓	
Negeri Sembilan	Seremban	✓				
	Port Dickson				✓	✓
THAILAND						
Pattani	Pattani City	✓				
Yala	Yala City	✓				
	Betong			✓		✓
Narathiwat	Narathiwat City	✓				
	Su-ngai Kolok			✓		
	Buketa			✓		
	Tak Bai		✓	✓		

BCP = border crossing point, CAP = capital, COM = commercial, MGP = maritime gateway port, TOUR = tourism.
Source: Study team.

Alternative Routes

There are two alternative routes in Malaysia from Kelantan. One passes through Terengganu, Pahang along the eastern coast, crossing to Selangor (EC2), Negeri Sembilan (EC2), Melaka (EC4) and onward to Johor (EC4); the other route links Kota Bharu (the start point of ECRL), passing through Perak, Selangor, up to Negeri Sembilan, Melaka, and with Johor as end point. These routes are henceforth referred to as EC6 Malaysia Route 1 (EC6-MR1), and EC6 Malaysia Route 2 (EC6-MR2). Both the EC6-MR1 and EC6-MR2 routes converge at Tanjung Bruas Port in Melaka for connectivity to the EC3 (Central Sumatera) and at Johor Bahru for connectivity to South Sumatera (Bangka Belitung and Riau Islands).

The EC6 route heading eastward will cover the east coast states of Peninsular Malaysia, namely Kelantan, Terengganu, and Pahang. These states are under the purview of the ECERDC. Meanwhile, the EC6 alternative route heading westward will cover several states on the west coast of Peninsular Malaysia, namely Perak, Selangor, and Negeri Sembilan.

The states of Terengganu, Pahang, and Johor[69] are not participating states under the IMT-GT cooperation framework. Therefore, the participation of these states must be agreed by the respective state governments and approved by the federal government. The IMT-GT states in the proposed EC6 route—Terengganu, Pahang, and Johor—can serve as a "bridge" for connectivity to southern Sumatera and the Riau Islands.

Route 1 Eastward: EC6-MR1

The EC6-MR1 route begins from Bukit Bunga BCP and traverses Kota Bharu, continues to Kuantan, and crosses to the west coast of Peninsular Malaysia via the East Coast Expressway (ECE) to Seremban and Port Dickson, heads toward the south to Tanjung Bruas Port and Melaka City, and finally ends in Johor Bahru. The distance from Bukit Bunga (Kelantan) to Johor Bahru (Johor) is almost 1,100 km via the state, federal and expressway roads. The expressways involved from Kota Bharu to Johor Bahru are the ECE 1 and 2, Kuala Lumpur–Karak Highway (E8), Seremban–Port Dickson Highway (E29) and E1–E2 (Table 73 and Map 19).

The key maritime gateway in EC6-MR1 is Kuantan Port (Pahang). Kuantan Port is the designated port for the PRC–Malaysia Belt and Road Initiatives and plays a strategic role in expanding trade with the PRC and Europe. Kuantan Port has maritime links to Songkhla Port in Thailand as well as the Southeast and Northeast Asian regions. There is no maritime connectivity between Kuantan Port (Pahang) and the ports in Sumatera, but it has connectivity with Laem Chabang Port in Bangkok.

---

[69] Terengganu and Pahang are not participating states in the IMT-GT. Johor is part of the Singapore-Johor-Riau Growth Triangle, established in 1994 by the governments of Malaysia, Indonesia, and Singapore. Johor has bilateral relations also with Singapore under the Malaysia–Singapore Joint Ministerial Committee for Iskandar Malaysia, which was established in 2007 to regulate the development of Iskandar Malaysia.

Table 73: EC6-MR1: Eastward Connectivity Routes

StartPoint	End Point	Route	Distance (km)	Traffic Lanes	Road Class
Bukit Bunga, Kelantan (BCP)		4, 8, D14,8	83	2	Federal and state road
Rantau Panjang, Kelantan (BCP)	Kota Bharu, Kelantan	AH18, 196, D23, 134, 3	40	2	Federal and state road
Pengkalan Kubor, Kelantan (BCP)		134, 3, 8	31	2	Federal road
Kota Bharu, Kelantan	Tok Bali, Kelantan	3, D10, D141	46	2	Federal and state road
Tok Bali, Kelantan	Kuala Terengganu, Terengganu	T3, 3685, T147, 3, 65	118	2	Federal and state road
Kuala Terengganu, Terengganu	Kemaman Port, Terengganu	14, E8, 3	157	2–4	Federal and state road
Kemaman Port, Terengganu	Kuantan Port, Pahang	3	45	2	Federal and state road
Kuantan Port, Pahang	Kuantan, Pahang	3	42	2	Federal road
Kuantan	Seremban (NS)	E8, E2/AH2	292	2–4	Federal road, and expressway
Seremban (NS)	Port Dickson* (NS)	E2/AH2, E29, 5	32	2–4	Federal road, and expressway
Port Dickson	Tanjung Bruas Port,* Melaka	5, N143	67	2	State and federal road
Tanjung Bruas Port,* Melaka	Melaka City / Melaka International Ferry Terminal*	141, 5	13	2	Federal road
Melaka City/Melaka International Ferry Terminal*	Johor Bahru	M31, M29, E2/AH2, 1	219	2–4	Federal road, state road, and expressway
Port of Port Dickson*			104 km (56 nm)	Ferry links	Passenger ferry terminal
Tanjung Bruas Port*	Dumai		177 km (96 nm)		
Melaka International Ferry Terminal*		Sea routes	107 km (58 nm)		
Tanjung Pelepas Port* (Gelang Patah/Stulang), Johor	Batam		97 km (52 nm)		
Johor Port* (Pasir Gudang), Johor	Batam		51 km (28 nm)		
	Tanjungpinang, Bintan Islands		99 km (54 nm)		

* = maritime gateway, BCP = border crossing point, EC = economic corridor, km = kilometer, MR1 = Malaysia Route 1, nm = nautical mile, NS = Negeri Sembilan. Source: Compiled by author.

Two other ports along this route are Kemaman Port (Terengganu) and Tok Bali Port (Kelantan). Kemaman Port is one of the deepest seaports in Malaysia and is fast-emerging as the new gateway to the Asia and Pacific region. Tok Bali Port (Kelantan) is a minor fishing port. Under the ECER Blueprint 2.0, this port will be expanded to serve as a feeder to Kuantan Port.

Map 19: Economic Corridor 6: Proposed Malaysia Route 1

Source: Asian Development Bank.

Route 2 Westward: EC6-MR2

From the BCPs in Kelantan, this route links with Kota Bharu—the start point of ECRL—and passes through Perak (Pengkalan Hulu, Ipoh, and Lumut Port), Port Klang, Seremban, Port Dickson, Tanjung Bruas Port and ends at Johor Bahru. This route has a westward orientation to Perak and converges southward to Melaka and Johor (Table 74 and Map 20).

The key maritime gateways in EC6-MR2 are Lumut Port (Pahang), Port Klang (Selangor), Port of Port Dickson (Negeri Sembilan), Tanjung Bruas Port (Melaka), Melaka International Ferry Terminal, Tanjung Pelepas Port (Pasir Gudang), and Johor Port (Pasir Gudang).

The maritime gateways to Central Sumatera (Dumai) are Lumut Port (Perak), Port Klang (Selangor), Port of Port Dickson (Negeri Sembilan), Tanjung Bruas Port (Melaka), and Melaka International Ferry Terminal (Melaka). Toward the south is Tanjung Pelepas Port (Gelang Patah or Stulang) and Johor Port (Pasir Gudang) in Johor Bahru, which have maritime connectivity with Batam Islands (Riau) via ferry links.

Table 74: EC6-MR2: Westward Connectivity Routes

Start Point	End Point	Route	Distance (km)	Traffic Lanes	Road Class
Kota Bharu	Pengkalan Hulu (BCP)	3, 196, 4, 76	213	2–4	Federal and expressway
Pengkalan Hulu (BCP)	Ipoh	76, E1/AH2	129	2–4	Federal and expressway
Ipoh	Lumut Port*	5,3145	79	2	Federal road
Lumut Port*	Port Klang*	5, 58, NSE1/AH2	250	2	Federal and state road
Port Klang*	Seremban	181, E5, E37, E2/AH2	95	2–4	Federal road and expressway
Seremban	Port Dickson	E2/AH2, E29, 5	32	2–4	Federal road and expressway
Port Dickson	Tanjung Bruas Port*	5, N143	67	2	State and federal road
Tanjung Bruas Port*	Melaka City/Melaka International Ferry Terminal*	141, 5	13	2	Federal road
Melaka City/Melaka International Ferry Terminal*	Johor Bahru	M31, M29, E2/AH2, 1	219	2–4	Federal road, state road, and expressway
Maritime Gateway					
Port Klang	Dumai	Sea routes	261 km (141 nm)	Ferry links	Passenger ferry terminal
Port of Port Dickson			172 km (93 nm)		
Tanjung Bruas Port			151 km (82 nm)		
Melaka International Ferry Terminal			151 km (82 nm)		
Tanjung Pelepas Port (Gelang Patah/Stulang), Johor	Batam		106 km (57 nm)		
Johor Port (Pasir Gudang), Johor	Batam		51 km (28 nm)		
	Tanjungpinang, Bintan Island		91 km (49 nm)		

* = maritime gateway, BCP = border crossing point, EC = economic corridor, km = kilometer, MR2 = Malaysia Route 2, nm = nautical mile.
Note: Maritime distance between ports were based on https://sea-distances.org/ and http://ports.com/.
Source: Compiled by author.

Map 20: Economic Corridor 6: Proposed Malaysia Route 2

SATUN

Satun

Kuah

Kangar

PERLIS

Pattani

SONGKHLA

Yala

PATTANI

Narathiwat

NARATHIWAT

Kota Bharu

INDONESIA–MALAYSIA–THAILAND GROWTH TRIANGLE

KEDAH

YALA

Bukit Bunga

Alor Setar

Butterworth

George Town

PENANG ISLAND

Kulim

Gerik

KELANTAN

Kuala Terengganu

Marang

PENANG

TERENGGANU

Kuala Sepetang

Gua Musang

Ipoh

PERAK

Lumut Port

Bagan Datuk

Strait of Malacca

Kuala Lipis

PENINSULAR MALAYSIA

Kemasik

PAHANG

Kuantan

Kisaran

SELANGOR

Shah Alam

KUALA LUMPUR

Port Klang

NORTH SUMATERA

Rantau Prapat

Dumai

Temerloh

NEGERI SEMBILAN

Seremban

Port Dickson

MELAKA

Melaka

Tanjung Bruas Port

MIFT

Muar

Mersing

JOHOR

Kota Tinggi

Johor Bahru

Johor Port

SUMATERA

Tanjung Pelepas Port

SINGAPORE

INDONESIA

Aek Kanopan

RIAU

Pekanbaru

RIAU ISLANDS

Legend:

⊛ National Capital
◉ Provincial/State Capital
● City/Town
▬ Economic Corridor (proposed)
▬ National Road
▬ Other Road
—·— Provincial Boundary
—··— International Boundary

MIFT = Melaka International Ferry Terminal
Boundaries are not necessarily authoritative.

This map was produced by the cartography unit of the Asian Development Bank. The boundaries, colors, denominations, and any other information shown on this map do not imply, on the part of the Asian Development Bank, any judgment on the legal status of any territory, or any endorsement or acceptance of such boundaries, colors, denominations, or information.

Source: Asian Development Bank.

Status of Physical Connectivity

Land

Road infrastructure between important nodes within the EC6 route is well-connected with state, federal, and expressway roads. The expressways involved in the EC6-MR1 route are the East Coast Highway, Kuala Lumpur–Karak Highway (E8), Seremban–Port Dickson Highway (E29), and the E1–E2. The expressways involved in the EC6-MR2 route, are the East–West Highway (4 and 185), E1–E2, and Seremban–Port Dickson Highway (E29). There is good road connectivity between major cities and hinterland areas through the state and federal road networks.

East Coast Expressway.[70] The ECE network is the primary mode of road transportation along the east coast of Peninsular Malaysia. It connects the east and west coasts and acts as a catalyst to spur the growth of the ECER states. The ECE is divided into three stages: the completed ECE1 and ECE2, as well as the proposed ECE3.

- ECE-1 begins from Karak (Pahang) to Jabor (Terengganu). The ECE1, which opened to road users in 2004, is an extension of the Kuala Lumpur–Karak Expressway that provides a link from the west coast to the east coast of Peninsular Malaysia.

- ECE-2 route is between Jabor and Kuala Terengganu and opened to road users in January 2015.

- The federal government has also proposed the ECE3 from Gemuruh to Tumpat in the 12th Malaysia Plan (2021–2025). The ECE-3 is an extension of the ECE2.

Rail Connectivity

KTMB East Line. Kelantan and Pahang are covered by the KTMB East Line. It runs from Tumpat, near the Thai border just north of Kota Bharu in Kelantan state, down to Gemas in Negeri Sembilan, where it joins up with the west coast line, which runs all the way from Singapore to Bangkok via Johor Bahru, Kuala Lumpur, and Penang. The East Line passes through the states of Kelantan, Pahang, and Negeri Sembilan (Table 75 and Map 21).

At present, there is no rail link between Kelantan and Narathiwat (Southern Thailand), in particular between Pasir Mas (Kelantan) and Su-ngai Kolok (Narathiwat). The railway service between the two stations, which has been in operation since 1954, was discontinued in 1982 for passenger services and in 2003 for cargo services due to widespread cross-border smuggling issues and security concerns.[71]

---

[70]   The information about East Coast Expressway was compiled from Anih Berhad found at http://www.anihberhad.com/?page_id=54.

[71]   Ministry of Transport Malaysia. 2018. *Capacity Building Workshop on Facilitation of International Railway Transport to Support Intra and Interregional Trade: Country Presentation: Malaysia.*

Table 75: Economic Corridor 6: KTMB East and South Line

KTMB Line	From		To	Distance (km)
East Line				
Kelantan	Tumpat	→	Wakaf Baru	14
	Wakaf Baru	→	Tanah Merah	38
	Tanah Merah	→	Pasir Mas	33
	Pasir Mas	→	Gua Musang	121
	Gua Musang	→	Merapuh	25
	Merapuh	→	Kuala Lipis	19
	Kuala Lipis	→	Jerantut	104
Pahang	Jerantut	→	Kuala Krau	25
	Kuala Krau	→	Mentakab	27
	Mentakab	→	Triang	32
	Triang	→	Kemayan	14
	Kemayan	→	Bahau	39
South Line				
Negeri Sembilan	Bahau	→	Gemas	37
			TOTAL	**528**

km = kilometer, KTMB = Keretapi Tanah Melayu Berhad or Malayan Railways Limited.
Source: Compiled by author from KTMB's various publication sources. http://www.ktmb.com.my/index.html.

There are plans to revive the railway service between Pasir Mas and Su-ngai Kolok[72] to connect Malaysia with the SKRL. The SKRL is a pan-Asian high-speed railway network being developed to connect the countries of Cambodia, the Lao PDR, Malaysia, Myanmar, the PRC, Singapore, Thailand, and Viet Nam. This will make Kota Bharu an important node connecting northeastern states of Malaysia, Southern Thailand, and the PRC under the BRI.

East Coast Rail Link.[73] The Malaysia Rail Link Sdn Bhd (MRLSB) operates and regulates the ECRL project. The cost of the ECRL project is RM44 billion. MRLSB has collaborated with the China Communications Construction Company Ltd. on the ECRL construction. The ECRL project is expected to be completed by the end of 2026 (Map 22).

---

[72] *Sinar Harian*. 2019. Baik pulih landasan kereta api Sungai Golok-Pasir Mas. 26 July. https://www.sinarharian.com.my/article/40098/EDISI/Kelantan/Baik-pulih-landasan-kereta-api-Sungai-Golok-Pasir-Mas.

[73] The information on East Coast Rail Link was compiled from Malaysia Rail Link Sendirian Berhad found at https://www.mrl.com.my/en/.

Map 21: Rail Routes in Malaysia

Legend:
- National Capital
- Provincial/State Capital
- SRT Southern Line
- KTMB West Coast Line
- KTMB East Coast Line
- KTMB Kargo Line
- National Road
- Other Road
- Provincial Boundary
- International Boundary

Boundaries are not necessarily authoritative.

State Railway of Thailand (SRT)
- Southern Line: Bangkok–Hat Yai–Padang Besar/Su-ngai Kolok

Keretapi Tanah Melayu Berhad (KTMB)/Malayan Railways Limited
- West Coast Line
  - North Line: Padang Besar–Tanjong Malim
  - Central Line: Tanjong Malim–Kuala Lumpur
  - South Line: Seremban–Woodlands
- East Coast Line: Tumpat–Gemas
- Kargo Line: Kuala Lumpur–Port Klang

This map was produced by the cartography unit of the Asian Development Bank. The boundaries, colors, denominations, and any other information shown on this map do not imply, on the part of the Asian Development Bank, any judgment on the legal status of any territory, or any endorsement or acceptance of such boundaries, colors, denominations, or information.

Source: Asian Development Bank.

Map 22: East Coast Rail Line

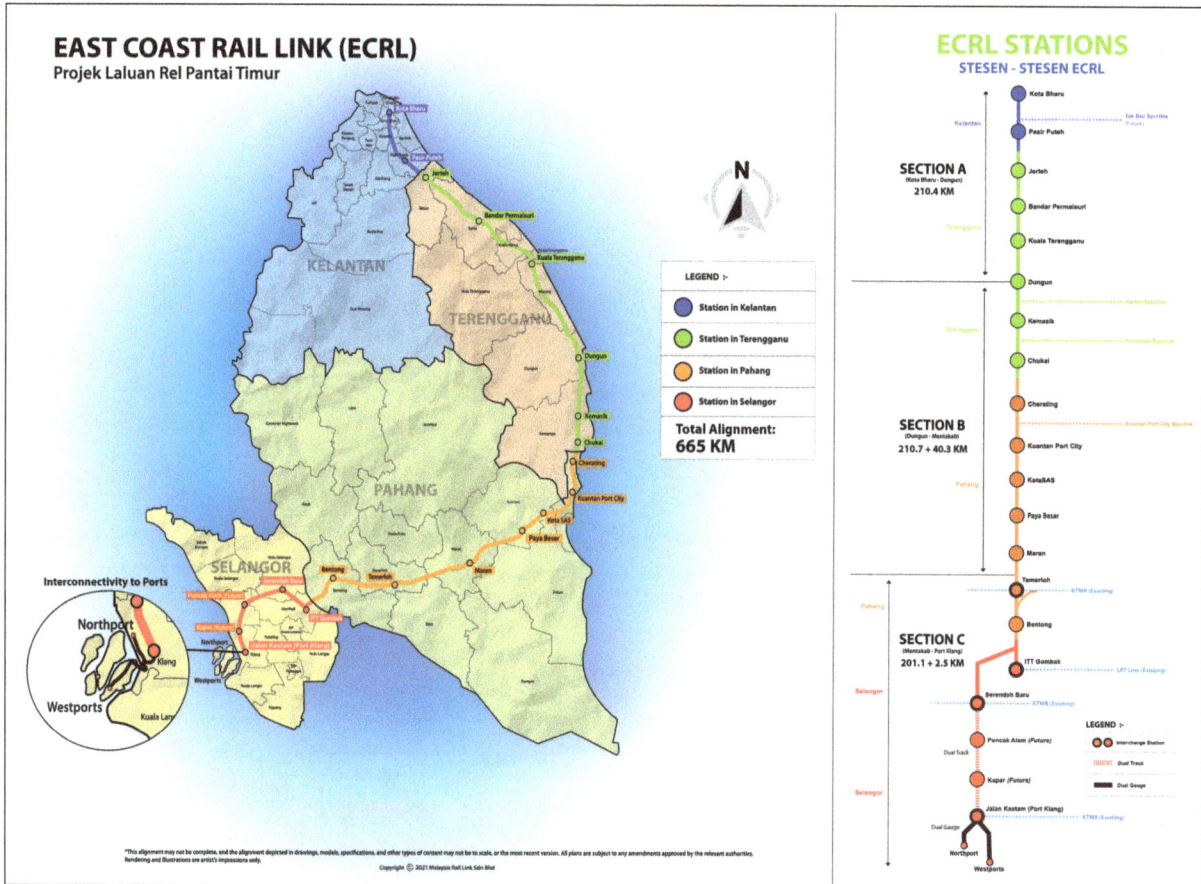

ECRL = East Coast Rail Line, km = kilometer.
Source: Malaysia Rail Link. Retrieved from: http://www.mrl.com.my/en/alignment/.

The ECRL was designed as such to provide much improved connectivity throughout the east coast region, as well as to the west coast. The project takes into consideration the potential growth of the industrial, commercial, and tourism sectors along the ECRL corridor. The ECRL also serves as a land bridge connecting Tok Bali, Kemaman Port, Kuantan Port, and Port Klang.

The ECRL service covers freight and passengers with a breakdown of the projected revenue ratio of 70% for freight and 30% for passengers. The passenger trains will travel at 160km/hour, cutting travel time from Kota Bharu to Putrajaya by approximately 4 hours, allowing for more convenient travel between the east and west coasts.

Maritime Connectivity

The main ports in the ECER states are Kemaman Port and Kuantan Port, which serve as major trade gateways to Cambodia, the Lao PDR, Thailand, Viet Nam, and northeast Asia. The primary objective of the ECER ports is to establish trading links with ports in East Asia. No trade ties with ports in Sumatera have been established.

- Kuantan Port is situated at Tanjung Gelang on the eastern seaboard of Peninsular Malaysia, about 25 km north of Kuantan, the state capital of Pahang. Kuantan Port is a multi-cargo deep seaport. The port is accessible by road via the ECE and the federal road networks. Strategically located in the heartland of the petrochemical industry, Kuantan Port has developed into a major container terminal for the east coast region. The port, which is linked to the world's major shipping lanes, serves as a gateway to Cambodia, the Lao PDR, the PRC, Viet Nam, the Far East, and the Pacific Rim.[74]

- The Kemaman Port is one of the deepest seaports in Malaysia and a fast-emerging port acting as a new gateway to the Asia and Pacific region. As a deep-sea port, it is capable of handling various types of cargo, ranging from general cargo, dry bulk, and liquid bulk. The port is also a regional center for transshipment activities as well as cargo consolidation and distribution activities. It will also serve as a feeder port for Kuantan Port, while serving the logistics requirements of the nearby Kemaman Heavy Industrial Park (KHIP). The port will be complemented by the ship building and repair facilities at KHIP, and will leverage the upstream and downstream developments within the oil and gas industry in nearby Kertih.[75]

The Tok Bali Port has also been identified as the regional distribution hub for the movement of goods from cross-border trade with neighboring countries. Tok Bali Port also serves as a halal export hub and as a supply base for offshore support activities in the oil and gas sector, playing the role as a one-stop center for multinationals operating in the Malaysia–Thailand Joint Development Area, the North Malay Basin,[76] and the Malaysia–Viet Nam Commercial Arrangement Area.[77]

Air Links

The airports located in the EC6-MR1 states are Sultan Ismail Petra Airport (Kota Bharu, Kelantan), Sultan Mahmud Airport (Kuala Terengganu), and Sultan Haji Ahmad Shah Airport (Kuantan, Pahang). Low-cost carriers operating in these airports serve only domestic routes to Kuala Lumpur, Subang, Penang, and Johor Baru. There are no international flights to Sumatera and Southern Thailand. Flights to Singapore are provided by Scoot Air (Table 76).

---

[74] Kuantan Port Consortium Sdn. Bhd. (KPC) was given the concession period of 30 years starting from 1998 to manage, operate, and develop Kuantan Port. KPC is jointly owned by IJM Corporation Berhad, a publicly-listed company on Bursa Malaysia and Beibu Gulf Holding (Hong Kong) Co. Ltd. on a 60:40 equity holdings with the Government of Malaysia having a special rights share. The profile of Kuantan Port was abridged from http://www.kuantanport.com.my/en_GB/about-us/corporate-profile/.

[75] The profile of Kemaman Port was abridged from EPIC found at https://www.epicgroup.com.my/index.php.

[76] The North Malay Basin is located approximately 300 km offshore the Terengganu Gas Terminal in the Gulf of Thailand. https://www.offshore-technology.com/projects/north-malay-basin-integrated-gas-development-project/.

[77] Malaysia–Viet Nam Commercial Arrangement Area involves the extraction of oil and gas from six different offshore fields located throughout a 1,350 km² area in the overlapping zone between Malaysia and Viet Nam. The production sharing between the two countries was signed in April 2016. Retrieved from: https://www.offshore-technology.com/projects/pm3/.

Table 76: EC6-MR1: Flight Routes

Airports	Airlines	Destinations
Sultan Ismail Petra Airport, Kota Bharu, Kelantan	Air Asia; MAS Firefly Malindo Air Scoot*	Kuala Lumpur Subang, Penang, Johor Bahru Subang Singapore (commenced in 2019)
Sultan Mahmud Airport, Kuala Terengganu, Terengganu	Air Asia, MAS Firefly, Malindo Air	Kuala Lumpur Subang
Sultan Haji Ahmad Shah Airport, Kuantan, Pahang	Air Asia, MAS Firefly Scoot*	Kuala Lumpur Penang Singapore

* International carrier, EC = economic corridor, MAS = Malaysia Airlines, MR1 = Malaysia Route 1.
Source: Compiled by author from the websites of relevant domestic and international airlines

Socioeconomic Profile

The ECER states of Kelantan, Terengganu, and Pahang are less-developed compared to the states along the west coast. Among the ECER states, Pahang had the highest GDP during 2014–2018, averaging $13 billion per year or 4% of Malaysia's GDP. In terms of per capita income, Kelantan had the lowest at an average of $3,200 per annum for 2014–2018. All three states recorded positive growth rates during the review period. The difference in GDP among them reflects the regional disparities among the less-developed states (Table 77).

Table 77: EC6–MR1: Selected Macroeconomic Indicators of Kelantan, Terengganu, and Pahang, 2014–2018

	2014	2018	Average (2014–2018)	Average Share to Malaysia (2014–2018), %	CAGR* (2014–2018), % (based in RM)
GDP (at constant 2015 prices, $ million)*					
Kelantan	6,273	5,972	5,714	1.8	4.1
Terengganu	9,108	8,629	8,254	2.6	4.0
Pahang	14,278	13,926	13,129	4.2	4.7
Malaysia	336,823	337,420	313,828		5.4
GDP per capita (at constant 2015 prices, $)*					
Kelantan	3,640	3,210	3,189	–	2.1
Terengganu	7,986	7,025	6,978	–	2.0
Pahang	8,970	8,365	8,069	–	3.5
Malaysia	10,968	10,420	9,939	–	4.0
Population (million)					
Kelantan	1.7	1.9	1.8	5.7	1.9
Terengganu	1.1	1.2	1.2	3.7	1.9
Pahang	1.6	1.7	1.6	5.2	1.1
Malaysia	30.7	32.4	31.6	–	1.3
Population Density (population/square kilometer)					
Kelantan	115	124	119	–	2.2
Terengganu	88	95	91	–	2.2
Pahang	44	46	45	–	1.5
Malaysia	93	98	96	–	1.3

– = not applicable, CAGR = compound annual growth rate, GDP = gross domestic product, RM = Malaysian ringgit.
* Calculation of CAGR based in local currency (Malaysian ringgit) to avoid erratic fluctuation in foreign exchange.
Source: Department of Statistics. 2019. *State's Socioeconomic Report (various states)*. Putrajaya: DOS Malaysia.

The development gap phenomenon is attributed to the state's economic structure. Terengganu and Pahang are driven by the manufacturing sector, whereas Kelantan is dominated by agriculture. The oil and gas industry, in particular, dominates Terengganu's manufacturing industry (Table 78).

Table 78: Share of Sector Value-Added to Gross Domestic Product by Economic Activity, 2018
(%)

	Agriculture (%)	Mining and Quarrying (%)	Manufacturing (%)	Construction (%)	Services (%)
Kelantan	22	1	5	1	69
Terengganu	8	1	37	3	50
Pahang	22	1	22	4	51
Malaysia	**7**	**8**	**22**	**5**	**57**

Source: Department of Statistics. 2019. *State's Socioeconomic Report (various states)*. Putrajaya: DOS Malaysia.

The ECER Blueprint 2.0 takes into account the state's development plan to move the state toward a high-income economy, thereby addressing the issue of regional imbalance (Table 79). The Blueprint 2.0 has identified seven key development areas (KDA); namely:

(i)   Cross-Border Development: Kota Bharu–Jeli–Besut

(ii)   Central Spine Development: Gua Musang–Lojing Highlands–Kuala Lipis

(iii)   West Pahang Growth Area: Bentong–Raub

(iv)   Pahang Tenggara Regional Development Authority: Jengka Temerloh–Mentakab–Maran–Bera

(v)   Kuala Terengganu Growth Triangle: Kuala Terengganu City Center–Kenyir–Dungun

(vi)   ECER Special Economic Zone: Kertih–Kuantan–Pekan

(vii)   Mersing–Rompin Growth Area

**Table 79: Economic Corridor 2: State and Regional Development Blueprint
of Kelantan, Terengganu, and Pahang**

EC6	State Development Blueprint	Regional Development Blueprint
Kelantan	Kelantan Sustainable Development Masterplan 2019–2023	ECER Blueprint 2.0 (2018–2025)
Terengganu	Terengganu Prosperity Masterplan 2030 (2019–2030)	
Pahang	Pahang Strategic Development Plan 2020–2025	

EC = economic corridor. ECER = East Coast Economic Region.
Source: Compiled by author from various state development blueprints.

Projects in Kelantan included in the IMT-GT IB (2017–2021) are Pengkalan Kubor–Tak Bai Bridge Link, Rantau Panjang–Su-ngai Kolok Second Bridge Link, and upgrading of Kota Bharu Airport. These projects are in various stages of planning and implementation.

The IMT-GT Plaza at Bukit Bunga, which was planned under the IMT-GT IB (2012–2016), was completed in November 2019. The plaza is a strategic commercial complex developed by the federal government through the ECERDC. The aim is to realize the potential of Bukit Bunga as a gateway to cross-border tourism and trade for Kelantan. The plaza is also a platform for traders from Indonesia, Malaysia, and Thailand to introduce, showcase, and market their products under one strategically located venue.[78]

Trade

There are three BCPs in Kelantan, bordering the provinces of Southern Thailand: (i) Bukit Bunga–Ban Buketa (Narathiwat), (ii) Rantau Panjang–Su-ngai Kolok (Narathiwat), and Pengkalan Kubor–Tak Bai (Narathiwat).

During 2015–2018, the Kelantan's cross-border trade averaged $147 million a year, with a surplus of $35 million. Kelantan's border trade with Thailand contributed 2% on average to Malaysia's total cross-border trade during 2015–2018. The Rantau Panjang BCP is the main trade gateway for cross-border trade between Kelantan and Southern Thailand. Kelantan–Thailand trade has been sluggish during 2015–2018 with an average growth rate of less than 1% (Table 80).

Table 80: Kelantan–Thailand Trade, 2015–2018
($ million)

	2015	2016	2017	2018	Average (2015–2018)	Average Share to All Malaysia–Thai BCPs, %	CAGR+ (2015–2018), % (based in RM)
Kelantan	147	152	145	145	147	2.3	0.7
Export	86	97	96	86	91	3.2	1.3
Import	61	55	49	59	56	1.5	(0.02)
Rantau Panjang	126	133	127	123	127	1.9	0.4
Export	82	92	90	80	86	3.0	0.5
Import	44	41	37	43	41	1.1	0.3
Bukit Bunga	1.9	2.8	3.7	6.4	3.7	0.1	50.8
Export	0.2	0.1	0.0	0.1	0.1	0.0	(15.1)
Import	1.7	2.7	3.7	6.2	3.6	0.1	55.8
Pengkalan Kubor	19	17	14	16	16	0.3	(5.6)
Export	4	5	6	6	5	0.2	16.1
Import	15	12	8	10	11	0.3	(12.7)
All Malaysia–Thai BCPs	6,515	6,420	6,574	6,620	6,532	–	1.6
Export	2,792	2,848	2,904	2,985	2,882	–	3.4
Import	3,723	3,572	3,670	3,634	3,650	–	0.3

– = not applicable, ( ) = negative, BCP = border crossing point, CAGR = compound annual growth rate.
Note: The CAGR was calculated using the local currency (Malaysian ringgit) to avoid erratic fluctuation in foreign exchange rates.
Source: Royal Malaysian Customs Department, 2019. Putrajaya: RMCD.

---

[78] NST Business. 2019. Plaza IMT-GT to Boost Cross-Border Trade and Socio-Economic Activities in Kelantan. The New Straits Times. 3 November. https://www.nst.com.my/business/2019/11/535439/plaza-imt-gt-boost-cross-border-trade-and-socio-economic-activities-kelantan.

Tourism

Kelantan and Pahang have no tourism development blueprints. These states adopt tourism plans designed by Plan Malaysia's State Structure Plan. Terengganu has a State Tourism Master Plan 2018–2025. ECERDC has integrated the tourism development plan prepared by Plan Malaysia and the state of Terengganu under the ECER Blueprint 2.0 (Table 81).

Table 81: East Coast Economic Region Tourism Project

State	Tourism Product
Kelantan	• IMT-GT Plaza Bukit Bunga • Integrated Tourism in Lojing • Water Village Tourism Development • Malaysian Tiger Trail in Kuala Krai (Stong, Dabong) • Malaysian Tiger Trail in Gua Musang
Terengganu	• Dungun Town Mainland Coastal Tourism • Kuala Terengganu City Centre including Airport Road • Lagoon-Style Marina Village (Pulau Besar Integrated Resort, Merang–Setiu) • Setiu and Marang Tourism and Island Gateway
Pahang	• Cherating Mainland Coastal Tourism • Kuantan Waterfront • Pekan Royal Town • Taman Negara Endau Rompin • Kuantan Museum Strip • Chini Lake • Malayan Tiger Trail in Lipis • Malayan Tiger Trail in Raub • Malayan Tiger Trail in Lanchang

IMT-GT = Indonesia–Malaysia–Thailand Growth Triangle.
Source: ECER Blueprint 2.0.

Present tourism development trends include archaeotourism, ecotourism, heritage tourism, and geotourism sectors, which are covered in the National Ecotourism Plan 2016–2025 and the National Tourism Policy 2020–2030. Under the ECER Blueprint 2.0, the tourism industry is one of five key economic drivers for promoting the ECER state economies. ECERDC has identified several subsectors in ECER's tourism cluster: coastal tourism, island tourism, ecotourism, and arts, culture and heritage tourism.

The intensity of the tourism industry is reflected in the number of tourist arrivals as hotel guests in each of the states that they visit. Pahang recorded the highest number of hotel guests of an average of 11 million tourists each year for 2014–2018 (Table 82). Hotel guests are dominated by domestic tourists. Kelantan, Pahang, and Terengganu recorded positive growth in tourist arrivals. In Kelantan, which borders with Narathiwat, approximately 95% of the foreign tourists are from Southern Thailand.[79]

---

[79]   Calculated from the international tourist entry into Kelantan. Data abstracted from Malaysia Open Data Portal. *Statistics of international tourist arrivals to the state of Kelantan.* https://www.data.gov.my/data/ms_MY/dataset/statistik-kemasukan-pelancong-antarabangsa-ke-negeri-kelantan.

Table 82: Hotel Guests in Kelantan, Terengganu, and Pahang, 2014 and 2018
(million)

	2014	2018	Average (2014–2018)	Share to State (2014–2018) %	CAGR (2014–2018), %
Kelantan	1.2	1.2	1.2	100	0.3
Foreign	0.06	0.05	0.06	5	(3.8)
Domestic	1.1	1.2	1.1	95	0.5
Pahang	10.4	11.6	10.7	100	2.9
Foreign	2.3	2.7	2.5	23	3.8
Domestic	8.1	9.0	8.3	77	2.7
Terengganu	1.6	1.9	1.8	100	3.8
Foreign	0.12	0.2	0.2	10	2.0
Domestic	1.5	1.7	1.6	90	4.0
Malaysia	71.7	82.4	75.0	100	3.6
Foreign	26.3	30.0	27.2	36	3.4
Domestic	45.4	52.4	47.9	64	3.7

( ) = negative, CAGR = compound annual growth rate.
Source: My Tourism Data Portal. Hotel Guests by States (2014-2018). http://mytourismdata.tourism.gov.my/.

Industrial Activities

Each state has established industrial parks as a strategy to attract investments. In 2018, Terengganu had 25 industrial parks; Pahang, 17; and Kelantan, 11 (Table 83). The state-owned agencies that develop and manage the industrial parks are the Kelantan State Economic Development Corporation, Terengganu State Economic Development Corporation, and Pahang State Economic Development Corporation in their respective states.

Apart from general industrial parks, there are also specialized parks, such as the halal parks in Pasir Mas (Kelantan), Chendering (Terengganu), and Gambang (Pahang). Other specialized parks include the Biopolymer Park in Kerteh (Terengganu) and the Automotive Park in Pekan (Pahang). The Kertih Biopolymer Park in ECER SEZ Terengganu, for example, has elevated Malaysia into a regional biotechnology hub with the presence of world biotechnology players like CJ Cheil Jedang, Arkema, and Gevo.[80]

---

[80] NST Business. 2018. CJ-Arkema Announces Additional Investment of RM 1.2b in Kertih Ops. *The New Straits Times.* 1 May. https://www.nst.com.my/business/2018/05/364280/cj-arkema-announces-additional-investment-rm-12b-kertih-ops.

Table 83: Industrial Parks in Kelantan, Terengganu, and Pahang
(as of end December 2018)

Kelantan	Terengganu	Pahang
1. Gua Musang Industrial Park	1. Gong Medang Industrial Area	1. Bentong Industrial Park (I, IIA, IIB)
2. Jeli Industrial Park	2. Sungai Baru Industrial Estate	2. Gebeng Industrial Park
3. Kemubu Industrial Park	3. Saujana Industrial Estate	3. Habour Park Industrial Park
4. Pengkalan Chepa I Industrial Park	4. Bukit Rakit Industrial Estate	4. Jerantut Industrial Park
5. Pengkalan Chepa II Industrial Park	5. Gong Badak Industrial Estate	5. Kechau Tui Industrial Park, Kuala Lipis
6. SME Bank Factory Complex Pengkalan Chepa I	6. Cendering Industrial Estate	6. Kuantan Port Industrial Area
7. SME Bank Factory Complex Pengkalan Chepa II	7. Bukit Khoe Industrial Estate, Marang	7. Malaysia China Kuantan Industrial Park
8. Staphonal Industrial Park	8. Wakaf Tapai Industrial Estate	8. Maran Industrial Park
9. Tanah Merah Industrial Park	9. Batu 7 Industrial Estate, Dungun	9. Muadzam Shah Industrial Area
	10. Pulau Serai Industrial Estate	10. Pahang Technology Park, Gambang
Specialized Park	11. Ajil Industrial Estate	11. Peramu Industrial Park
10. Tok Bali Integrated Fisheries Park	12. Kerteh Industrial Estate	12. Rompin Industrial Park
11. Pasir Mas Halal Park	13. Lot P Industrial Estate	13. Semambu Industrial park
	14. Bukit Labohan Industrial Estate	14. Tanjung Agas Oil and Gas Logistic Industrial Park
	15. Teluk Kalong Industrial Estate and Kemaman Heavy Industry Park	15. Temerloh Industrial Park
	16. Jakar I, II, & III Industrial Estate	
	17. Mak Lagam Industrial Estate	**Specialized Park**
	18. Perasing Industrial Estate	16. Gambang Halal Park
	19. Bukit Besi Industrial Estate	17. Pekan Automotive Park
	20. Al-Muktafi Billah Shah Industrial Estate	
	21. Ketengah Jaya Industrial Estate	
	22. Ceneh Baru Industrial Estate	
	23. Cherul Industrial Estate	
	Specialized Park	
	24. Kerteh Biopolymer Park	
	25. Terengganu Halal Park	

Source: Malaysian Investment Development Authority. 2018. Industrial Park in Malaysia. Kuala Lumpur: MIDA.

The industrial parks in the ECER states have good connectivity with their respective seaports through the federal roads and expressways, as well as the rail network when the ECRL project is completed. Industry players located in industrial parks can easily access Kuantan Port and Kemaman Port to export their products to the international markets in East Asia.

Both ECE and ECRL form the transport backbone and link with seaports on the west coast through multimodal transport, providing opportunities for industries in the ECER states to export their products to Sumatera, South Asia, Middle East, and Europe. Industries on the west coast can also utilize the Kuantan Port and Kemaman Port to export their products to northeast Asia. For industry players in the southern regions of the EC2 and EC4 Extended, they can use SIP (Segamat, Johor) as a satellite terminal to Kuantan Port for exporting their products to Eastern Asia.

Manufacturers in the industrial parks also have direct access to the markets in Southern Thailand through the road transport network, namely via AH18, which connects the Rantau Panjang-Su-ngai Kolok BCP.

Bridging the EC6 Gaps

Southern Thailand and South Sumatera are relatively far apart, and ECER states can serve as a bridge between the provinces. Aside from transportation, Southern Thailand and southern Sumatera can be linked through interregional linkages between SEZs by creating industrial clusters such as KRC. An industry cluster represents the entire value chain of a broadly defined industry, from suppliers to end products, including supporting services and specialized infrastructure. Therefore, investment from the private sector is critical for the development of the interregional industrial cluster.

Rubber belt. Indonesia, Malaysia, and Thailand are among the world's leading producers and exporters of natural rubber, with each country establishing a rubber city. The four rubber city sites in the IMT-GT corridor that will form the rubber belt are Bukit Ketapang SEZ, Kedah (Malaysia), Songkhla SEZ (Southern Thailand), Tanjung Api-Api SEZ (Southern Sumatera), and Sei Mangkei SEZ (North Sumatera) (Map 23). These sites will venture into downstream activities and the manufacture of high value-added rubber products. For the KRC, a project implementation team at the IMT-GT level has been created to supervise the development of the rubber city, which comprises NCIA (Malaysia), the Thai Rubber Association (Thailand), and Kemenko Perekonomian (Indonesia). The rubber belt concept, if successfully realized, is a supply chain model that can be applied to other industries. This can be done through industrial integration (in the form of backward or forward linkages) between the SEZs. Each country could identify its specializations in hi-tech downstream activities to determine the complementary supply chain activities.

Palm oil belt. The interregional industrial cluster in the rubber industry can also be applied to the palm oil industry and halal food, where the ECER states, Southern Thailand, and South Sumatera have competitive advantages in those industries. A palm oil development belt and halal belt may be considered to link the Southern Thailand with South Sumatera, with the ECER states acting as a "bridge" to link these areas.

Indonesia, Malaysia, and Thailand are the world's largest producers of palm oil. An interregional industrial cluster and supply chain can be established by developing industrial linkages between the existing SEZs in Kelantan with Narathiwat, and Johor (Tanjung Langsat) with southern Sumatera (Tanjung Api-Api). Industries in each country would need to re-strategize and work together to identify the downward activities that will be mutually beneficial in building competitiveness and a sustainable interregional supply chain.

Halal belt. Indonesia, Malaysia, and Thailand have their own specialized halal parks. They are competing to be the world's leading halal food producer. To avoid competition, a halal belt may be considered covering Kelantan–Narathiwat–Pattani, and Johor–Riau Islands. This could be carried out through interregional industrial linkages between halal parks in the ECER states, Narathiwat, Pattani, and Riau Islands (Batamindo Industrial Park, Batam Island).

Map 23: Proposed Rubber, Palm Oil, and Halal Belt

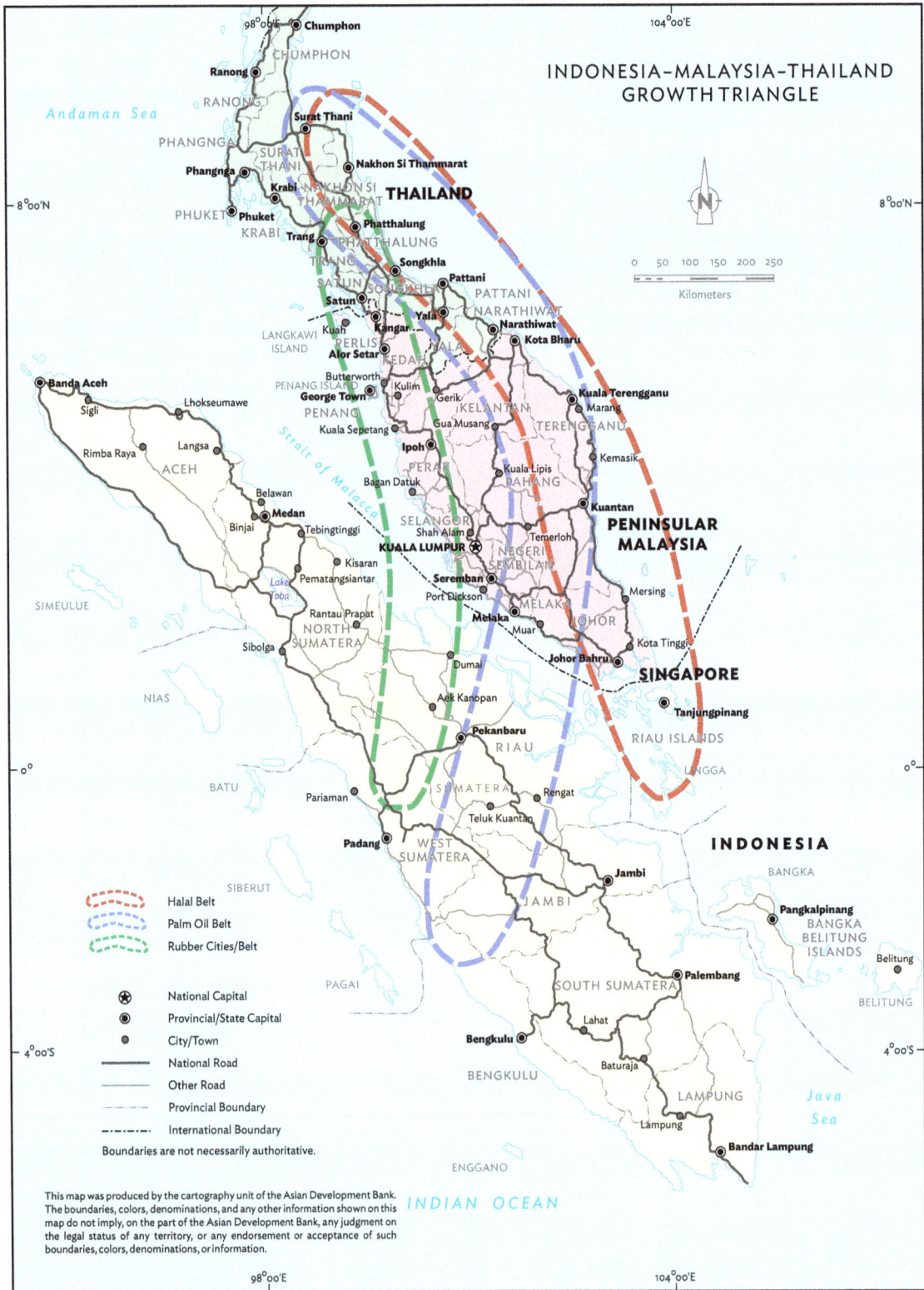

Source: Asian Development Bank.

Recommendations

Rail connectivity between Pasir Mas and Su-ngai Kolok, which was discontinued in 1982 for passenger services and in 2003 for cargo services, should be revived. The rail link will complete the connection along the route from Kunming–Bangkok–Su-ngai Kolok and Pasir Mas–Tumpat–Kota Bharu and via the ECRL to Port Klang. This will form a land bridge mainly from Bangkok to Port Klang and ports in Johor Bahru. This land bridge service can reduce logistics costs for manufacturers in Thailand who wish to export their products to Sumatera and Malaysia.

Melaka and Johor will play important roles in EC6 in enabling connectivity with provinces in central and southern Sumatera. The implementation of the Melaka–Dumai Ro-Ro project will further boost exports and imports of cargo freight between Malaysia and Sumatera. Johor Port (Pasir Gudang) has trade links with ports in Palembang (South Sumatera) and Belawan (North Sumatera). There are also ferry links to Batam (Riau Islands).

The ECRL is a game changer and gives a new perspective on the connectivity links in IMT-GT. It will link Malaysia's east and west coasts through Port Klang which is the main trade gateway of the country. ECRL will also become part of the SKRL and Trans-Asia Railway if the connectivity between Su-ngai Kolok and Pasir Mas can be revived by the Malaysian and Thai governments. The link between Su-ngai Kolok and Pasir Mas and SKRL will expand trading potential with Cambodia, the Lao PDR, the PRC, and Viet Nam.

Once the RTS between Johor Bahru and Singapore is implemented, the ECRL will also connect the east coast with South Sumatera and the Riau Islands. Johor Bahru will be the main gateway from South Sumatera and the Riau Islands, via Singapore, thus completing the southward connectivity route with EC3 in Sumatera.

Therefore, the proposal for establishing the EC6 corridor is highly feasible since it has the potential to create trade and investment opportunities through the ECRL that facilitates seamless connectivity within the northeastern states of Malaysia and with Southern Thailand, southern Sumatera, and the Riau Islands via two alternative pathways, i.e., EC6-MR1 (eastward) and EC6-MR2 (westward). EC6 will be named as the **Southeastern Thailand–Eastern Malaysia–Southern Sumatera Economic Corridor**.

CHAPTER

5

THE NETWORK OF IMT-GT ECONOMIC CORRIDORS

Revisiting the Economic Corridor Concept

The concept of economic corridor. Economic corridors are developed along a major transport route to provide production units with access to markets though distribution centers and gateway ports. A transport corridor is the foundation for developing an economic corridor. As the corridor develops, the "narrow" transport corridor expands as urban infrastructure, industrial parks, and other agglomeration spaces emerge as part of development plans.

Economic corridor development in IMT-GT traverses national borders and as such, requires collaboration between countries to ensure that goods and people move seamlessly across national boundaries. These require measures such as transport and trade facilitation in order to transform national corridors that are merely juxtaposed at the borders, into fully functioning cross-border economic corridors. Deliberate and collaborative planning between countries is critical to optimize spatial use by taking advantage of new production, growth and logistics centers, expanded connectivity, and access to gateways. As discussed in the economic corridor chapters of this study, this approach to economic corridor development has not fully materialized in IMT-GT. For the most part, Indonesia, Malaysia, and Thailand have been pursuing strategies, programs, and projects in their respective country segments of the IMT-GT economic corridors rather than as a result of a collaborative and deliberate planning at the subregional level.[81]

Corridor nodes. As part of the review, the study identified specific nodes in each corridor. For a given corridor, the relationship and continuity between the different nodes is important to help delineate core areas, i.e., the growth and catalytic centers from which spillovers are expected to radiate (peripheral areas). The nodes identified were the points or areas that perform catalytic roles in the corridor influence areas, with the potential to contribute to trade and economic growth by leveraging on infrastructure connectivity.

The nodes identified in this study were classified as follows:

- **Capital city**: the main urban and administrative center in a province or state; the area is compact, transit-oriented, and densely populated, and where high concentrations of residential, employment, retail, and key services are located.

- **Border crossing point (BCP)**: the point where border areas between two countries in the corridor converge and where customs, immigration, and quarantine (CIQ) facilities are provided to enable the entry and exit of goods across the borders.

- **Commercial node**: an area with a high concentration of economic activity such industrial parks, SEZs, distribution centers; usually accompanied by redevelopment around the area that includes residential, retail, and services facilities.

- **Maritime gateway port**: an area for the transport of cargo and/or passengers to external markets and/or destinations comprising a land domain (the port's region and its locality) and the maritime domain which services ships for global trade.

- **Tourism node**: an area with a medium-to-high density of tourists having the full range of facilities, services, and amenities, usually part of a cluster of destinations where tourists can engage in a variety of activities beyond visiting a single attraction or tourist site.

---

[81] C. S. Guina. 2023. *Review and Assessment of the Indonesia–Malaysia–Thailand Growth Triangle Economic Corridors: Integrative Report.* Manila: Asian Development Bank. The contents of this section was based on the integrative report, which is published as a separate publication.

Interlink corridors. The additional provinces or states and nodes under the reconfigured corridors in Chapter 3 expanded the existing corridors significantly, resulting in interlink corridors. An interlink corridor is the "route that connects two or more points in different corridors." Interlink corridors enable corridors to function as a network, rather than as single corridors. Corridors functioning as a network can change the pattern of mobility for both goods and people. They can facilitate access to a larger and more diverse base of inputs (raw materials, parts, energy or labor) and broader markets for diverse outputs (intermediate and finished goods).

The concept of economic corridors as networks rather than as point-to-point connections implies that spatial development would need to be more deliberate and coordinated. At present, economic corridor projects are typically national projects located in a corridor; and the mere collation of these projects would be considered as the set of projects for the corridor. In a network perspective, this piecemeal approach may have to give way to a more comprehensive spatial planning aimed at reducing economic distance and overcoming trade barriers in the corridors to promote complementarities in production and trade and realize scale economies for enhanced competitiveness.

Interlink Corridors in Malaysia

The interlink corridors that have emerged from the expansion of the existing corridors are illustrated in the ensuing paragraphs (Map 24).

Interlink Corridor A

The maritime route that connects Langkawi (EC5) to Penang Port at George Town (EC1); Kuala Kedah, Kedah (EC1); and Kuala Perlis, Perlis (EC2) via ferry serves as an interlink corridor (**Interlink Corridor A**). Penang Port, Kuala Kedah and Kuala Perlis are the tourist gateways to Langkawi Island with Kuah Jetty Terminal as the entrance point. Penang and Langkawi are positioned along the cruise liner routes in the Andaman Sea and Strait of Malacca. The interlink corridor generates synergies within the tourism industry.

Interlink Corridor B

The westward route in EC6 (EC6-MR2) functions as an interlink corridor (**Interlink Corridor B**). This interlink corridor traverses Kota Bharu, Kelantan (EC6), Penang Port at Butterworth (EC1/2), Padang Besar, Perlis (EC1/2) via the East–West Highway; and Port Klang (EC2) via E1–E2. Both Penang Port and Port Klang function as a maritime gateway for manufacturers in the EC6, particularly in Kelantan.

Interlink Corridor C

The eastward route in EC6 (EC6-MR1) also functions as an interlink corridor (**Interlink Corridor C**). It connects Kota Bharu, Kelantan (EC6) with Port Klang, Selangor (EC2), and Johor Bahru, Johor (EC4) via ECE, Kuala Lumpur–Karak Highway and E1–E2.

The rail links—ECRL (which is under construction) and KTMB—will connect Kuantan and Kemaman Ports in EC6 with Port Klang, Tanjung Pelepas Port, and Johor Port (EC2–EC4).

The road link connects EC6 with Port Dickson, Negeri Sembilan (EC2) and Tanjung Bruas Port, Melaka (EC4). Connectivity to the maritime gateways in the west coast will enable manufacturers in EC6 to have an alternative route for their shipments to Sumatera, South Asia, Middle East, Africa, and Europe.

Both interlink corridors B and C generate synergies in logistics, tourism, oil and gas, manufacturing, and agriculture, that are prevalent in ECs 1, 2, 4, 5, and 6. The synergies created in these corridors can help narrow the development gap between the less-developed states in the east coast and the more-developed states in the west coast through labor and resource mobility resulting from the development of growth nodes and conurbation areas.

Map 24: Interlink Corridors in Malaysia

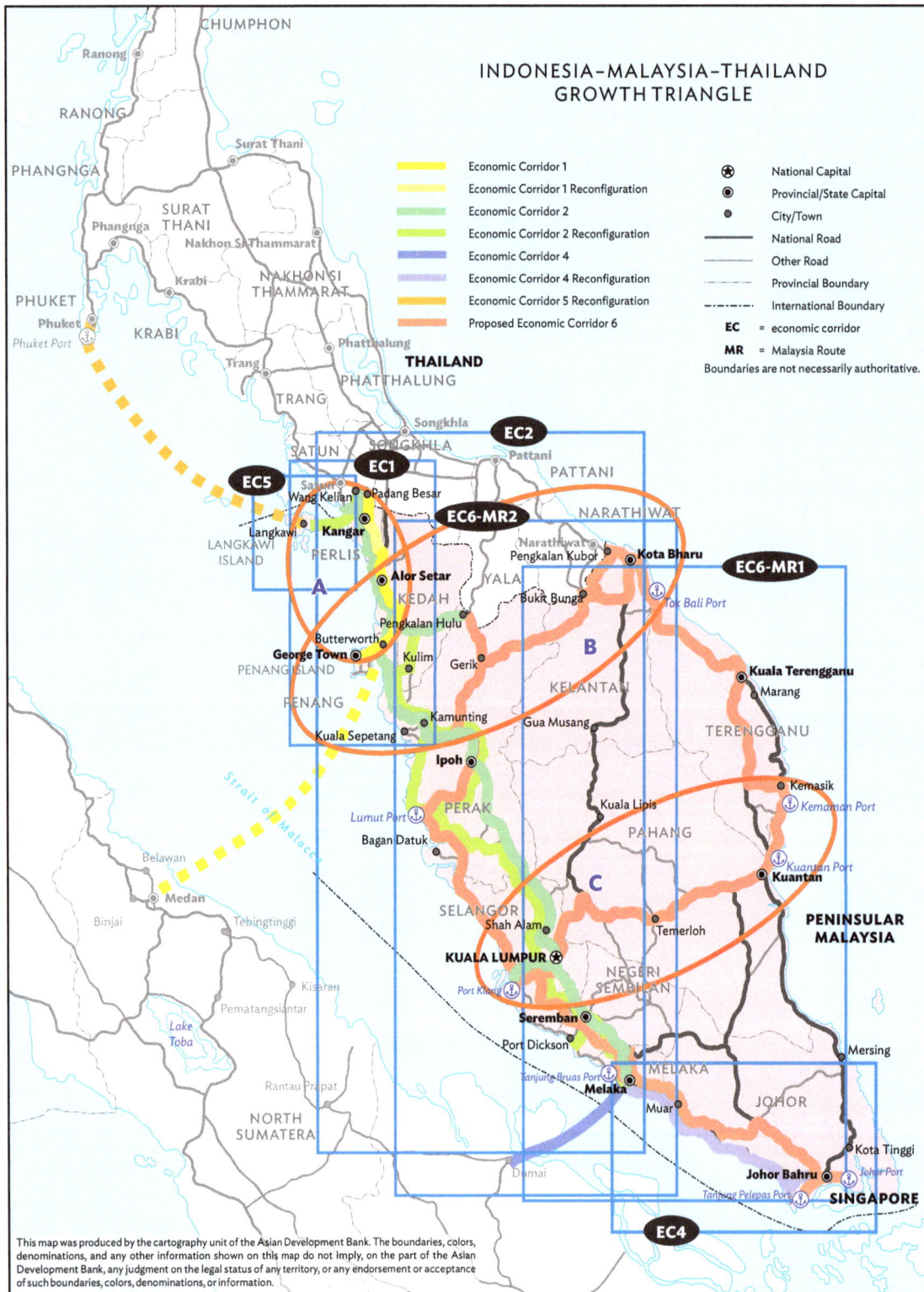

Source: Asian Development Bank.

ECONOMIC CORRIDORS FROM A VALUE CHAIN PERSPECTIVE

Introduction

The development of value chain linkages is a key motivation for economic corridor development. This chapter looks at the value chain[82] of three major products in IMT-GT—palm oil, rubber, and halal foods—to get a broad perspective on the geography of their production, processing, and distribution components. Value chains can be facilitated by efficient physical infrastructure to facilitate movement of goods between its various stages. Value chains can also be impacted by the location of SEZs and industrial clusters, which are crucial for attracting investments, and creating the density required to enable logistics services to operate efficiently.

The role of economic corridors can be better appreciated when seen as a part of the country's or the region's value chain. The study thus examined the value chain of three products of strategic importance to the IMT-GT countries—palm oil, halal food, and rubber. The study looked at the spatial dimensions of the different stages of these value chains focusing on the role of economic corridors.

Economic Corridors Involved in the Value Chains

The states in Malaysia that are part of the IMT-GT economic corridors have comparative advantages in the agriculture, manufacturing, and tourism sectors. Industries with potential value chain linkages to Sumatera and Southern Thailand are (i) palm oil, (ii) halal food, and (iii) rubber (Table 84). The states in ECs 1, 2, 4, and 6 play important roles in these three industries. Johor and Kedah are the largest producers of crude palm oil (CPO) and rubber, respectively, in Malaysia.

Table 84: Potential Supply Chain in the Economic Corridors

Potential Industries	EC1	EC2	EC4	EC5	EC6
Palm oil and palm-based products	Kedah, Penang/ Seberang Perai	Perak, Selangor, Negeri Sembilan	Melaka, Johor	–	Kelantan, Terengganu, Pahang
Halal food	Perlis, Kedah, Penang	Perak, Selangor, Negeri Sembilan, Selangor	Melaka, Johor	–	Kelantan, Terengganu, Pahang
Rubber and rubber products	Kedah	Perak, Selangor, Negeri Sembilan, Selangor	Melaka, Johor	–	Kelantan, Terengganu, Pahang

– = not applicable, EC = economic corridor.
Source: Compiled by author.

---

[82] In this study, the distinction between the terms **value chain** and **supply chain** is not strictly applied. It is noted that a value chain is the process by which a company adds value to its raw materials to produce products eventually sold to consumers; while the supply chain represents all the steps required to get the product to the customer. https://www.investopedia.com/ask/answers/043015/what-difference-between-value-chain-and-supply-chain.asp#:~:text=The%20value%20chain%20is%20a,the%20product%20to%20the%20customer.

Palm Oil

Production

Malaysia is one of the leading producers of palm oil in the world. In 2018, Malaysia contributed 26% to the world palm oil production. Indonesia contributed 58%. The two countries combined accounted for 84% of the world's palm oil production. Thailand is the world's third-largest producer of palm oil; accounting for 4% of the world palm oil production (Table 85).

Table 85: World's Top Three Palm Oil Producers, 2018

Rank	Producer	'000 tonnes	Share to World Production, %
1	Indonesia	42,700	58
2	Malaysia	19,516	26
3	Thailand	2,775	4
	Others	9,181	12
	World	**74,172**	**100**

Source: Malaysian Palm Oil Board. 2019. *Malaysian Oil Palm Statistics 2018*. Bangi: MPOB.

The palm oil value chain is depicted in Figure 1. In 2018, there were 0.7 million hectares of palm oil plantations, with the state of Johor (EC4) having the largest area in the ECs, accounting for 13% of the total palm oil area planted (Table 86). Of the palm oil plantations in Johor, 44% are owned by private estates, 29% by independent smallholders, and the remaining are owned by state-owned enterprises (e.g., Johor Corporation) and government-linked companies (e.g., Federal Land Development Authority, Federal Land Consolidation and Rehabilitation Authority).[83] At the national level, 61% of the palm oil plantation area is owned by the private sector and 8% by independent smallholders. The palm oil industry is led by the private sector.

At the upstream level, the production of palm fruit (fresh fruit bunch [FFB]) received by FBB or palm oil mills was 98 million tonnes in 2018 with Johor being the largest FFB producer in Peninsular Malaysia. with production of 16 million tonnes or 13%, of the total FFB production. There are 451 FFB mills operating in the country with Johor having 61 mills (14%), which is the largest in Peninsular Malaysia. These palm oil fruits will be processed by FFB mills near the estate to produce CPO and palm kernels.[84] See Table 86 for CPO production, palm kernel, palm kernel oil, and palm kernel cake in 2018 and the number of related factories by state.

---

[83] Johor Corporation (JCorp) was established as a public enterprise and a statutory body via Johor Enactment No. 4 1968 (as amended under Enactment No. 5, 1995). As a state-owned conglomerate, JCorp through its group of companies is involved in core businesses encompassing plantation, specialist healthcare, food and restaurant services and real estate. The Federal Land Development Authority (FELDA) is a Malaysian government agency founded to handle the resettlement of rural poor into newly developed areas and to organize smallholder farms growing cash crops. Federal Land Consolidation and Rehabilitation Authority (FELCRA) is a corporate organization wholly owned by the Malaysian government, incorporated under the Minister of Finance. FELCRA's objective to develop rural areas by helping the rural community to join in economic activities and improve their living standards. Its goal is to create a dynamic, attractive, and profitable rural sector. It became a company in 1997, and as of October 2018, was reported to be managing 220,086 hectares of plantation and farmland of 111,684 FELCRA settlers and their families, and 30,189 hectares of FELCRA's own land.

[84] Carotino Sdn Bhd is selected as an example. This leading palm oil company in Malaysia was founded in 1981 and is headquartered in Pasir Gudang (Johor), Malaysia. This top palm oil manufacturer in Malaysia has a storage and production capacity of between 4 to 5 million tonnes of palm oil and owns a plantation area of more than 35,000 hectares. This best palm oil supplier in Malaysia has 4 CPO mills, 5 plantations, and 12 estates for palm oil in Malaysia. Retrieved from Carotino Group. Retrieved from www.carotino.com.

Figure 1: Palm Oil Value Chain

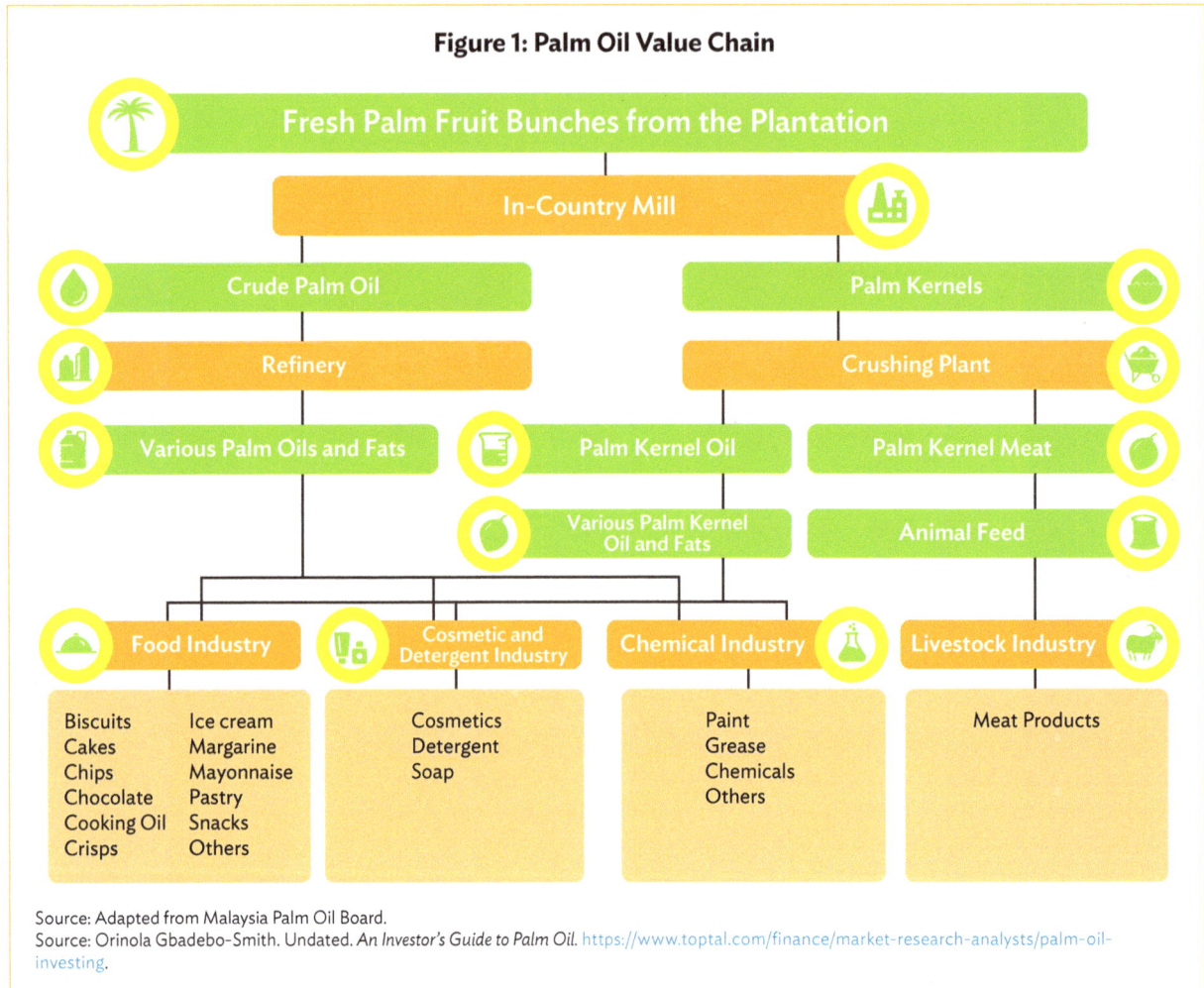

Source: Adapted from Malaysia Palm Oil Board.
Source: Orinola Gbadebo-Smith. Undated. *An Investor's Guide to Palm Oil.* https://www.toptal.com/finance/market-research-analysts/palm-oil-investing.

Crude palm oil. The production of CPO from FFB was 20 million tonnes in 2018 with Johor producing 3 million tonnes of CPO in 2018. Johor was the largest producer of CPO contributing 16% of the total CPO production. Johor has the largest palm oil terminal in the world located in Johor Port in Pasir Gudang. Johor Port has seven bulking installations with storage capacity of 644,000 tonnes in 2018.[85]

---

[85]   Bulking installations are facilities for the storage of crude and refined palm oils in port tanks until they are ready to be piped directly into the tankers which berth at nearby jetties in the port.

Table 86: Malaysia: Production of Palm Oil, 2018

State	Oil Palm Plantation		Input Supplier			Upstream			
						Crude Palm Oil		Palm Kernel	
	Area Planted '000 hectares	Share %	Fresh Fruit Bunches received by Mills '000 tonnes	Share %	No. of FBB mills	'000 tonnes	Share %	'000 tonnes	Share %
Existing IMT-GT State									
Perak (EC2)	413	7	9,725	10	45	1,861	10	528	11
Negeri Sembilan (EC2)	187	3	3,530	4	16	679	3	191	4
Kelantan (EC6)	155	3	1,428	1	10	295	2	73	2
Selangor (EC2)	136	2	2,742	3	16	520	3	149	3
Kedah (EC1/2)	90	2	1,331	1	6	266	1	71	1
Melaka(EC2/4)	57	1	–	–	–	–	–	–	–
Penang (EC1/2)	15	0*	–	–	–	–	–	–	–
Perlis (EC1/2)	1	0*	–	–	–	–	–	–	–
Proposed IMT-GT States									
Pahang (EC6)	756	13	14,079	14	70	2,754	14	729	15
Johor (EC4)	748	13	15,858	16	61	3,113	16	877	18
Terengganu (EC6)	169	3	2,436	2	13	486	2	124	3
Non IMT-GT States									
Sabah	1,549	26	25,044	25	128	5,139	26	1,180	24
Sarawak	1,572	27	21,111	21	81	4,179	21	875	18
Total (Malaysia)	**5,849**	**100**	**98,410**	**100**	**451**	**19,516**	**100**	**4,859**	**100**

– = not available, * = very negligible, EC = economic corridor, FBB = fresh fruit bunches, IMT-GT = Indonesia–Malaysia–Thailand Growth Triangle.
Sources: Department of Agriculture Malaysia. 2019. *Industrial Crop Statistics Malaysia 2018.* http://www.doa.gov.my/index/resources/aktiviti_sumber/sumber_awam/maklumat_pertanian/perangkaan_tanaman/perangkaan_tnmn_industri_2018.pdf; Ministry of Primary Industries Retrieved from https://www.mpi.gov.my/mpi/statistik/muat-turun-data-set; Malaysian Palm Oil Board. 2019. *Malaysian Oil Palm Statistics 2018.* Bangi: MPOB.

Palm kernels and palm kernel cake. Johor was the leading producer of palm kernels accounting for 18% of the total palm kernels produced in the country. Palm kernel crusher plants will process palm kernels into palm kernel oil and palm kernel cake.

Processing

In 2018, there were 26 palm kernel crushers plants in Peninsular Malaysia, 4 in Sarawak and 13 in Sabah. Meanwhile, for palm oil refineries, 34 plants are in the Peninsular Malaysia, 10 in Sabah, and 6 in Sarawak (Table 87). Most of these factories operate in the industrial parks provided by the state government.

Table 87: Palm Oil Plants by State and Type, 2018

State	Palm Kernel Crushers	Refineries	Oleochemical	Biodiesel
Johor (EC4)	8	13	6	5
Selangor (EC2)	9	13	8	5
Perak (EC2)	5	4	0	0
Other States	4	4	5	4
Peninsular Malaysia	**26**	**34**	**19**	**14**
Sabah	13	10	0	0
Sarawak	4	6	0	0
Malaysia	**43**	**50**	**19**	**14**

EC = economic corridor
Source: Malaysian Palm Oil Board. 2019. *Malaysian Oil Palm Statistics 2018.*

Midstream activities. At the midstream activities level, there are 43 palm crusher plants in Malaysia (Table 88). Of that total, Johor has 8 plants. These crushing plants will produce palm kernel oils and palm kernel cakes. Selangor was the largest producer of palm kernel oil and palm kernel cake in the ECs with 24% and 23% of the total palm kernel oil and palm kernel cake production in the country in 2018. Johor was the second-largest manufacturer in the production of these palm oil products.

Table 88: Production of Palm Kernel Oil, Palm Kernel Cake, 2018

Economic Corridor	State	No. of Palm Kernel Crusher Plants	Midstream			
			Palm Kernel Oil		Palm Kernel Cake	
			'000 tonnes	Share (%)	'000 tonnes	Share (%)
EC4	**Johor**	**9**	**443**	**19**	**485**	**19**
EC2	Perak	4	221	10	241	9
EC2	Selangor	9	543	24	602	23
	Sabah	13	554	24	673	26
	Sarawak	4	378	16	414	16
	Other States	4	160	7	180	7
Total (Malaysia)		**43**	**2,299**	**100**	**2,595**	**100**

EC = economic corridor
Source: Malaysian Palm Oil Board. 2019. *Malaysian Oil Palm Statistics 2018.* Bangi: MPOB.

Downstream activities. In 2018, there were 51 refinery plants in Malaysia, with Johor and Selangor each having 13 plants. The plant processes CPO into various palm oils and fats—refined, bleached, and deodorized (RBD) palm oil, RBD palm olein, RBD palm stearin, cooking oil, crude palm olein, palm fatty acid distillate (PFAD), and CP stearin—for the use of local industries, especially industries in the food industry (food), cosmetic and detergents, chemical industry, and livestock industry. Among the processed products, RBD palm oil and RBD palm olein, accounted for 42% and 30% of the production of processed palm oil products, respectively in 2018 (Table 89).[86]

---

[86]   RBD palm oil is now the most widely used vegetable oil in the world, a key component of foods ranging from baked goods to salad dressings to ice cream. RBD palm olein is also used as cooking oil as well as frying oil for the food industries such as salad and cooking oils in households, industrial frying fat of instant noodles, potato chips, donuts, condensed milk, snack food, and ready-to-eat food. It is also used as a raw material for margarine and shortening.

Table 89: Malaysia: Processed Palm Oil Products, 2018

Processed Palm Oil Products	Total (tonnes)	Share, %
RBD Palm Oil	14,940,999	49
RBD Palm Olein	10,595,104	35
RBD Palm Stearin	2,966,425	10
Cooking Oil	558,317	2
CP Olein	588,373	2
PFAD	782,048	3
CP Stearin	91,758	0
TOTAL	**30,523,024**	**100**

CP = crude palm; PFAD = palm fatty acid distillate; RBD = refined, bleached, and deodorized.
Source: Malaysian Palm Oil Board. 2019. *Malaysian Oil Palm Statistics 2018*. Bangi: MPOB.

End user. Processed palm oil products are part of the input in the production of food, cosmetic and detergents, chemicals, and animal feed. Increased production of these products directly increases the demand for processed palm-based products. Table 90 presents the industries that utilize palm oil products in the production of their final goods. The size of the industry related to palm-based products was small, with only 4% of the total sales of manufactured products in 2018.

Table 90: Malaysia: Manufacturing Sector Sales Value of Own Manufactured Products, Ex-Factory, 2018

Industry Code	Industry Using Palm-Based Products	Sales ($ million)	Share to All Manufacturing %
10404 and 10406	Manufacture of crude and refined vegetable oil & Manufacture of compound cooking fats	1,517	0.7
10800	Manufacture of prepared animal feeds	1,478	0.7
10502	Manufacture of condensed, powdered and evaporated milk and evaporated milk	1,269	0.6
10732 and 10733	Manufacture of chocolate and chocolate products & Manufacture of sugar confectionery	1,094	0.5
20231 and 20232	Manufacture of soap and detergents, cleaning and polishing preparations & Manufacture of perfumes and toilet preparations	807	0.4
20221	Manufacture of paints, varnishes and similar coatings ink and mastics	666	0.3
10712	Manufacture of bread, cakes and other bakery products	647	0.3
10711	Manufacture of biscuits and cookies	550	0.3
10713	Manufacture of snack products	318	0.2
TOTAL		**8,345**	**4.1**
All Manufacturing		**204,421**	

Source: Department of Statistics. 2020. Monthly Manufacturing Statistics. December 2019. Putrajaya: DOS Malaysia.

Distribution

Malaysia produced approximately 20 million tonnes of CPO (including processed palm oil) in 2014 and 19.5 million tonnes in 2018 (Table 91). During this period, local consumption of CPO (including processed palm oil) increased from 14% to 20%. This has indicated a rise in the downstream industry activities for palm-based products to meet domestic demand.

Table 91: Malaysia: Production, Export, Import and Consumption of Crude Palm Oil
('000 tonnes)

Item	2014	2018
Production	19,667	19,516
Import	486	841
Export	17,306	16,488
Domestic Consumption	**2,846**	**3,870**
Domestic Production (%)	**14**	**20**

Note: Data includes processed palm oil.
Source: Malaysian Pam Oil Board. 2020. *Malaysian Palm Oil Board: Statistics 2019*. Bangi: MPOB.

Johor, Sabah, and Sarawak, are the major contributors to Malaysia's position as a major exporter of palm oil in the world. In 2018, Malaysia contributed 32% to world palm oil exports, second to Indonesia's contribution of 57% (Table 92). The two countries combined accounted for almost 90% of the world's palm oil production. Thailand was the seventh-largest exporter accounting for 1% of the world palm oil production.

Table 92: World's Top Three Exporters of Palm Oil, 2018

Rank	Exporter	Export '000 tonnes	Export Share, %	Production '000 tonnes	Export/ Production (%)
1	Indonesia	27,900	57	41,000	68
2	Malaysia	16,488	32	19,516	84
3	Guatemala	770	2	830	93
	Others	4,887	10	–	–
	World	**50,045**	**100**	**72,087**	**69**
7th	Thailand [1]	390	1	2728	14

– = not available
Note: [1] Thailand is the world's third largest producer of palm oil.
Source: Department of Statistics. 2020. *Monthly manufacturing statistics December 2019*. Putrajaya: DOS Malaysia.

In terms of production to export ratio, Malaysia exports 84% of its total production compared to Indonesia with 69%. This would indicate that upstream activities still dominate the palm oil industry. The bulk of Thailand's production is for the domestic market with only 14% of its production exported. This reflects Thailand's focus on downstream activities.

Palm oil products. Among the palm oil products exported, processed palm oil was the main export, accounting for 51% of the total exports in 2018 (Table 93). The second most important palm oil product was CPO followed by oleochemicals. Based on the export pattern of palm oil products, the country's palm oil industry is still concentrated in the intermediate products and less in downstream activities especially in the production of end products. This is also reflected in the value chain structure in the country's palm oil industry which tends toward upstream activities compared to intermediate products.

Table 93: Malaysia: Exports of Oil Palm Products, 2018

Palm Oil Product	Volume (tonnes)	Share (%)	Exports $ million	Share (%)
Crude Palm Oil	3,425,422	14	1,957	12
Processed Palm Oil	13,062,123	53	8,214	51
Palm Oil (CPO+PPO)	**16,487,546**	**66**	**10,172**	**63**
Crude Palm Kernel Oil	334,746	1	317	2
Processed Palm Kernel Oil	587,682	2	698	4
Palm Kernel Oil (CPKO+PPKO)	**922,429**	**4**	**1,015**	**6**
Palm Kernel Cake	2,292,144	9	272	2
Oleochemicals	3,091,710	12	3,535	22
Finished Products	615,136	2	682	4
Biodiesel	515,467	2	357	2
Others	952,340	4	179	1
Total	**24,876,769**	**100**	**16,212**	**100**

CPKO = crude palm kernel oil, CPO = crude palm oil, PPKO = processed palm kernel oil, PPO = processed palm oil.
Note: Totals may not sum precisely because of rounding.
Source: Malaysian Palm Oil Board. 2019. *Malaysian Oil Palm Statistics 2018.* Bangi, MPOB.

Export markets. For palm oil and palm kernel oil products, the main markets include India, the European Union (EU), Pakistan, the Philippines, the PRC, Turkey, and the United States (US). Malaysia also exports to Indonesia, specifically palm kernel oil products. Palm oil exports to the world was 16 million tonnes and palm kernel oil, 0.9 million tonnes in 2018 (Table 94).

Table 94: Malaysia: Top Five Export Markets for Palm Oil and Palm Kernel Oil, 2018

	Palm Oil	2018 (tonnes)	Share (%)		Palm Kernel Oil	2018 (tonnes)	Share (%)
Rank	Destination			Rank	Destination		
1	India	2,514,008	15	1	EU	240,167	26
2	EU	1,911,800	12	2	PRC	157,813	17
3	PRC	1,859,748	11	3	India	82,754	9
4	Pakistan	1,161,278	7	4	US	79,571	9
5	Philippines	689,290	4	5	Turkey	64,321	7
	Others	8,351,432	51		Indonesia	493	0.05
	World	16,487,556	100		Others	297,802	32
					World	922,428	100

EU = European Union, PRC = People's Republic of China, US = United States.
Source: Malaysian Palm Oil Board. 2019. *Malaysian Oil Palm Statistics 2018.* Bangi, MPOB.

Exports to Indonesia. The major markets for palm-based oleochemicals were the PRC, EU, the US, Japan, and India. For biodiesel, its major markets were the EU, the PRC, Indonesia, Peru, and Japan. Malaysia also exports biodiesel and palm-based oleochemicals to Indonesia (Table 95).

Table 95: Malaysia: Top Five Export Markets for Palm-Based Oleochemicals and Biodiesel, 2018

		Palm-based Oleochemicals				Biodiesel	
Rank	Destination	2018 (tonnes)	Share (%)	Rank	Destination	2018 (tonnes)	Share (%)
1	PRC	531,910	17	1	EU	253,940	49
2	EU	438,276	14	2	PRC	164,007	32
3	US	331,970	11	3	Indonesia	40,882	8
4	Japan	244,700	8	4	Peru	27,944	5
5	India	182,115	6	5	Japan	9,487	2
	Indonesia	69.724	2		Others	19,207	4
	Others	1,362,739	44		World	515,467	100
	World	3,091,710	100				

EU = European Union, PRC = People's Republic of China, US = United States.
Source: Malaysian Palm Oil Board. 2019. *Malaysian Oil Palm Statistics 2018*. Bangi, MPOB.

Imports from Indonesia and Thailand. Although Malaysia is one of the world's leading producers of palm oil, it still imports from Thailand and Indonesia to meet the demand of local industries. Malaysia imported 1 million tonnes of palm oil from Indonesia, accounting for 89% of the country's total imports, followed by Thailand, with 9%, in 2018 (Table 96).

Table 96: Malaysia: Import of Palm Oil from Thailand and Indonesia, 2018

	(tonnes)				Share, %			
Origin	Palm Oil	Palm Kernel Oil	Palm Kernel	Total Palm Products	Palm Oil	Palm Kernel Oil	Palm Kernel	Total Palm Products
Indonesia	819,823	157,541	58,024	1,035,388	97	65	73	89
Thailand	8,044	82,546	12,387	102,977	1	34	16	9
Others	13,585	939	8,887	23,411	2	0*	11	2
Total	**841,452**	**241,026**	**79,298**	**1,161,776**	**100**	**100**	**100**	**100**

* very negligible
Note: Totals may not sum precisely because of rounding.
Source: Malaysian Palm Oil Board. 2019. *Malaysian Oil Palm Statistics 2018*. Bangi, MPOB.

Ports. There is a bulking installation for CPO before it can be exported. Among the important ports are Port Klang, Penang Port, and Johor Port. Johor Port had a storage capacity of 644,000 tonnes in 2018 (Table 97).

Table 97: Major Ports: Status of Port Bulking Installation, 2018

Corridor	Port	Number of Installations	Storage Capacity ('000 tonnes)	Quantity Received ('000 tonnes)	Domestic Distribution ('000 tonnes)	Exports ('000 tonnes)
EC2	Port Klang	14	417	2,039	1,004	957
EC1/2	Penang Port	5	141	802	284	479
EC4	Johor Port, Pasir Gudang	7	644	6,377	2,752	3,558
EC6	Kuantan Port	3	225	1,312	535	772
	Peninsular Malaysia	29	1,429	10,529	4,575	5,766
	Sabah and Sarawak	13	531	4,848	751	4,016

EC = economic corridor.
Source: Malaysian Palm Oil Board. 2019. *Malaysian Oil Palm Statistics 2018.* Bangi, MPOB.

Among the major ports, Port Klang accounted for 23% of the total palm oil exports by all domestic ports in 2018, followed by Johor Port (Pasir Gudang) with 20%. Johor Port and Tanjung Pelepas Port registered high growth rates of 6.2% and 7.4%, respectively in the volume of palm oil exports. All the major ports are easily accessible by manufacturers through road and rail connectivity (Table 98).

Table 98: Exports of Palm Products by Major Ports

Corridor	Port	(tonnes) 2014	(tonnes) 2018	Share, % 2014	Share, % 2018	CAGR, % 2014–2018
EC2	Port Klang	5,154,101	5,682,597	21	23	2.5
EC1/2	Penang Port	978,472	797,651	4	3	(5.0)
EC2	Lumut Port	357,773	335,627	1	1	(1.6)
EC4	Johor Port	3,822,888	4,857,989	15	20	6.2
EC4	Tanjung Pelepas Port	786,079	1,046,358	3	4	7.4
EC6	Kuantan Port	2,076,585	997,651	8	4	(16.7)
	Others	603,665	578,777	2	2	(1.0)
	Peninsular Malaysia	13,779,563	14,296,650	55	57	0.9
	Malaysia	25,072,102	24,876,780	100	100	(0.2)

( ) = negative, CAGR = compound annual growth rate, EC = economic corridor.
Note: * Includes palm oil, palm kernel oil, palm kernel cake, palm-based oleochemicals, biodiesel, finished products, and other oil palm products.
Source: Malaysian Palm Oil Board. 2019. *Malaysian Oil Palm Statistics 2018.* Bangi: MPOB.

Overland border trade. Trading of palm oil products between Malaysia and Thailand is by road through the Malaysia–Thailand borders and also by train via the land bridge rail service from Tanjung Pelepas Port, Johor Port, Port Klang, and Penang Port to Hat Yai, and subsequently Bangkok via Padang Besar Station. The total trade of vegetable products (including palm products) was 4% of the Malaysia–Thailand trade volume in 2018 (Table 99). The bilateral trade balance in vegetable products (including palm oil products) was in favor of Thailand.

**Table 99: Palm Oil Products Trade between Malaysia and Thailand
at Malaysia–Thai Border Checkpoints, 2018**

HS-Code	Product Description	Export, ('000 $)	Share, %	Import ($ '000)	Share, %
06-15	Vegetable Products (including palm products)	110,831	4	147,390	4
	Other Commodities	2,874,336	96	3,487,015	96
	Total	2,985,167	100	3,634,405	100

Source: Royal Malaysian Customs Department, 2019. Putrajaya. RMCD.

Findings and Recommendations

Comparative advantage of EC states. ECs 1, 2, 4, and 6 have a comparative advantage in the palm oil industry, with the state of Johor as the largest producer of palm oil in Malaysia. Most of the palm oil plantations are located in hinterland areas. While the processing industries for palm oil, especially downstream activities, are mostly concentrated in industrial estates or industrial parks.

Access to ports. The road and rail networks facilitate the palm oil value chain in their respective corridors and also between ECs 1, 2, 4, and 6. The ports in these corridors, namely Port Klang, Penang Port, Lumut Port, Tanjung Pelepas Port, Johor Port, and Kuantan Port are accessible by road and rail.

Seamless connectivity. To support palm oil value chain development, planning for economic corridors should focus not only on the main transport backbone, but also on transport links that enhance the efficiency of logistics services, which are crucial for value chains.

- Last-mile connectivity—both gateway-based and hinterland-based—could help facilitate transport and bring down logistics costs at various stages of the value chain.

- Improved connectivity from industrial estates to seaports will facilitate exports of products to international markets and can contribute to the competitiveness of the products.

- Railway spur lines are being planned to be built in the ECs for ports that do not have direct rail links with major economic centers. The proposed railway spur lines are from Bukit Kayu Hitam in Kedah to Arau in Perlis (EC1 and EC2) (footnote 43) and ICT to Lumut Port in Perak (EC2) (footnote 44). This will improve transport connectivity and support product value chain development.

- The role of inland ports in the ECs needs to be further enhanced. The existing inland ports in the ECs are ICT (Perak), NIP (Negeri Sembilan), SIP (Johor), and BPCT (Johor). Inland ports will allow many supply chain functions to take place further inland and offer better access to inland markets.[87]

The role of EC6. The EC6's states—Kelantan, Terengganu, and Pahang—are among the major producers of palm oil. The ECRL route from Kota Bharu to Port Klang and the East Coast Highway from Tumpat to Kuala Lumpur will develop a road-rail-ports intermodal link, particularly to Kemaman Port and Kuantan Port, that will support the development of value chains in the region. Both ports in the EC6 serve as trade gateways for manufacturers to export their products to East Asia. Manufacturers in the EC6 can also use this overland route as a land bridge to export their products by using ports on the west coast, such as Port Klang and Tanjung Bruas Port.

---

[87]   Jean-Paul Rodrigue, Jean Debrie, Antoine Fremont, and Elisabeth Gouvernal. 2010. Functions and Actors of Inland Ports: European and North American Dynamics. *Journal of Transport Geography*. 18(4). July. pp. 519–529.

Industrial clusters for palm oil should be promoted. An industry cluster represents the entire value chain of a broadly defined industry, from suppliers to end products, including supporting services and specialized infrastructure. Industry clusters are geographically concentrated and interconnected by the flow of goods and services, which is stronger than the flow linking them to the rest of the economy. While the concept of industrial clusters is different from that of industrial estates, industrial clusters can be developed alongside, or in proximity to, industrial estates. Johor has a dedicated industrial estate to support palm oil value chain activities with the development of the Tanjung Langsat Palm Oil Industrial Cluster. This economic zone is connected to Johor Port (Pasir Gudang) and Tanjung Pelepas Port (Gelang Patah) by road.

Halal Food

As of 2010, there were 1.6 billion Muslims around the world, representing 23% of the world population. This makes Islam the world's second-largest religion. Muslims are expected to grow twice as fast as the overall global population. Consequently, Muslims are projected to rise from 23% of the world's population in 2010 to 30% in 2050.[88] Thus, there is a high market potential for halal food. The actual global halal food market value could be substantially higher if the growing numbers of non-Muslims who consume halal food are taken into account.

Halal is an Arabic word which means lawful or permissible by Islamic laws. In Malaysia, the use of the term *halal* referred to in the Trade Descriptions 1975 can be applied to food. The term *Ditanggung Halal* indicates that a Muslim is allowed to consume the products as permitted by Islam. The halal concept is not only confined to food but also covers the process of handling, packaging, storing, and delivering. The concept of halal is not only introduced to the food sectors, but also to the nonfood sectors such as pharmaceuticals, cosmetics, and financial services.[89]

The vegetable and animal oils, fats, and food processing industry and beverage industry were selected as examples to analyze the halal food value chain in the country. Figure 2 presents the supply chain in the halal food industry. The value chain which involves livestock, will be required to conduct the Islamic slaughtering process to obtain recognition as halal food.[90]

---

[88] Data on Muslim population were compiled from Pew Templeton. Global Religious Future. http://www.globalreligiousfutures.org/religions/muslims.

[89] Emi Normalina Omar and Harlina Suzana Jaafar. 2011. *Halal Supply Chain in the Food Industry - A Conceptual Model*. Paper presented at IEEE Symposium on Business, Engineering and Industrial Applications (ISBEIA), Langkawi, Malaysia, September.

[90] Most of the statistics published on the halal food industry are at the national level. Information published according to the breakdown by state is also available, however, only at the production stage. The latest statistics for the halal food industry published by the Department of Statistics Malaysia was in 2017; *Economic Census 2016; Halal Statistics.*

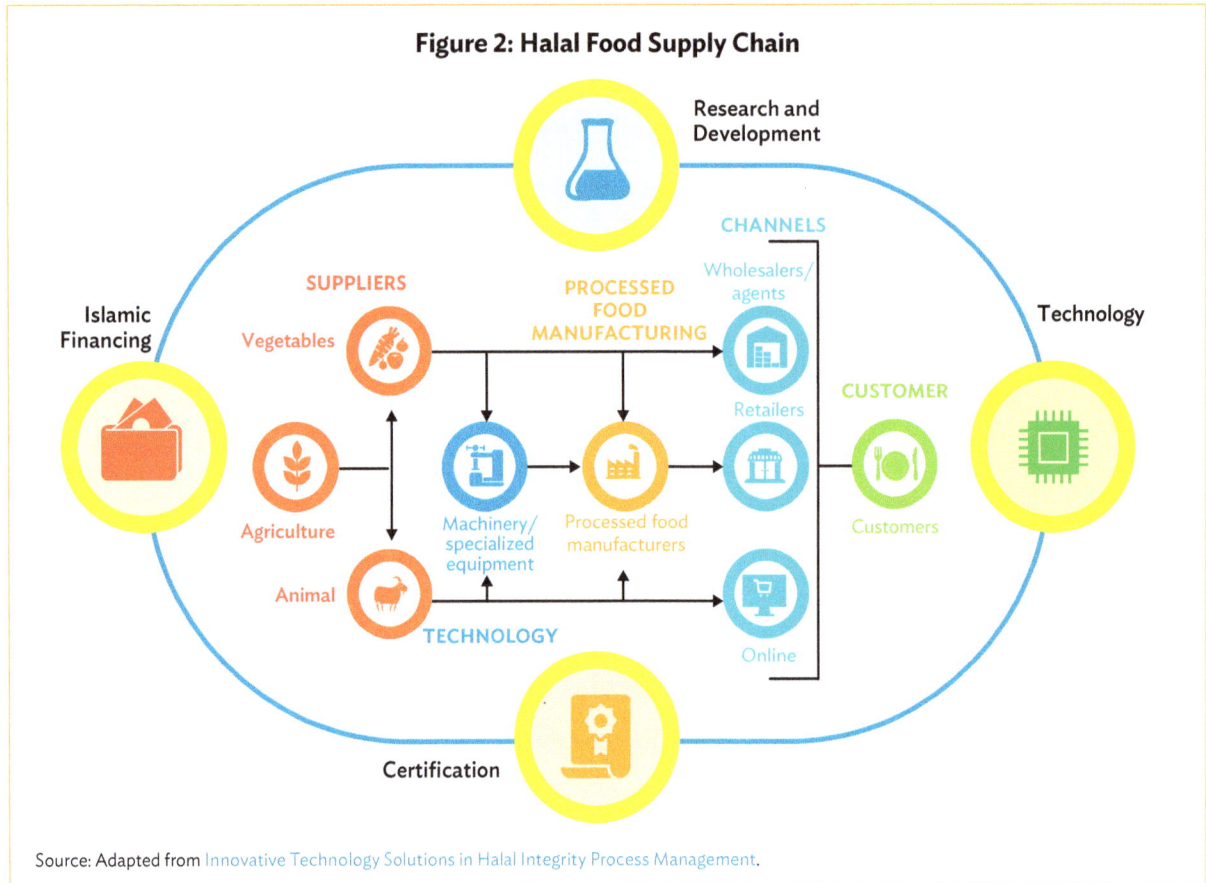

Figure 2: Halal Food Supply Chain

Source: Adapted from Innovative Technology Solutions in Halal Integrity Process Management.

Halal Certification

Halal certification. The Department of Islamic Development Malaysia (JAKIM) is the Malaysian government agency that issues halal certificates. For the purpose of halal certification, JAKIM has to ascertain the halal status of the product at every stage and at every process involved by carrying out an official site inspection on the plants purposely to examine how the halal status of the raw material is maintained and monitored at all times. There are three types of certification schemes available which cover (i) consumable and nonconsumable products, (ii) food premises, and (iii) abattoirs and slaughterhouses.[91]

JAKIM also verifies the halal status of imported products with a foreign halal certificate by sending its members to verify the halal status of these products. All imported food and goods marketed in Malaysia cannot be described as halal unless the imported food and goods comply with the requirements or certified as halal by the foreign halal certification body recognized by JAKIM.

The Malaysia halal logo is recognized and well-accepted worldwide. Malaysia is the only country in the world where the government provides full support in promoting the halal certification process on products and services. Halal certification bodies in other countries are either developed by the individual provinces or states or backed by nongovernment organizations.

---

[91]   The information about Halal Certification was abridged from Department of Islamic Development Malaysia (Jabatan Kemajuan Islam Malaysia). 2015. Manual Procedure for Malaysia Halal Certification (3rd. Revision 2014. Putrajaya).

Production

Examples of input suppliers for halal food industry include (i) fruit crops, (ii) cash crops, (iii) industrial crops, (iv) rice, and (v) crude palm oil sectors. These types of crops are grown by individual farmers, smallholder farmers and estates. In these sectors, the halal concept also covers the cultivation process with good practices and Sharia compliant,[92] such as not utilizing fertilizer from swine products. These crops will be processed further into vegetable and animal oils and fats, and food and beverages products, by local factories. Factory owners can apply for halal certification and status from the government to be recognized as halal establishments. There are also factories operating in halal parks provided by the government. To date, 14 halal parks have been built by the government to support the halal industry.

Table 100 presents the input suppliers according to the type of crop and the size of the area planted. The production volume of crop types depends on the crop area. CPO production was almost 20 million tonnes in 2015 with a crop area of almost 6 million hectares compared to cash crops production of 227,000 tonnes from a crop area of 19,000 hectares.

Table 100: Input Suppliers for Halal Food, 2015

State	Area Planted ('000 hectares)					Production ('000 tonnes)				
	Fruit Crops [1]	Cash Crops [2]	Industrial Crops [3]	Paddy [4]	Palm Oil [5]	Fruit Crops [1]	Cash Crops	Industrial Crops	Rice	Crude Palm Oil
Existing IMT-GT States										
Perlis	3	0.04	0.4	52	1	na	0	1	161	na
Kedah	11	1	2	215	90	71	5	7	621	266
Penang	2	0.1	0.1	26	15	na	1	0	97	na
Perak	12	2	9	82	413	127	41	106	223	1,861
Selangor	2	1	10	38	136	16	23	104	156	520
Negeri Sembilan	7	0.5	2	2	187	65	8	10	6	679
Melaka	5	1	2	3	57	43	6	18	7	na
Kelantan	22	1	8	72	155	137	19	52	192	295
Proposed IMT-GT States										
Terengganu	6	1	2	16	169	49	7	8	52	486
Pahang	30	1	5	12	756	201	14	28	25	2,754
Johor	45	4	13	3	748	515	57	105	8	3,113
Non IMT-GT States										
Sabah	16	2	19	39	1,549	139	15	52	75	5,139
Sarawak	33	4	76	121	1,572	150	30	210	145	4,179
(Malaysia)	**194**	**19**	**149**	**682**	**5,849**	**289**	**227**	**702**	**1,767**	**19,516**

ECER = East Coast Economic Region, HALMAS = Halal Malaysia, IMT-GT = Indonesia–Malaysia–Thailand Growth Triangle, na = not available.
Sources: [1] Department of Agriculture. 2016. *Fruits Crops Statistics Malaysia 2015*. Putrajaya. DOA Malaysia, [2] Department of Agriculture. 2019. *Vegetables and Cash Crop Statistics: Malaysia 2018*. Putrajaya. DOA Malaysia, [3] Department of Agriculture. 2016. *Industrial Crops Statistics Malaysia 2015*. Putrajaya. DOA Malaysia, [4] Department of Agriculture. 2016. *Paddy Statistics of Malaysia 2015*. Putrajaya. DOA Malaysia, [5] Ministry of Primary Industries Retrieved from https://www.mpi.gov.my/mpi/statistik/muat-turun-data-set.

---

[92] Sharia compliant refers to an act or activity that complies with the requirements of the Sharia, or Islamic law. Halal is a Quranic term that means permissible and lawful. According to Sharia, all issues concerning Halal or non-Halal (Haram) should be referred to Quran and Sunnah. It includes foods, all good services, entertainments, finance, and all aspects of human life that come under the judgment of halal and haram. The Sunnah refers to the sayings and practices of the Prophet Muhammad (pbuh) and is the second source of knowledge for Muslims.

Processing

In 2015, there were 2,151 halal establishments that had halal certification to process crop inputs (Table 102). Of the 2,151 halal establishments, 115 of them were involved in the vegetable, animal oils and fats, and food processing industry and 1,737 halal establishments were involved in the beverage industry in 2015. The value of the halal output produced by vegetable, animal oils and fats, and the food processing industry was $20 billion while the beverage industry produced halal output worth $13 billion (Table 103). Table 101 shows the halal parks with Halal Malaysia (HALMAS) status from the Halal Development Corporation and Non-HALMAS status, as well as the operator that manages the Halal Park.

Table 101: Malaysia: Halal Park by Operator

State/Corridor	Halal Parks	Operator
Existing IMT-GT States		
Perlis (EC1/2)	Perlis Halal Park*	Perlis State Government
	MARA Halal Park Kuala Perlis*	MARA
Penang (EC1/2)	Penang International Halal Park	PIHH Sdn Bhd
	PERDA Halal Park	Lembaga Kemajuan Wilayah Pulau Pinang (PERDA)
Kedah (EC1/2)	Kedah Halal Park*	Kedah State Government
Perak (EC2)	MARA Halal Park Tambun*	MARA
Selangor (EC2)	Selangor Halal Hub	Central Spectrum (M) Sdn Bhd
	Port Klang Free Zone (PKFZ) National Halal Park	PKFZ (M) Sdn Bhd
Kelantan (EC6)	ECER Pasir Mas Halal Park	East Coast Economic Region Development Council (ECERDC)
	Pengkalan Chepa Halal Park*	Kelantan State Government
Negeri Sembilan (EC2)	Techpark@enstek	THP Enstek Development Sdn Bhd
	Pedas Halal Park	MIDF Property Berhad
Melaka (EC4)	Melaka Halal Park	Melaka Halal Hub Sdn Bhd
Additional States in Reconfigured Economic Corridors as well as EC6		
Johor (EC4)	Palm Oil Industrial Cluster Tanjung Langsat	TPM Technopark Sdn Bhd
	Iskandar Halal Park	Iskandar Halal Park Sdn Bhd
Pahang (EC6)	ECER Gambang Halal Park	ECERDC
Terengganu (EC6)	Terengganu Halal Park*	Terengganu State Government
Non-IMT-GT States		
Sarawak	MARA Halal Park Kuching*	MARA
	Tanjung Manis Halal Food Park	Tanjung Manis Food & Industrial Park Sdn Bhd
Sabah	Labuan Hub Distributive Hub*	Labuan Corporation, Ministry of Federal Territory and Marditech Corporation Sdn Bhd.
	Kota Kinabalu Industrial Park	K.K.I.P Sdn Bhd
	Palm Oil Industrial Cluster Lahad Datu	Palm Oil Industrial Cluster Sdn Bhd

EC = economic corridor, ECER = East Coast Economic Region, HALMAS = Halal Malaysia, IMT-GT = Indonesia–Malaysia–Thailand Growth Triangle.
* Non-HALMAS status.
Source: Halal Development Corporation. http://www.halalpark.com.my/publisher/halal_park_companies.

Table 102: Statistics of Halal Establishments in the Manufacturing Sector by State, 2015

Economic Corridor	State	No.of Halal Establishment in Manufacturing Sector based on Halal Certification, 2015	Economic Sector			
			Vegetable and Animal Oils and Fats and Food Processing Sector		Beverages Products Sector	
			No. of Halal Establishment, 2015	Value of Halal Gross Output, 2015 ($ billion)	No. of Halal Establishment, 2015	Value of Halal Gross Output, 2015 ($ billion)
Existing IMT-GT States						
EC2	Selangor	549				
EC2	Perak	233				
EC1/2	Penang	230				
EC1/2	Kedah	126				
EC4	Melaka	94	–	–	–	–
EC2	Negeri Sembilan	78				
EC6	Kelantan	64				
EC1/2	Perlis	6				
Proposed IMT-GT States						
EC6	Johor	398				
EC6	Pahang	65	–	–	–	–
EC6	Terengganu	35				
Non IMT-GT Region						
	FT Kuala Lumpur	102				
	FT Labuan	3	–	–	–	–
	Sarawak	85				
	Sabah	83				
	Malaysia	**2,151**	**115**	**20**	**1,737**	**13**

– = not available, EC = economic corridor, FT = federal territory, IMT-GT = Indonesia–Malaysia–Thailand Growth Triangle.
Source: Department of Statistics. 2016. *Economic Census 2016: Halal Statistic Malaysia*. Putrajaya: DOS Malaysia.

Services. Other services industries are also involved in supporting the halal food value chain, including the sectors of distributive trade, food and beverages, accommodation, transportation, and storage. Table 103 presents the number of halal establishments involved in the services industry in 2015. The percentage of halal establishments in each industry is less than 1%, except in the accommodation subsector with a share of 6%. The distributive trade subsector, generated a significant output value of $2.5 billion in 2015.

Table 103: Malaysia: Halal Establishment in the Services Industry, 2015

Services Industry – Sub-industry	Number of Establishments	Number of Halal Establishments	Share of Halal Establishments, %	Value of Gross Halal Output ($ billion)
Distributive Trade	418,569	934	0.2	2.5
Food and Beverage	167,490	2,606	0.0*	2
Accommodation	4,377	263	6.0	1
Transport and Storage	54,190	33	0.1	0.8

* very negligible.
Source: Department of Statistics Malaysia. 2016. *Economic Census 2016: Halal Statistic Malaysia.* Putrajaya: DOS Malaysia.

Distribution

The export value of halal products in 2015 was $17 billion, accounting for 9% of the country's total exports. This indicates that the contribution of halal product exports is still small and can be further developed in the future through programs and promotions conducted by the Halal Development Corporation (Table 104).

Table 104: Malaysia's Export of Halal Products by Commodity, 2015

Commodity Section (SITC)	Product Description	Total Export Value ($ billion)	Export Value of Halal Establishments ($ billion)	Export Value of Halal Establishments Share, %
All (SITC 0–9)	**Total**	**194**	**17**	**9**
SITC 0	Food	7	5	69
SITC 1	Beverage and tobacco	1	0.3	22
SITC 4	Animal and vegetable oils and fats	12	12	74

SITC = Standard International Trade Classification.
Source: Department of Statistics Malaysia (2016). Economic Census 2016: Halal Statistic Malaysia. Putrajaya: DOS Malaysia.

Export markets. The value of the country's halal exports was $10 billion in 2015, accounting for 5% of the country's total exports (Table 105). Halal exports are mostly shipped through Penang Port and Port Klang. Halal products are also exported via overland routes that traverse through the Malaysia–Thailand border via BCPs Padang Besar, Bukit Kayu Hitam, and Rantau Panjang.

The top five countries for Malaysia's halal exports were the PRC, Singapore, the US, Indonesia, and Japan. Thailand was ranked 6th. In the context of IMT-GT, there is an opportunity to create a halal corridor belt between Indonesia, Malaysia, and Thailand as discussed in Chapter 4.

Table 105: Malaysia's Export of Halal Products by Destination, 2015

Rank	Export Destination	Total Export Value ($ million)	Halal Export Value ($ million)	Halal Export Share (%)
1	PRC	25,384	1,192	4.7
2	Singapore	27,097	979	3.6
3	US	7,276	680	9.4
4	**Indonesia**	**18,171**	**613**	**3.4**
5	Japan	18,171	553	3.0
6	**Thailand**	**11,097**	**461**	**4.2**
7	Australia	7,020	420	6.0
8	Philippines	3,294	410	12.5
9	Netherlands	5,849	360	6.2
10	India	7,915	345	4.4
	Worldwide Total	**194,339**	**9,860**	**5.0**

PRC = People's Republic of China, US = United States.
Source: Department of Statistics Malaysia. 2016. *Economic Census 2016: Halal Statistic Malaysia.* Putrajaya: DOS Malaysia.

Findings and Recommendations

Comparative advantage. ECs 1, 2, 4, and 6 have a comparative advantage in the halal food industry, with the state of Selangor having the highest number of halal establishments in Malaysia. All states in the ECs have halal parks that are largely developed by state governments or federal-owned agencies. Manufacturers involved in the halal food industry or halal services require a certificate from JAKIM to operate in the halal parks or industrial estates.

Weak integration. Malaysia has a relatively developed halal ecosystem and a strong halal brand. However, the integration of the halal value chain between input suppliers, manufacturers, logistics providers, wholesalers, and retailers is still weak. This is reflected in the low number of participating halal establishments in the halal food value chain.

Seamless connectivity. Transport links play an important role in enhancing the efficiency of logistics. These include last-mile connectivity between hinterlands and gateways, connectivity from industrial estates to seaports, and railway spur lines that link ports to economic centers. Inland ports need to be enhanced to allow many value chain functions to take place further inland to benefit both producers and consumers.

The role of EC6. The states of Kelantan, Pahang, and Terengganu are among the major producers of halal food products. The ECRL route from Kota Bharu to Port Klang and the East Coast Highway from Tumpat to Kuala Lumpur will develop a road–rail–ports intermodal link particularly to Kemaman Port and Kuantan Port. Manufacturers in the EC6 can use this overland route as a land bridge to export their products by using ports on the west coast, such as Port Klang and Tanjung Bruas Port.

Regional halal certification. One of the concerns raised in the IMT-GT IB 2017–2021 is the gap in halal certification practices between IMT countries. The agencies responsible—JAKIM, the Central Islamic Council of Thailand, and the Indonesian Council of Ulama—are currently coordinating the certification practices through the IMT-GT Working Group on Halal Products for the IMT's halal logo to be recognized and well-accepted globally. This will help the IMT expand its regional and global trade of halal products.

Halal cluster network. At the Malaysia International Halal Showcase 2019 in Kuala Lumpur, the Modern Halal Valley (Indonesia) and Iskandar Halal Park (Malaysia), Penang International Halal Hub (Malaysia), and Cluster Halal Córdoba (Spain) launched the Halal Cluster Network. The Halal Cluster Network links local, regional, and international halal clusters together, as the full potential of halal parks can only be achieved when working together. The goal of this global initiative is to achieve synergy advantages for halal clusters and its industries based in a halal cluster. Areas of collaboration include halal assurance, sourcing, market access, joint promotion, and research and development, among others.[93] The Halal Cluster Network concept can be applied to the EC6 and EC2.

Rubber and Rubber Products

Production

The rubber and rubber industry is selected as an example to discuss the potential of value chain in the EC1 (Figure 3). This is based on the proposal to create Rubber Cities at the IMT-GT level, which involves the provinces in the EC1 (Kedah and Southern Thailand) and the EC3 (Sumatera). The rubber cities comprise the KRC (Padang Terap, Kedah), Rubber City in the Special Economic Zone Tanjung Api-Api (South Sumatera), Sei Mangkei (North Sumatera), and Hat Yai's Southern Regional Industrial Estate.

Indonesia, Malaysia, and Thailand were among the world's leading producers and exporters of natural rubber. Malaysia was the fifth-largest natural rubber producer in the world in 2018, accounting for 4% of the world's natural rubber production (Table 106). Thailand was the leading producer, followed by Indonesia.[94] Malaysia was the third-largest exporter of natural rubber in the world in 2018, accounting for 9% of the world's total exports. Indonesia was the leading exporter, followed by Thailand.

Table 106: Top Five Producers and Exporters of Natural Rubber in the World, 2018

Production ('000 tonnes) [1]				Exports ($ billion) [2]			
Rank	Country	Production ('000 tonnes)	Share to Total Production, %	Rank	Country	Exports ($ billion)	Share to World Export, %
1	Thailand	5,145	37	1	Indonesia	4.8	33
2	Indonesia	3,486	25	2	Thailand	4.8	33
3	Viet Nam	1,142	8	**3**	**Malaysia**	**1.3**	**9**
4	People's Republic of China	811	6	4	Ivory Coast	0.9	6
5	**Malaysia**	**6,03**	**4**	5	Viet Nam	0.7	5
	World Production	13,887	100		World Export	14.7	

Sources:
[1] Tridge. Market Intelligence. https://www.tridge.com/intelligences/natural-rubber/export.
[2] Ministry of Primary Industries and Commodities, Malaysia. https://www.mpic.gov.my/mpi/en/statistic/download-set-data.

---

93   M. Ti. 2019. Malaysia: Halal Cluster Network with Halal Clusters in Indonesia, Malaysia, and Spain. *Halal Focus*. 4 April. https://halalfocus. net/malaysia-halal-cluster-network-with-halal-clusters-in-indonesia-malaysia-and-spain/.

94   The Association of Natural Rubber Producing Countries. http://www.anrpc.org/ and Department of Statistics Malaysia. 2019. Monthly Rubber Statistics: Malaysia. December 2018.

Figure 3: Rubber Value Chain

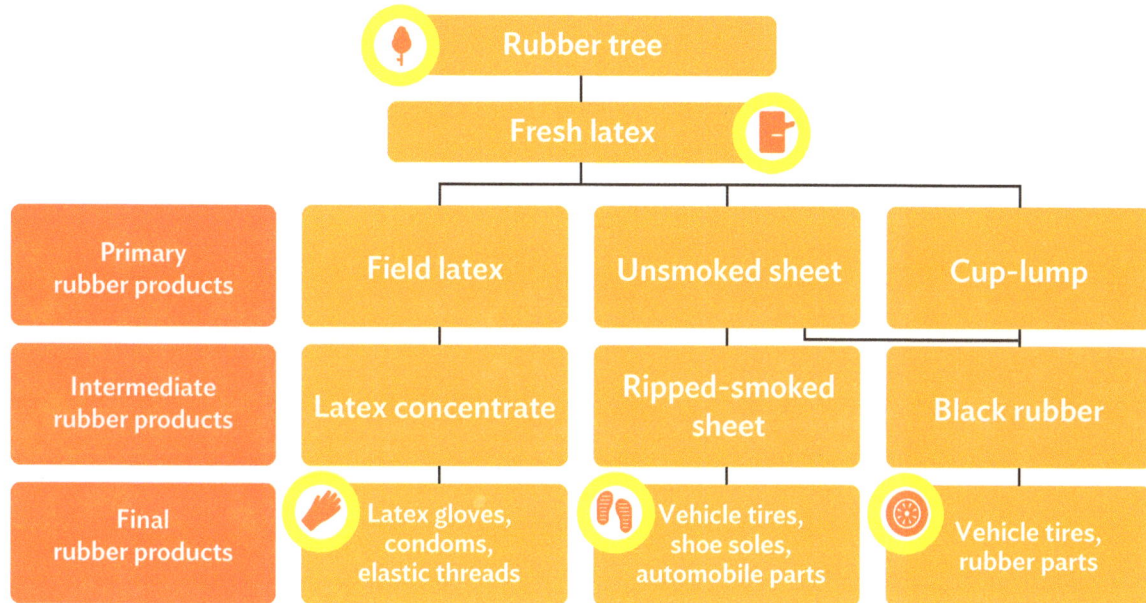

Source: Adapted from Chanchaichujit J., Saavedra-Rosas J.F. 2018. The Elements of the Natural Rubber Industry Supply Chain. *Using Simulation Tools to Model Renewable Resources*. Palgrave Macmillan, Cham.

In 2016, the participating states in the economic corridors produced 38,131 tonnes of natural rubber from a 52,000-hectare rubber plantation area. The state of Kedah is the largest producer of natural rubber in the country with a production volume of almost 18,600 tonnes, accounting for 27% of the country's natural rubber production (Table 107).

The rubber estates are owned by state-owned enterprises, federal government-linked companies such as Federal Land Development Authority (FELDA), Federal Land Consolidation and Rehabilitation Authority (FELCRA), and RISDA, and private companies. An example of a private company is the Tradewinds Plantation Berhad in Kedah, which is involved in the KRC project. This company owns 6,940 hectares of rubber plantations.[95] Kedah State Development Corporation, a state-owned enterprise, owns 3,277 hectares of rubber plantations.[96]

---

[95] The information of the company was abstracted from Tradewinds Plantation Berhad found at https://www.tpb.com.my/page/170/Rubber/.

[96] The information was adapted from Kumpulan Ladang-Ladang Perbadanan Kedah Sdn Bhd (KLPK) found at https://www.klpk.com.my/about/.

Table 107: Malaysia: Planted Area and Production in Rubber Estates, 2016

State	Area (hectare)	Area Share, %	Natural Rubber Production (tonnes)	Production Share, %	Rubber Product Manufacturers (Number of plants) [1]
Existing IMT-GT States					
Kedah and Perlis	18,567	24	14,285	27	39 (Kedah-35 Perlis-4)
Perak	7,447	10	5,344	10	67
Negeri Sembilan	7,009	9	8,302	16	20
Selangor	4,915	6	2,684	5	187
Melaka	707	1	804	2	19
Penang*	–	–	–	–	35
IMT-GT States in reconfigured economic corridors and EC6					
Kelantan** and Terengganu	12,850	17	8,252	16	1 (Kelantan-1 Terengganu-0)
Johor	7,243	9	6,762	13	45
Pahang	6,345	8	6,548	12	3
Non-IMT-GT States					
Sabah and Sarawak	12,322	16	56	0	3 (Sabah-1 Sarawak-2)
Kuala Lumpur	–	–	–	–	9
Total (Malaysia)	**77,405**	**100**	**53,037**	**100**	**428**

– = not available. IMT-GT = Indonesia–Malaysia–Thailand Growth Triangle. EC = economic corridor.
Notes:
* No estates were recorded in Penang.
** Kelantan is existing IMT-GT State.
Sources: Department of Statistics. 2017. *Annual Rubber Statistics 2016*. Putrajaya: DOS Malaysia, [1] Ministry of Plantation Industries and Commodities. Directory of Rubber Product Manufacturers. https://www.mpic.gov.my/mpi/en/data-terbuka.

There are 425 rubber products manufacturing plants in Malaysia, of which 92% (393 plants) are located in the economic corridors. Selangor, which is close to Port Klang, accounted for 44% of the total number of rubber products manufacturers. Kedah, Perlis, Penang, and Perak, which are close to Penang Port, in aggregate, accounted for 32% (138 plants) of the total number of rubber product manufactures. All these plants operate in the industrial parks provided by the government and receive fiscal incentives for investing in the relevant states.

Malaysia also imports natural rubber from Thailand and Indonesia as well as other countries to meet the demand of the domestic industry. In 2018, approximately 480,000 tonnes and nearly 4,000 tonnes of natural rubber were imported from Thailand and Indonesia, accounting for 47% and 0.5% of the country's total imports of natural rubber, respectively (Table 108).

Table 108: Malaysia's Imports of Natural Rubber by Country of Origin, 2018
(tonnes)

Rank	Origin	2018 Volume (tonnes)	Share to Total Import (%)
1	Thailand	480,053	47
2	Ivory Coast	256,715	25
3	Philippines	98,186	10
	Other Countries	179,829	18
	Total Imports	1,014,783	100
Memo Item			
	Indonesia	3,997	0.4

Sources: Malaysia Rubber Board. 2020. Natural Rubber Statistics. Kuala Lumpur: MRB, Department of Statistics Malaysia. 2019. *Monthly Rubber Statistics Malaysia.* December 2018. Putrajaya: DOS Malaysia.

Processing

The production of natural rubber in the country and those imported from abroad will be processed by the factories in the following sub-industries:

- Rubber gloves
- Rubber remilling and latex processing (including other products of natural or synthetic rubber, unvulcanized)
- Rubber tires for vehicles
- Rubber footwear (including leather footwear)
- Interchangeable tire treads and retreading rubber tires
- Other rubber products

The total sales value of processed rubber and rubber products was $7 billion in 2018, accounting for 4% of the total sales value of the manufacturing industry. In the rubber and rubber industry, the rubber glove sector accounted for 53% of the total sales value of the industry (Table 109).

Table 109: Malaysia: Sales Value of Manufactured Rubber Products by Industry, 2018

Sub-Industry	Sales value (Ex-factory) ($ million)	Share of Total Sales Value of Rubber Products (%)
Rubber gloves	3,790	53
Rubber remilling and latex processing (including other products of natural or synthetic rubber, unvulcanized)	1,397	19
Rubber tires for vehicles	555	8
Rubber footwear (including leather footwear)	102	1
Interchangeable tire treads and retreading rubber tires	42	1
Other rubber products	1,278	18
Total	**7,163**	**100**
All Manufacturing Sectors	**204,421**	
Share of Rubber Products in the Manufacturing Sector, %	**4**	

Source: Department of Statistics Malaysia. 2019. *Monthly Rubber Statistics Malaysia.* December 2018. Putrajaya: DOS Malaysia.

Distribution

Malaysia produced approximately 669,000 tonnes of natural rubber in 2014 and 603,000 tonnes in 2015 (Table 110). During this period, local consumption of natural rubber increased from 57% to 84%. This indicates an increase in downstream activities for natural rubber-based products to meet local market demand.

Table 110: Malaysia: Production, Export, Import and Consumption of Natural Rubber

('000 tonnes)

Item	2014	2018
Production	668.6	603.3
Import	904.9	1,014.8
Export	1,191.0	1,108.7
Domestic Consumption	**382.5**	**509.4**
Domestic Production, %	**57**	**84**

Source: Malaysian Rubber Board. 2019. *Natural Rubber Statistics 2018*. Kuala Lumpur. MRB.

The rubber products manufactured by the industries include tires (pneumatic), inner tubes, catheters, gloves, footwear, rubber bands, rubber sheets, and condoms. These rubber products are exported to the international market. Rubber gloves are a major rubber export product, accounting for 74% of the total rubber products exports in 2018 with an export value of $4 billion (Table 111).

Table 111: Malaysia's Exports of Selected Rubber Products, 2018

Rubber Products	($ million)	Share, %
Gloves, other than surgical gloves	4,013	74.3
Surgical gloves	384	7.1
New tires	297	5.5
Tubes, pipes, and hoses	239	4.4
Latex thread	142	2.6
Catheters	87	1.6
Condoms	84	1.6
Seals and gaskets	53	1.0
Foam products	29	0.5
Precured treads	25	0.5
Floor coverings and mats	23	0.4
Fenders	13	0.2
Structural bearings	9	0.2
Total	**5,397**	**100.0**

Source: Malaysian Rubber Export Promotion Council (MREPC). http://www.mrepc.com/industry/malaysia_export.php.

The major markets for rubber products were the US and the PRC, which accounted for 22% and 19%, respectively, of total rubber products exports in 2018 (Table 112). Malaysia also exports rubber products to Thailand and Indonesia with a share of 3% and 2%, respectively, of the country's total rubber products exports. Penang Port is the main maritime gateway for exports of rubber and rubber products to the international market while Bukit Kayu Hitam and Padang Besar BCPs are the main overland gateways for trade between Thailand and Malaysia. Rubber and rubber products are also exported via Port Klang, but the contribution is small compared to Penang Port as rubber production is largely concentrated in the northern states of Malaysia. Furthermore, Penang Port is also a trade gateway for rubber producers in Southern Thailand.

Table 112: Malaysia's Major Export Markets of Rubber and Rubber Products, 2018

Rank	Destination	($ million)	Share of Total Export, %
1	United States	1,735	22
2	People's Republic of China	1,474	19
3	Germany	514	7
4	Japan	349	4
5	**Thailand**	**215**	**3**
13	**Indonesia**	**122**	**2**
	Rest of the World	3,412	44
Total Exports		**7,821**	**100**

Sources: Malaysia Rubber Board. 2020. *Natural Rubber Statistics*. Kuala Lumpur: MRB, Department of Statistics Malaysia. 2019. *Monthly Rubber Statistics Malaysia*. December 2018. Putrajaya: DOS Malaysia.

Penang Port. In 2018, a total of 3 million tonnes of rubber and latex products were exported by Penang Port, which accounted for 21% of all commodities it exported. While its imports are almost 0.6 million tonnes with rubber and latex products accounting for 3% of its total imports (Table 113).

Table 113: Penang Port: Key Commodity Traded, 2018
(FWT)

Product	Cargo		Share of all Commodities	
	Export (Loaded)	Import (Unloaded)	Export (Loaded)	Import (Unloaded)
Rubber and latex	3,218,862	617,071	21	3
All Commodities	**15,080,897**	**18,657,712**		

FWT = freight weight tonnes
Source: Penang Port Commission. 2019. *Commodities Loaded and Unloaded by Type 2014-2018*. George Town: PPC.

Port Klang. Port Klang also exports rubber and rubber goods to the international market. In 2018, the total export of Port Klang to the world market was 35 million tonnes, of which the share of rubber and rubber goods was about only 1% (Table 114).

Table 114: Port Klang: Export and Import of Rubber and Rubber Goods

Port Klang	Cargo (FWT)		Share (%)	
	Export (Loaded)	Import (Unloaded)	Export (Loaded)	Import (Unloaded)
Rubber	**13,493**	**118,304**	**4**	**97**
Rubber Goods	**311,268**	**3,193**	**96**	**3**
Sum of Above	324,761	121,497	100	100
Share to all Commodities	0.9%	0.4%		
All Commodities	34,839,429	34,458,514		

FWT = freight weight tonnes
Source: Port Klang Authority. 2018. *Statistical Bulletin 2018*. Klang: PKA.

Malaysia's trade with Indonesia and Thailand. Table 115 shows the rubber and rubber products traded with Thailand and Indonesia. Bilateral trade with Thailand in rubber and rubber products in 2018 was in favor of Thailand. Imports of rubber and rubber products from Thailand was $1 billion, accounting for 30% of Malaysia's total rubber and rubber products imports. This shows a high dependence on rubber and rubber products from Thailand compared to Indonesia which accounts for only 3% of the total rubber and rubber products imported by Malaysia.

Table 115: Malaysia's Trade with Thailand and Indonesia of Rubber and Rubber Products, 2018

Country/ SITC	Products	$ million				Share to:		
		Imports	Exports	Total Trade	Balance of Trade	Imports, %	Exports, %	Total Trade, %
World	All Commodities (SITC 0-9)	218,043	248,720	466,764	30,677	–	–	–
	Rubber and Rubber products	3,662	3,084	6,745	(578)	–	–	–
Thailand	**Rubber and rubber products**							
231	**Natural rubber, natural gums, in primary forms**	**710**	**2**	**713**	**(708)**	**65**	**2**	**57**
232	Synthetic rubber; reclaimed rubber, waste, parings, and scrap of unhardened rubber	64	78	142	14	6	48	11
621	Materials of rubber	13	10	23	(3)	1	6	2
625	Rubber tires, interchangeable tire treads, inner tubes, and tire flabs	256	51	307	(205)	23	31	24
629	Articles of rubber, nes	48	22	70	(27)	4	13	6
	Subtotal	1,092	163	1,255	(929)	100	100	100
	Share of Thailand to world rubber and rubber products, (%)	30	5	19	–	–	–	–
	Share of Thailand to all commodity (SITC 0-9), (%)	0.5	0.1	0.3	–	–	–	–
Indonesia	**Rubber and rubber products**							
231	Natural rubber, natural gums, in primary forms	6	0	6	(6)	5	0	3
232	Synthetic rubber; reclaimed rubber, waste, parings, and scrap of unhardened rubber	6	41	46	35	5	46	23
621	Materials of rubber	5	22	27	16	5	24	14
625	**Rubber tires, interchangeable tire treads, inner tubes, and tire flabs**	**79**	**16**	**95**	**(64)**	**73**	**18**	**48**
629	Articles of rubber, nes	13	11	24	(2)	12	12	12
	Subtotal	109	89	198	(20)	100	100	100
	Share of Indonesia to world rubber and rubber products, (%)	3.0	2.9	2.9	–	–	–	–
	Share of Indonesia to all commodity (SITC 0-9), (%)	0.1	0.04	0.04	–	–	–	–

– = not applicable, ( ) = negative, nes = not elsewhere specified, SITC = Standard International Trade Classification.
Source: Department of Statistics Malaysia. 2021. Retrieved from Malaysia External Trade Statistics Online. https://metsonline.dosm.gov.my/.

In comparison with Thailand's import patterns, Malaysia imports more natural rubber than rubber intermediary products. Malaysia's imports from Thailand lean toward upstream activities. Natural rubber products account for 65% of the total rubber and rubber products imports from Thailand. This scenario differs from the pattern of imports from Indonesia, whereby Malaysia imports more intermediate inputs, e.g., rubber tires, interchangeable tire treads, inner tubes and tire flabs, which account for 73% of the total imports of rubber and rubber products from Indonesia. The bilateral trade between Malaysia and Indonesia was in favor of Indonesia in 2018 and the import pattern inclined toward downward activities.

Malaysia–Thailand border crossing points. Among the eight borders, Bukit Kayu Hitam and Padang Besar are the main trade routes for rubber and rubber products. Rail connectivity is via the land bridge rail between Songkhla and Penang Port through Padang Besar Station. Total exports of rubber and plastic products to Thailand traversing through all borders in Malaysia was $319 million in 2018. Of that amount, Bukit Kayu Hitam BCP accounted for 77% of the total cross-border exports to Thailand, followed by Padang Besar at 23%. Bukit Kayu Hitam accounted for 84% of the total rubber and plastic products imported through all Malaysia–Thailand borders in 2018 (Table 116).

Table 116: Malaysia–Thailand Bilateral Trade of Rubber and Plastic (HS 39-40) by Border Crossing Points, 2018

BCPs	Exports, 2018 ($ '000)	Share, %	BCPs	Import, 2018 ($ '000)	Share, %
Bukit Kayu Hitam	244,639	77	Bukit Kayu Hitam	809,251	84
Padang Besar (road mode)	73,181	23	Pengkalan Hulu	68,280	7
Pengkalan Hulu	673	0	Padang Besar (road mode)	66,371	7
Pengkalan Kubor	191	0	Rantau Panjang	14,553	2
Rantau Panjang	64	0	Bukit Bunga	4,560	0
Wang Kelian	10	0	Padang Besar (Railway)	264	0
Durian Burung	7	0	Pengkalan Kubor	190	0
Bukit Bunga	5	0	Durian Burung	81	0
Padang Besar (Railway mode)	0	0	Wang Kelian	1	0
Total Export of HS Code 39-40	**318,770**	**100**	**Total Import HS Code 39-40**	**963,550**	**100**

BCP = border crossing point. HS = harmonized system
Source: Royal Malaysian Customs Department, 2019. Putrajaya. RMCD.

Penang Port. Penang Port also handles cargo from Southern Thailand for export to the international markets. Traders in Thailand utilize Penang Port as their main export platform due to lower logistics costs and time-saving factor compared to ports in Thailand such as Songkhla Port or Bangkok Port. Penang Port handled 70,236 tonnes of rubber and rubber products annually from Southern Thailand for 2014–2018, which accounted for 30% of all commodities it handles. Rubber and rubber products are the second most important commodity operated by the Penang Port (Table 117).

Table 117: Penang Port: Cargo Loaded by Commodity from Southern Thailand
(FWT)

Commodity	FWT							
	2014	2015	2016	2017	2018	Average (2014–2018)	Average Share to Total Cargo, %	CAGR (2014–2018) %
Sawn timber	77,983	91,584	116,044	134,361	113,544	106,703	45	9.8
Rubber	55,945	61,369	61,771	69,496	68,063	63,329	27	5.0
Rubber products	11,886	8,679	5,253	4,340	4,380	6,908	3	(22.1)
Wood moldings	13,811	22,945	37,587	22,877	24,244	24,293	10	15.1
Latex	17,511	18,903	21,969	21,596	22,695	20,535	9	6.7
Other manufacturing products	2,1922	16,348	19,681	14,951	7,192	16,019	7	(24.3)
Total	**199,058**	**219,828**	**262,305**	**267,621**	**240,118**	**237,786**	**100**	**4.8**

( ) = negative, CAGR = compound annual growth rate, FWT = freight weight tonnes.
Source: Penang Port Commission. 2019. *Commodities Loaded and Unloaded by Type 2014–2018*. George Town: PPC.

Findings and Recommendations

Comparative advantage. ECs 1, 2, 4, and 6 have comparative advantages in the rubber and rubber products, where most plantations are located in the hinterlands. Kedah is the major producer of natural rubber in Peninsular Malaysia, with most processing facilities, especially for downstream activities, are mostly concentrated in industrial estates.

Accessibility to ports. The road and rail network in ECs facilitate the transport of rubber and rubber products along the value chain. International gateway ports in the ECs are accessible by road and train. Bukit Kayu Hitam BCP and Padang Besar BCP in EC1 are the main border trade gateways for rubber and rubber products to Thailand. Thai traders in Southern Thailand also use the border trade gateways to export rubber products to Malaysia and the international market via Penang Port.

Seamless connectivity. Transport links that enhance the efficiency of logistics services are crucial for value chains. Last-mile connectivity—both gateway-based and hinterland-based—could help facilitate transport and bring down logistics costs at various stages of the value chain. Improved connectivity from industrial estates to seaports will facilitate exports of products to international markets and can contribute to the competitiveness of the products.

Inland ports. The role of inland ports in the ECs needs to be further enhanced as they allow many supply chain functions to take place further inland and offer better access to inland markets. The related inland ports in the ECs are ICT (Perak), NIP (Negeri Sembilan), SIP (Johor), and BPCT (Johor).

Rail links. Railway spur lines are being planned to be built in the ECs for ports that have no direct rail links with major economic centers. Railway spur lines that are being proposed in the ECs are Bukit Kayu Hitam in Kedah to Arau in Perlis (EC1 and EC2),[97] ICT to Lumut Port in Perak (EC2),[98] and Pulau Sebang or Tampin to Tanjung Bruas Port in Melaka (EC4).[99]

The role of EC6. Kelantan, Pahang, and Terengganu are among the major producers of natural rubber. The ECRL route from Kota Bharu to Port Klang and the ECE from Tumpat to Kuala Lumpur will develop a road–rail–ports intermodal link particularly to Kemaman Port and Kuantan Port that will support the development of value chains in the region. Both ports in the EC6 serve as trade gateways for manufacturers to export their products to East Asia. Manufacturers in the EC6 can also use this overland route as a land bridge to export their products by using ports in the west coast, such as Port Klang and Tanjung Bruas Port.

Industrial clusters. Industrial clusters for rubber and rubber products should be promoted. KRC in EC1 is an example of a rubber and rubber product industry cluster and is currently an IMT-GT project with the participation from Indonesia and Thailand. The implementation of the KRC project needs to be accelerated as a model for developing and advancing the rubber city concept in other ECs.

---

[97] *Free Malaysia Today*. 2019. Kedah-Perlis rail link better than ECRL to boost trade. 9 January. Retrieved from https://www.freemalaysiatoday.com/category/nation/2019/01/09/kedah-perlis-rail-link-better-than-ecrl-to-boost-trade-expert-says/.

[98] *Perak Today*. 2010. Railway Link to Lumut. 21 September. https://peraktoday.com.my/2010/09/railway-link-to-lumut/.

[99] Under Melaka's State Structure Plan 2015–2035 (Melaka 2035), a proposal was made to build a railway connecting Tanjung Bruas Port with the Inland Port to be developed in Taboh Naning (Alor Gajah, Melaka). The Taboh Naning Inland Port will be built by the state government in collaboration with the federal government. This inland port will be connected to Pulau Sebang or Tampin Railway Station. However, the proposal to build the Inland Port Taboh Naning, in Alor Gajah (Melaka) and the railway is still in the planning phase.

ADDRESSING GAPS IN INSTITUTIONAL MECHANISMS FOR ECONOMIC CORRIDOR DEVELOPMENT

Coordination at the Subregional Level

IMT-GT is a subregional cooperation initiative formed by the governments of the three countries— Indonesia, Malaysia, and Thailand—in 1993 to accelerate speed the economic transformation in their least-developed provinces and states. The cooperation seeks to promote the welfare and economic growth of the people living in the areas covered by the IMT-GT.

Figure 4 shows the IMT-GT institutional coordination mechanism structure. The institutional coordination mechanism for IMT-GT programs and project adopts a bottom–up and top–down approach involving working groups at the regional level and the national secretariats. The IMT-GT Senior Officials Meeting (SOM) determines the implementation priorities and provides directions and advice on IMT-GT's programs and projects to ensure coordination and integration of its guiding approaches, key measures, and strategies. The IMT-GT Ministerial Meeting provides overall guidance and advice on overall strategy and direction of IMT-GT cooperation at the policy level and performs an oversight function on IMT-GT programs and projects. The ministerial meeting also provides guidance on key issues and challenges of common interest among the member provinces and states and sets the policy directions to achieve the vision and goals of IMT-GT.

The Chief Ministers and Governors Forum (CMGF) provides policy inputs to and collaborates closely with SOM and the ministerial meeting for effective implementation of IMT-GT's programs and projects at local government level. It sensitizes the participating local governments on the goals, objectives, programs, and projects of IMT-GT.

The IMT-GT Leaders' Summit which is attended by the heads of state of the three countries, is the highest decision-making body. It sets the overall policy direction and areas of collaboration among the member countries. It fosters consensus on joint approaches to promote economic growth and social development. It meets once a year in conjunction with the Association of Southeast Asian Nations (ASEAN) Summit. A joint statement on agreements reached is issued by the leaders at the close of their summit meeting.

The Centre for IMT-GT Subregional Cooperation (CIMT) is the subregional secretariat of IMT-GT. It supports member countries in coordinating and facilitating the planning, implementation, and monitoring of programs and projects. Its mandate include strengthening coordination mechanisms and consultation processes among IMT-GT institutions; providing an institutional framework to support public and private sector activities; and facilitating the evaluation, implementation, and monitoring of projects; and other subregional initiatives. It represents the IMT-GT in establishing and enhancing external relations with development partners, investors, and other institutions for potential collaboration. It establishes databases to provide the required information for policy decisions.[100]

---

[100] The information on coordination at the subregional level was abridged from CIMT-GT. 2016. *Implementation Blueprint 2017–2021*. Putrajaya: CIMT. pp. 26–31.

Figure 4: IMT-GT Institutional Coordination Mechanism Structure

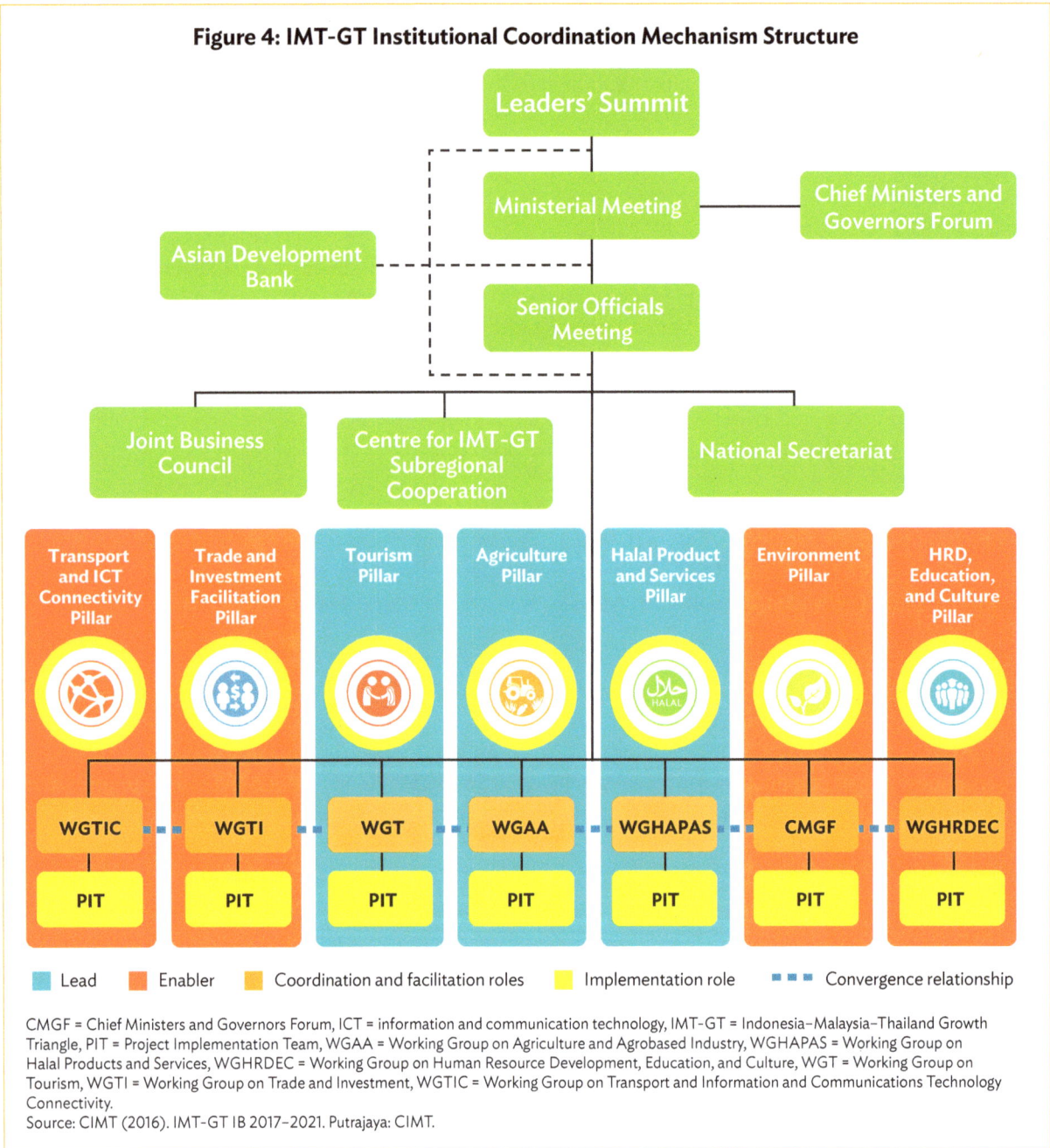

CMGF = Chief Ministers and Governors Forum, ICT = information and communication technology, IMT-GT = Indonesia–Malaysia–Thailand Growth Triangle, PIT = Project Implementation Team, WGAA = Working Group on Agriculture and Agrobased Industry, WGHAPAS = Working Group on Halal Products and Services, WGHRDEC = Working Group on Human Resource Development, Education, and Culture, WGT = Working Group on Tourism, WGTI = Working Group on Trade and Investment, WGTIC = Working Group on Transport and Information and Communications Technology Connectivity.
Source: CIMT (2016). IMT-GT IB 2017–2021. Putrajaya: CIMT.

Coordination at the Country Level

National secretariats have been established in the three countries to coordinate IMT-GT activities at the national level. The National Secretariat in Malaysia (NS Malaysia) is represented by the Economic Planning Unit (EPU), Regional Development Division (RDD). NS Malaysia is headed by the Director of RDD. Other members include deputy director RDD, principal assistant RDD, and assistant director RDD. The portfolio of this division includes the Brunei Darussalam–Indonesia–Malaysia–Philippines East ASEAN Growth Area (BIMP-EAGA),

Malaysia–Thailand Joint Development Strategy for Border Areas, and the Malaysia–Singapore Joint Ministerial Committee for Iskandar Malaysia (JMCIM).

The NS Malaysia supports the SOM in the operationalization of the IMT-GT's programs and projects embodied in the implementation blueprints issued every 5 years, and Vision 2036. It ensures that these projects are included and prioritized in the national and subnational development plans and supported by adequate policy and funding support from the federal government. The NS Malaysia involves the state governments, private sector and other stakeholders in project identification, planning and implementation in accordance with the bottom-up approach advocated under the implementation blueprint 2017–2021 and Vision 2036.

IMT-GT projects proposed to the federal government are coordinated by NS Malaysia. In the case of the KRC for example, NS Malaysia will propose the project to the Working Group Trade and Industry (WGTI) at the national level for deliberation before this is presented at WGTI at the subregional level where Indonesia and Thailand are also represented. The position of WG chair rotates among the countries every 2 years. The working group structure at the national level mirrors the structure at the IMT-GT level; i.e., there are also seven working groups (Tables 118 and 119). The private sector and other stakeholders are consulted on projects that involve them. Once a project has been agreed upon, the working group will set up the project implementation team (PIT) to ensure the successful implementation of the project. The Box at the end of this chapter illustrates the process of project planning from the state to the federal levels using the case of the KRC project.[101]

Table 118: Working Group Focal Ministries at National and IMT-GT Level

Working Group	Responsible Ministry in Malaysia
Transport and Information and Communication Technology	Ministry of Transport
Trade and Investment	Ministry of International Trade and Industry
Tourism	Ministry of Tourism, Arts and Culture
Halal Product and Services	Ministry of International Trade and Industry
HRD, Education and Culture	Ministry of Human Resource
Agriculture and Argo Based Industry	Ministry of Agriculture and Food Industries
Environment	Ministry of Environment and Water

HRD = human resource development, Indonesia–Malaysia–Thailand Growth Triangle.
Source: CIMT. 2016. *Implementation Blueprint 2017–2021*. Putrajaya: CIMT.

The national secretariats of the three countries meet at least four times a year, usually before the Strategic Planning Meeting (SPM), SOM, ministerial meeting, and leaders' summit. The national secretariat meetings are held to finalize the agenda and identify the important issues to be discussed during the SPM, SOM, ministerial meeting, and leaders' summit. The JBC is involved in all these meetings up to the ministerial meeting level.[102]

---

[101] The information on the coordination at the country level was compiled from consultation with NS Malaysia on 24 August, 2020.

[102] The IMT-GT JBC acts as the focal point of the private sector with objectives of encouraging the private sector to pursue trade and investment opportunities created by Vision 2036. It will enlarge its membership base to include micro, small, and medium-sized enterprises, small and medium-sized enterprises, social enterprises, and high caliber players and representatives of large corporations. It will solicit, consolidate, and prioritize policy inputs and project ideas from its diverse membership base for achieving the inclusive objective of Vision 2036 and IB 2017–2021. JBC members will be key implementer of Vision 2036 projects and IB 2017–2021. As a key member of the project implementation team, JBC will engage in regular dialogue with working groups, national secretariat, SOM, and ministerial meeting to ensure issues and challenges related to the implementation of Vision 2036 and ADB IB 2017–2021 are properly and promptly dealt with. (IMT-GT Vision 2036).

The SPM, which is attended by senior officials and the national secretariat, is held at the beginning of each year to discuss and implement the decisions of the leaders' summit. During the SPM, the working groups review the status and progress of their activities, propose new initiatives based on the directives of the leaders' summit, and prepare a forward schedule of activities. These are then presented to the senior officials for further guidance and concurrence.

Table 119: Ministry and/or Agency Representation at the National and IMT-GT Level

Malaysia		IMT-GT			
NS Malaysia	**Working Group Composition**	**Working Group Lead Ministries**	**Senior Official Meeting**	**Ministerial Meeting**	**Leaders' Summit**
EPU – Regional Development Division • Director (Head) • Deputy Director • Principal Assistant • Assistant Director	• Headed by Relevant Ministry • NS Malaysia (Secretariat) [1] • Other relevant Ministries / Agency (by invitation) • State Government • Private Sector (by invitation)	• Transport and ICT • Trade and Investment • Tourism • Agriculture and Agro-Based Industry • Halal Product and Services • Environment • HRD, Education and Culture	• Secretary General of EPU	• Minister in The Prime Minister's Department (Economy)	• Prime Minister

EPU = Economic Planning Unit, HRD = human resource development, ICT = information and communication technology, IMT-GT = Indonesia–Malaysia–Thailand Growth Triangle, NS Malaysia = National Secretariat Malaysia.
Note: [1] The NS serves as the Secretariat for all IMT-GT meetings.
Source: Compiled by author from consultation with NS Malaysia on 24 August 2020.

Coordination with Line Ministries

The national-level working groups are headed by line ministries responsible for the IMT-GT's priority sectors of cooperation. The members include representatives from the national secretariat, the state government, other relevant ministries (by invitation), and the private sector (by invitation) (Table 120).

Table 120: Working Group at National and IMT-GT Level

Working Group	Line Ministry
Transport and Information and Communication Technology	Ministry of Transport [1]
Trade and Investment	Ministry of International Trade and Industry [2]
Tourism	Ministry of Tourism, Arts and Culture [3]
Halal Product and Services	Ministry of International Trade and Industry
HRD, Education and Culture	Ministry of Human Resource [4]
Agriculture and Argo Based Industry	Ministry of Agriculture and Food Industries [5]
Environment	Ministry of Environment and Water [6]

HRD = human resource development, IMT-GT = Indonesia–Malaysia–Thailand Growth Triangle.
Note: For the line ministries' functions, refer to the following links:
[1] MOT Malaysia website https://www.miti.gov.my; [2] MITI Malaysia website, https://www.miti.gov.my; [3] MOTAC Malaysia website, http://www.motac.gov.my; [4] MOHR Malaysia website, https://www.mohr.gov.my ;[5] MAFI Malaysia website, https://www.mafi.gov.my; [6] DOE Malaysia website, https://www.doe.gov.my/
Source: Compiled by author from consultation with CIMT deputy director (Malaysia) on 15 July 2020.

Coordination with State Governments

The subnational level comprises the state government, state government development agencies, and the local authorities. The coordination and communication flow between the federal government (represented by EPU Putrajaya) and state government is top-down and bottom-up with regard to IMT-GT projects.[103]

At the state government level, the evaluation process for proposed projects involves the SEPU, State Economic Council, State Executive Council, District Office, and the State Planning Committee. The state government would invite the state development agencies (e.g., the State Economic Development Corporation), development agencies at the federal level (e.g., NCIA, ECERDC, and IRDA), and private sector representative to provide inputs on planned projects. An important line agency is the district office that evaluates the proposed projects within its administrative jurisdiction. The district office's evaluation will be forwarded to the SEPU and eventually to the State Planning Committee, chaired by the chief minister. This committee meets about six times a year.

The State Planning Committee's decision will be forwarded to the federal government (EPU, Putrajaya) for project approval and funding from the Ministry of Finance. If the project has a potentially significant impact on the IMT-GT region, the national secretariat forwards the project to the relevant working group as a proposed IMT-GT project. This is the coordination mechanism in place between the national secretariat and the state government for a project categorized as an IMT-GT-based project.

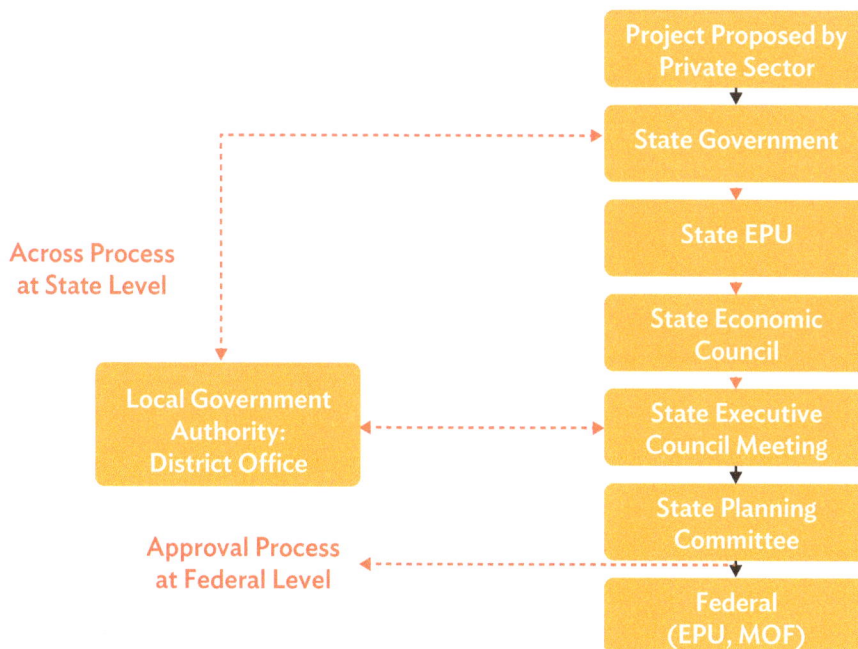

Figure 5: Planning Process from the State to the Federal Government

EPU = Economic Planning Unit, MOF = Ministry of Finance.
Source: Compiled by author from consultation with the Kedah State Economic Planning Unit on 16 July 2020.

[103] The information on coordination with state governments was based on consultation with the Kedah State Economic Planning Unit on 16th July, 2020

Coordination between Government and the Private Sector

The private sector may propose projects to the state and federal governments in line with the policy to promote partnerships with the private sector. The state and federal governments will invite stakeholders and relevant private sector representatives to provide inputs on the proposed project's development impact. At the IMT-GT level, national secretariats, in coordination with CIMT, will invite JBC to provide their inputs on the proposed project.

Coordination for Economic Corridor Development

There is no formal mechanism at the state or federal levels that focuses on the development of IMT-GT economic corridors. However, national projects located in the IMT-GT economic corridors are evaluated taking into account the potential synergies and spillovers that could result from their location in the corridor. The development blueprints formulated by the NCIA, ECERDC, and IRDA also take into consideration the development strategies, programs and projects of neighboring countries, including those in IMT-GT, in mapping out their spatial approach. This notwithstanding, an occasional forum can be organized to promote greater awareness of developments in IMT-GT economic corridors. This forum can be held once a year before the CMGF to sensitize the chief ministers on the developments in the IMT-GT.

Findings and Recommendations

Coordination between federal, state, and provincial government. There is close collaboration and coordination between the federal, state, and local governments, as well as line ministries and agencies in the different levels that ensure the effective implementation of the state and federal projects. Coordination and communication in the planning and management of these projects is through a top–down and bottom–up approach that reflects a highly consultative process among various stakeholders.

Private sector. The private sector is an active partner in the development process. In IMT-GT, this is reflected through the mechanism of the JBC, which participates in the meetings of working groups, senior officials, and ministers. Private sector stakeholders are invited to provide inputs on IMT-GT initiatives and projects that include those related to economic corridor development. Malaysia supports the plan to give JBC legal status to enhance its effectiveness as a regional coordinating body.

National secretariat. The national secretariats' capacity for coordinating regional cooperation programs could be further enhanced. At present, the national secretariat's staff is limited considering that it is coordinating a wide portfolio of subregional programs, which includes the BIMP-EAGA, Malaysia–Thailand Joint Development Strategy for Border Areas, and Malaysia–Singapore JMCIM. Additional human resources in the national secretariat is needed so that it can better support Malaysia's participation in IMT-GT as well as other subregional programs and initiatives.

Chief Ministers and Governors Forum. At the subregional level, the CMGF is the platform for representing the interests of the provinces and states in IMT-GT. It reports directly to the IMT-GT ministers and, working closely with the senior officials, provides policy inputs at the local government level for the effective implementation of the 5-year implementation blueprints to realize Vision 2036. While the CMGF has been a useful venue for presenting development opportunities in IMT-GT provinces, it has not functioned as a mechanism for coordinating the strategies for economic corridor development at the IMT-GT level. To address this gap, a regional forum on economic corridor development may be organized on a regular basis during the day prior to the regular meeting of the CMGF. This regional forum would involve representatives from the provinces and states participating in IMT-GT. This forum could be a venue for generating greater awareness on economic corridor development and providing the latest updates on economic corridor development.

Coordination for economic corridor development. In the absence of a formal mechanism focusing on economic corridor development, the national secretariat could organize occasional forums to promote greater awareness of economic corridors among local government officials and stakeholders. These could be done through a series of learning events for different stakeholder groups. The NS could also encourage regular meetings of clusters of provinces and states in a given corridor to plan for cross-border initiatives; The establishment of a CMGF secretariat should be supported.

Box: Kedah Rubber City: From State-Based to IMT-GT-Based Project

The case of Kedah Rubber City (KRC) highlights the coordination of the project planning between the state government and federal government as well as national secretariats' collaboration at the Indonesia–Malaysia–Thailand Growth Triangle (IMT-GT) level. Originally, the KRC project was a state-based project that has been upgraded by the National Secretariat, Malaysia as an IMT-GT project with the inclusion and participation of Thailand and Indonesia.

The KRC project was a private sector initiative proposed by Tradewinds Plantation Bhd to the state and federal governments. At the state government level, the KRC project planning began with the State Economic Planning Unit (BPEN), which held the role of secretariat to the KRC project. BPEN invited government-led development agencies and the private sector to obtain inputs on the impacts of the project on the state's economy. The outcomes of the discussions with the private and public sectors were presented to the Kedah Economic Council (KEC), chaired by the chief minister, for approval under the State Development Blueprint. Other KEC members are representatives from the Kedah State Finance and Treasury Department, BPEN, Public Works Department, Department of Irrigation and Drainage, Department of Land and Mines, State Legal Advisor Office, and Federal Department of Town and Country Planning (Plan Malaysia).

KEC forwarded the feasibility of the KRC project to the Kedah State Executive Council (State Exco) for approval. Since this KRC project was proposed for implementation at Padang Terap, it also required approval from the local authority, i.e., the Padang Terap District Council (MDPT). The approval from MDPT was presented to the State Exco chaired by the chief minister.

The State Exco decisions related to KRC projects are forwarded to the State Planning Committee (SPC) Meeting chaired by the chief minister. The SPC's decision was forwarded to the federal government (Economic Planning Unit, Putrajaya) for project approval as well as funding from the Ministry of Finance (MOF).

An important line agency in the SPC is the Plan Malaysia. The role of Plan Malaysia, which is the secretariat to the SPC, is to determine whether the KRC project is in line with the Third National Physical Plan (NPP3). The State Development Blueprint should conform to the NPP3 and the Kedah State Structure Plan. In addition, district local plans and special area plans are also consulted on the relevance of the project to the district or area concerned.

In parallel with the KRC project planning at the state government level, BPEN and Northern Corridor Implementation Authority (NCIA) has established the Kedah Rubber City Implementation Committee (KRCIC) with the main objective of determining the direction of KRC development and its potential on the Kedah's economy. The KRCIC is chaired by the chair of the Kedah State Industry and Investment Standing Committee, and is composed of permanent member representative from BPEN, NCIA, MDPT, Plan Malaysia, Malaysian Investment Development Authority (MIDA), and Invest Kedah.

continued on next page

Box (continued)

The KRC project's progress is periodically discussed at the State Steering Committee (SSC) Meetings, chaired by the chief minister of Kedah and the NCIA is secretariat to the SSC. Other members of the SSC include the State Secretary of Kedah, MOF, EPU (Putrajaya), BPEN, chief minister of Kedah Incorporated, Department Land and Mines, Kedah, Kedah State Development Corporation (PKNK), and Plan Malaysia. The frequency of meetings between the state government and the NCIA is four times a year.

The NCIA which is a federal-led development agency, presents the latest development of the KRC project for approval to the NCIA Council, chaired by the prime minister. The NCIA Council members consist of the prime minister (chair), deputy prime minister, the chief ministers of Perlis, Kedah, and Penang, two federal ministers, two private sector representatives, one public sector representative, and the NCIA chief executive (secretary).

The KRC project has been listed under the Kedah Transformation Plan 2013–2018 and the Kedah Development Plan 2020–2035. It has also been integrated into the Northern Corridor Economic Region Blueprint 2.0 (2016–2025). At the IMT-GT level, the KRC project is under the IMT-GT Implementation Blueprint 2017–2021.

At the IMT-GT level, National Secretariat, Malaysia would present the KRC project to the Working Group Trade and Industry (WGTI) led by the Ministry of International Trade and Industry (MITI). The National Secretariat, Malaysia invites other stakeholders (e.g., the Ministry of Plantation Industries and Commodities (MPIC), NCIA, Malaysia Rubber Board (MRB), Plan Malaysia, and the Joint Business Council representing the private sector in discussing the feasibility and impact of the project at the regional level. A project implementation team has been created for the KRC, composed of NCIA (Malaysia), the Thai Rubber Association (Thailand), and Kemenko Perekonomian (Indonesia).

Source: Compiled by author from consultation with the Kedah State Economic Planning Unit on 16 July 2020 and Northern Corridor Implementation Authority on 11 June 2020.

SUMMARY OF FINDINGS AND RECOMMENDATIONS

Extend IMT-GT economic corridors to include the states of Johor, Terengganu, and Pahang. The reconfigured economic corridors 1, 2, 4, and 5, as well as the proposed route for EC6, has established an "internal corridor" in Malaysia where segments of IMT-GT corridors in the 11 states are contiguous or adjacent to each other. The east and west coasts are now connected by highway, railway, and air links. Langkawi Island, as part of EC5 is connected with the mainland through maritime and air links. At the subregional level, the economic corridors in Malaysia are connected to economic corridors in Sumatera via the maritime and air links. Economic corridors in Southern Thailand are connected with Malaysia by roads and railways traversing the northern states of Malaysian–Thai borders gates (Map 25).

The states of Terengganu, Pahang, and Johor are not participating states under the IMT-GT cooperation framework. Therefore, the participation of these states should be agreed by the respective state governments and approved by the federal government. The nonparticipating IMT-GT states in the proposed EC6 route— Terengganu, Pahang, and Johor—can serve as a "bridge" for connectivity to South Sumatera and the Riau Islands.

Upgrade and expand expressways, federal, and state roads for better land connectivity. Economic corridors are well-connected by roads, especially through expressway networks. Road connectivity provided by federal and state roads are adequate. Expressways, federal, and state roads would need to be expanded or upgraded to meet the increasing demand of road users and establish last-mile connectivity between the urban and hinterland areas in the less-developed economic corridors.

Strengthen regional air connectivity collaboration. Air links are adequate for connecting major cities or capitals within the economic corridors. Air travel provides vital links for promoting the country's tourism industry. In this regard, government needs to upgrade and expand domestic airports to meet the increasing demand. At the IMT-GT level, air links to Sumatera and Southern Thailand are still limited. To strengthen regional air links and promote regional tourism, the Government of Malaysia with cooperation from their counterparts in Thailand and Indonesia, can increase the frequency of scheduled flights in the existing airports.

The ECRL should be completed as planned, and the RTS proposal should be realized to enhance regional connectivity. KTMB railway networks are adequate for connectivity between major cities, especially those along the west coast economic corridors. The east and west coast economic corridors will become more well-connected when the ECRL project is completed since it will be linked to the main KTMB railway line. ECRL is a game changer because it establishes the railway networks within the Malaysian economic corridors as part of the Singapore–Kunming Rail Link (SKRL) and the PRC's BRI. In addition, the revival of the passenger and cargo railway services between Su-ngai Kolok and Pasir Mas will connect the SRT Southern Line and the KTMB east line with the ECRL. This will further strengthen connectivity between ECs in Malaysia and Southern Thailand which is weak at present. Stronger regional railway links will boost Malaysia–Thailand cross-border trade. Railway connectivity with SKRL will open Malaysia's access to new markets in Cambodia, the Lao PDR, Myanmar, the PRC, and Viet Nam. The proposed Johor Bahru–Singapore RTS project, when completed, will further improve connectivity between southern Malaysia, southern Sumatera, and Riau Islands. Singapore will serve as a bridge between southern Peninsular Malaysia and the southern Sumatera or Riau Islands.

With the ECRL—KTMB rail link, seaports along the east coast economic corridor (EC6) can also access Sumatera's seaports via Port Klang which will be the main trade gateway for Kemaman Port and Kuantan through multimodal transport. This will provide opportunities for traders in the EC6 to access new markets in Sumatera, including the Riau Islands.

Build new railway spur lines for secondary ports facing last-mile connectivity. The collaboration between KTMB and SRT has established a cost-effective multimodal transport between Malaysia and Thailand. However, only major ports—Penang Port, Port Klang, Tanjung Pelepas Port, and Johor Port—provide land bridge services to Bangkok. Multimodal transport needs to be extended to secondary ports facing last-mile connectivity problems. At present, secondary ports can only be accessed via roads. This issue can be overcome by building railway spur lines to related secondary ports, i.e., (i) ICT to Lumut Port, (ii) Seremban Railway Station to Port of Port Dickson, and (iii) Pulau Sebang or Tampin to Tanjung Bruas Port. The establishment of a new land bridge service will incentivize more traders to utilize multimodal transport, thus increasing the competitiveness of rail transport relative to road transport.

Develop Malaysia–Thailand multimodal connectivity to enhance cross-border trade. Even though the contribution of cross-border trade along the Malaysia–Thailand border averaged almost 30% annually during 2015–2018, growth has been sluggish at less than 1% annually. To boost cross-border trade, it is recommended to construct the Penang–Songkhla land bridge, which is a railway spur line from Songkhla Port–Hat Yai–Bukit Kayu Hitam–Arau–Penang Port, to lower the logistics costs and transit time to the Strait of Malacca. Malaysia–Thailand cross-border trade can be also strengthened with the construction of new bridges. i.e., (i) Bukit Putih (Kuala Perlis) and Tammalang (Satun), (ii) Rantau Panjang–Su–ngai Kolok, and (iii) Pengkalan Kubor–Tak Bai. These efforts can contribute toward increasing cross-border trade between Malaysia and Thailand via the well-connected bridges.

A blueprint for inland ports is needed to enhance their role in economic corridors. Inland port services are underutilized because rail freight and inland port capacity is limited, as well as having to face the problem of last-mile connectivity to seaports. This has made road transport the more dominant mode in freight transport. Linking the rail–road system for seaport–hinterland freight transport in Malaysia is crucial. Presently, none of Malaysia's inland ports are categorized as an integrated seaport-based dry port and as a result, seaports tend to use inland ports only for customs clearance without any other extensive value-added services. Thus, a coherent effort is needed to enable Malaysian inland ports to play a more significant role in facilitating the nation's growing trade. The 'last-mile connectivity' of seaports must also be improved to attract companies and shipping lines. The government would need a national plan to develop inland ports in a comprehensive and systematic manner.

Resolve regulatory gaps related to vehicle mobility between Melaka–Dumai for the Ro-Ro ferry project to succeed. As of 2021, the planned Ro-Ro ferry link between Dumai and Melaka has yet to materialize as there are still outstanding physical infrastructure and regulatory issues that need to be harmonized. Both the governments of Malaysia and Indonesia need to address the cross-border formalities, procedures, and rules governing the movement of road vehicles that currently impede the progress of this project. Once operational, the Ro-Ro ferry link can open economic opportunities in the trade and tourism sectors between the economic corridors in southern Malaysia and Sumatera.

Provide fiscal and nonfiscal incentives to strengthen halal supply chain. There is a weak integration of the halal value chain between input suppliers, manufacturers, logistics providers, wholesalers, and retailers. This is reflected in the low number of participating halal establishments in the halal food supply chain. The Halal Development Corporation needs to provide incentives and implement a more coherent program to increase the participation of halal establishments at different stages of the supply chain. This will help the halal industry to become more integrated and establish Malaysia as a key player in the global halal industry.

Focus more on downstream activities for higher value-added supply chain. The rubber and palm oil industries are still focused on upstream actives at present. These primary industries need to focus more on downstream actives through research and development and innovation in high-end rubber-based and palm-based products with higher value-added in the supply chain. Specializing in these downstream activities can establish Malaysia to become a key player in processed rubber-based and palm-based products, and not just as the main world producer of natural rubber and palm oil. Hence, the strategy to increase downstream activities needs to be further designed by the Malaysian Rubber Board and the Malaysia Palm Oil Board, which are the custodians of the rubber and palm oil industries, respectively, according to the pattern of global demand for rubber and palm oil-based products.

Formalize federal and state coordination for economic corridor development. There is no formal mechanism at the state or federal levels that focuses on the development of IMT-GT economic corridors. In the absence of a formal mechanism focusing on economic corridor development, the national secretariats could organize forums and workshops to promote greater awareness of economic corridors among state government officials, the private sector and various stakeholders. The national secretariats could also encourage regular meetings among state governments in a given corridor to plan for cross-border initiatives and projects. This could also contribute to narrowing the development gap between states and economic corridors.

Strengthen EC6 through interregional industrial clusters. Malaysia, Southern Thailand, and South Sumatera are well-connected via land, rail, and maritime links in EC6. However, Southern Thailand and South Sumatera are relatively far apart. The ECER states can serve as a bridge between these two areas through the development of interregional industrial clusters involving SEZs located near the borders. An industry cluster represents the entire value chain of a broadly defined industry, from suppliers to end products, including supporting services and specialized infrastructure. The interregional industrial clusters would be private sector-driven. Opportunities for developing industry clusters include (i) a palm oil development belt involving SEZs in Narathiwat–Kelantan and Tanjung Langsat (Johor)–Tanjung Api-Api (South Sumatera), and (ii) a halal belt involving halal parks in ECER–Narathiwat–Pattani and Johor–Batam that could link with Southern Thailand and southern Sumatera. Interregional industrial clusters with ECER states serving as a bridge will strengthen the development of the EC6.

Map 25: Six Indonesia–Malaysia–Thailand Growth Triangle Economic Corridors

Source: Asian Development Bank.

www.ingramcontent.com/pod-product-compliance
Lightning Source LLC
Chambersburg PA
CBHW041428270326
41932CB00031B/3499

9 789292 697686